31
H468 H
7311h

D0742126

CHRISTIAN
HERITAGE
COLLEGE
LIBRARY

PRESENTED BY

Mr. and Mrs. Harry R. Newland

HEINE
A Biography

HEINRICH HEINE

HEINE

A Biography

By

FRANÇOIS FEJTÖ

Translated by Mervyn Savill

KENNIKAT PRESS
Port Washington, N. Y./London

HEINE

First published in 1946
Reissued in 1970 by Kennikat Press
Library of Congress Catalog Card No: 78-103187
SBN 8046-0824-5

Manufactured by Taylor Publishing Company   Dallas, Texas

CONTENTS

39015

CONTENTS

LIST OF ILLUSTRATIONS

ERRATA

Illustration facing page 64. Caption should read : " Charlotte Embden, Heine's sister."

Illustration facing page 65. Caption should read : " Rachel Varnhagen."

Page 69. For E. T. W. Hoffmann, read E. T. A. Hoffmann.

Page 297 (Index). For E. T. W. Hoffmann, read E. T. A. Hoffmann.

To my aged Father, deported in 1944 and disappeared. He loved Heine. And to my two Brothers, also disappeared.

FOREWORD

IN 1938, while an emigrant student in Paris, I was to have met my friend and countryman Odon de Horvath, who had just come to the notice of the French reading public through the translation of his poignant novel *Youth without a God*. Our meeting-place was to have been the George V Café, but on that very day a large branch from a tree in the Avenue Matignon, struck by lightning, fell upon and killed the young writer.

This untimely end reminded me of that meeting which had taken place a century ago between Heine and Börne in the Jardin des Plantes, and which, too, had almost ended in tragedy for the two German writers. On this occasion also, a sharp squall snapped off a branch which fell between the two friends, but they escaped with minor grazes. This coincidence led me to study in the Bibliothèque Nationale the exiled years of that great European, Heine. Ever since my childhood days his chequered life has fascinated me profoundly. In France I now had the chance to be living where that many-sided genius had spent the most fruitful years of his life. Thanks to my status of emigrant I was able to perfect my knowledge of the poet.

War and the Armistice took me to Cahors, where, for a livelihood—paradoxical enough for an anti-Nazi Hungarian—I gave lessons in the German language and literature. The only German books that I could find in the local libraries were the complete works of Heine. The French students were enchanted by his poems and astounded by his philosophy that revealed to them quite another side of Germany. This side was mysterious and magical, while the other, that they knew, was warlike, mail-fisted and was in process of desecrating their country. Everything that suggested bitter criticism of this second Germany aroused their interest. I was forced to delve into the most intimate details of his life to satisfy the insatiable curiosity of my young audience, and this led me to undertake a basic study of Heine and finally to write his biography. The essay I had written after the death of Horvath and which I had mislaid in my travels served as a foundation.

So many episodes of the poet's frenzied life are fraught with such contradiction and inconsequence that they have astonished and deceived many writers. I was therefore obliged to ask myself the question : would it enhance Heine's reputation to be revealed in all the phases of his existence ? Would it not be more respectful to cover his nakedness ? This weighty question decided me to go deeper into the subject and to ask myself whether Biography as a literary form does not detract from Art ?

Furthermore, Heine himself more than once protested against those who tried to explain the sorrowful magic of his poems by stressing *ad nauseam* the details of his love affair with his cousin, Amélie. Koestler, in his *The Yogi and the Commissar* seems—quite rightly to me—to defend the thesis that the life and work of an artist develop on two different planes, and that the latter must be the final yardstick. A work should be self-explanatory— if explanation is necessary. However, I continue to feel strongly that it is impossible to separate the work from the man, from whom in the ultimate analysis it is an emanation.

The work as defined is a reflection of the man and only enhanced by the frame in which it has been conceived. This is especially true in the case of Heine, inasmuch as for him artistic creation was, in the literal sense of the word, only one expression of his love of life.

Heine, while defending the autonomy of art, during the whole of his life tried to integrate it with reality. For him, poetry, love, literature, politics and pleasure comprised the whole, which must be developed in every direction. He despised dreamers and recluses who stood aside from their epoch. He felt himself capable of living his own period and being able to portray it for future generations. He imposed upon himself the task of expressing its struggles, rivalries and the divergent tendencies of his contemporaries. He was among those who most definitely *thought* in terms of the nineteenth century . . . the same nineteenth century that Leon Daudet has defined as " stupid," but which we persist in believing to be one of the most fecund and, despite its vagaries, one of the most enlightened in the history of the human race.

In this book I have not tried to analyse the mysterious charm of the *Lieder*. I have endeavoured to achieve a more modest and far-reaching result : to explain the personality who produced that masterpiece, and to write a living history of the thoughts and activities of that strange man who appears to us such a mixture of the erotic, mean, hateful and cynical. I have written these pages for those who seek in a biography that measure of superiority and wretchedness that are the very essence of the man. Heine, perhaps, does not gain by being known, by those who attach too much importance to an illusory image of greatness ; but the readers who seek the truth will be the richer for knowing him . . . and may, perhaps, grow to love him.

CHAPTER ONE

BETTY VAN GELDERN

SEVEN Grecian towns hotly contested for the honour of being Homer's birthplace. Düsseldorf, the birthplace of Heinrich Heine, has never boasted of the fact nor been able to deny it. The reasons for this indifference have nothing to do with poetry. It is not the place, but the date of his birth, that has caused disagreement among his biographers. They are faced with three possible clues. The first, given by the poet himself as January 1, 1800, appears to be the least probable. Heine had put this about, not altogether seriously, so as to be able to say : " I am one of the first men of the century." His niece and biographer, Princess della Rocca, believed this to be true—or pretended to believe it. She does, however, mention that Heine's mother gave the date as December 13, 1799, and several family documents actually confirm this date. Finally Heine assured his French friends that he was born two years earlier—that is to say, on December 13, 1797. His parents, he explained, had falsified his age after Waterloo to prevent his being conscripted for the Prussian army. The truth was difficult to unravel, for during the French occupation of Düsseldorf the civil registers were destroyed by fire.

Some years ago a young research worker unearthed a document which enables us to specify not only the date of Heine's birth, but also the reasons why his parents had recourse to make him out younger than he really was. The document is none other than the private diary of Grimm, the Protestant Pastor of Heiligenstadt. It was he who baptised Heine in 1825. In his diary he records having asked Heine the date of his birth and also that of his parents' marriage. He describes how the poet blushed scarlet with embarrassment and confessed to having been born in December, 1797, contrary to the entries on the documents and several months before the marriage. His parents, wishing to remove all trace of this stigma, had changed his birthdate after the fire.

The riddle is solved, and the biographer may rest assured that the author of the *Buch der Lieder*, the singer of sweet love songs, was the fruit of non-conjugal love. Moreover, it is interesting to trace the affinity between the circumstances of his birth and the subsequent outstanding traits in his character. It is well known that love-children are more delicate, tender and susceptible to illusion and suffering than those conceived and born in wedlock. Heine's life could undoubtedly be taken as a proof of this contention.

It would, however, be incorrect to portray Heine's mother Betty—or *Peierchen* as she was nicknamed in the family—as either a woman of easy virtue or a passionate lover. She was the daughter of a Jewish doctor, Gottschalk Geldern of Düsseldorf, and had been carefully brought up and given an education consistent with the knowledge of the period. The letters that she wrote to her girl friends before she met Samson Heine suggest that she was a reasonable and logical young woman, capable of self-criticism, and on the whole rather too intellectual. She had lost her mother when quite young, and had taken her place for both her young brothers and her father.

This would account for the streak of independence in her character. She was twenty-four when her father died, and almost immediately after she lost her eldest brother Juszpa. She was then left with no one but her brother Simeon, a timid and unsociable youth who spent days on end shut up in the library. *Peierchen* felt useless and abandoned. Her aunts and uncles never tired of telling her that it was time she got married. Although she did not oppose them in principle, as one of her letters proves, she had very definite ideas about marriage, which did not in the least conform with those of her co-religionists or with those of her family. She had read *La Nouvelle Héloïse* and *Werther* and studied *Émile*, and she believed that the natural human sentiments, if not actually the passions, should be inviolate. Despite uncles and aunts the daughter of Doctor Gottschalk had firmly decided to turn down the most alluring offers of *Schadchen* (the Jewish marriage intermediary), and to await the blossoming of that imperious sentiment known as love. It was useless to introduce her to rich and charming Jewish boys ; even though they were cultured and well

Amélie Heine (1830), *called Molly, daughter of Salomon Heine,*
the Poet's first love

[*To face p.* 14

Mathilde Heine

[*To face p.* 15

brought up she remained adamant. She waited obstinately for the *coup de foudre*—and at long last it came. She met Samson Heine from Hanover, and fell immediately under the spell of his velvety winning voice, clear thoughtful eyes and impeccable manners. His distinguished, almost aristocratic bearing contrasted strangely with his humble station and origin. Betty was so obviously attracted to the stranger that he was received with the gravest suspicion by the small Jewish community of Düsseldorf. The Geldern family, frightened by the favour she showed this " interloper," looked askance at Samson Heine.

Although Betty herself was not rich, she came from one of the great German Jewish families. They suspected Samson of paying court to her in order to gain admission into the family and with their support to set himself up in the town. The young couple ignored their disapproval and decided to present the family with a *fait accompli*. One day at a family meeting Betty raised her hand : a wedding-ring glittered on her finger. " I am Samson's wife," she announced in a voice that trembled a little.

According to an old Jewish custom, which Heine refers to in his *Rabbi von Bacharach* (incidentally this fragment contains many references to the history of his parents and of his own youth), a young man who places a wedding-ring on the finger of a virgin, repeating the words " By the Law of Moses and Israel I take thee for my wife," makes her, in fact, his wife. But the Geldern family was apparently already too modern and too emancipated to accept such a charming old custom as valid. Her relations were not content with reprimanding Betty and her seducer, but prevailed upon the Rabbi of Düsseldorf to refuse his blessing on the marriage. When Samson approached the Municipality for a permit of residence, the Jewish community, which was consulted as usual, gave an unfavourable report.

Betty rebelled against the tyranny of her family. If people refused to agree to her marriage, she would go through with it on her own account. This was not done in passion, but after sober reflection. She set herself deliberately to oppose the bigoted traditions of family and community. She made no secret of her " affair," and some months later was walking as proudly as ever through the streets of Düsseldorf in an advanced state of pregnancy. When the outcasts repeated their request to the Municipality for permission to reside, it was granted out of regard for Betty's condition.

On December 13, 1797, the courageous young woman gave birth to Heinrich. Her proud and dignified behaviour had gained her the sympathy of several of her co-religionists. The Rabbi revised his opinion and decided to give them his blessing ; the family also became reconciled to the position. Things became normal once more, and everyone agreed to forget the past. In the course of time Samson and Betty thought no more of this romantic episode in their life, which gradually became no more than a legend. Jewish families have an amazing aptitude for forgetting the immediate past ; their memory only retains that which is far distant, such as the glorious memorials of their race. Beyond this, only the future is important to them.

The former outlaws now settled down as peaceful and respected citizens. The conflagration that destroyed the town erased all traces of their adventure. Who can reproach Heine's parents for this mild forgery to justify their moral concepts ?

The child, whose birth had been a spirited challenge to strict and bigoted Judaism, retained to the end of his life the spirit of rebellion that had once actuated his parents. But the poet, who had no respect for authority, guarded the secret of Betty and Samson until his death—apart from this one admission to the pastor who had accepted him into the Christian fold. He knew, however, that even if the truth were generally known it would in no way have diminished the respect in which his mother was held. There is nothing immoral or frivolous in this story of Betty. The love which she bore the man who became her life companion was pure, deep and well balanced. The love affairs of her son were to follow very different paths . . .

CHAPTER TWO

THE MATERNAL FAMILY

AN Hungarian authority on Heine, David Kaufman, discloses in his work the family history of the poet's mother from the middle of the seventeenth century. The facts are taken from registers in the Pressburg archives. A Pressburg Jew, Simon Michael, founded the dynasty. He figures in the archives as a purveyor of gold and silver to the Imperial Mint in Vienna. He served the Emperor Leopold I with zealous fidelity—that same Leopold who in 1663 had issued a notoriously severe edict against the Jews forbidding " that useless and evil doing people " to reside in Vienna or any other town of his empire.

Jews bear less resentment than is popularly supposed. When the Hungarian nobility, under the aegis of Prince Rakoczy, rebelled against Habsburg absolutism, Simon Michael, known to the authorities of the monarchy in 1699 as the " representative of the Transdanubian Jewish Community," did not hesitate for an instant as to whom to support. It was, above all, thanks to his personal influence that the Western Hungarian Jews rallied to the Emperor as one man. They put their funds at the disposal of the Treasury and rendered great services to the Army Commissariat.

Simon Michael did not resent the persecution of his fellows. Despite bullyragging and humiliation, he was fully aware of the bonds of interest between absolute power and the financier. His great-grandson, Heinrich Heine, believed in quite a different community of interests. When the Hungarian Landowners in 1848 brought out once more the Rakoczy flags of liberation, the poet (although certain contemporaries saw the hidden hand of Metternich) saluted the heroes of liberty in the following pathetic couplet :

> *Wenn ich den Namen Ungarn hör'*
> *Wird mir das deutsche Wams zu enge.*

The ideals of Simon Michael were very different from those of his great-grandson. Liberty had no place in his dreams : he aspired much more modestly and with greater realism to open in Pressburg—with Imperial sanction—an exchange bureau or *Wechsel-stube*, to facilitate international commerce. But he died before the reactionary Viennese Government had grasped the importance of such an institution. He at least had the satisfaction of being able to die in Vienna : in recognition of his services to the dynasty the Imperial capital had opened its gates to the old Jew. During the last years of his life he had procured permission, for his family and for himself, valid for ten years, to reside in the city of Vienna.

Simon Michael's daughter, Sarah Lea, married a young man, Lazarus van Geldern of Düsseldorf, who had arrived in Vienna about 1715 in the course of his travels. His father, Joseph van Geldern (the prefix *van* is not a title of nobility but simply indicates that the family originated from the little Westphalian town of Geldern), filled almost the same role in the Principality of *Jülich und Berg* as Simon Michael at the Court of Vienna. The *Hoffactor* enjoyed the titles and office of Purveyor to the Court, worked for the Mint and the Treasury Bank, and negotiated all sorts of purchases and sales. A contemporary chronicle reports that Joseph van Geldern was summoned to appear before a tribunal to answer the accusation of one of his race on a charge of debasing the currency. He emerged from the action without a stain on his character, but he was completely ruined. On his death his son Lazarus inherited his appointment and his debts.

Düsseldorf was one of the few German towns that were relatively tolerant towards the Jews. The Düsseldorf Jews, who were estimated at the end of the eighteenth century to total about three hundred, were not forced to live behind ghetto walls. The life of that picturesque little town was reminiscent of the Low Countries, which was natural enough as it had very close business relations with the Dutch towns. Her trade was very brisk ; Dutch traveller rubbed shoulders with English trader, French merchant offered choice fabrics to Austrian buyer ; French books were also in circulation. In the hostelries religion and politics were eagerly discussed. Nowhere along the whole length of the Rhine were such gay fairs to be found, nowhere was the carnival so boisterous and colourful. As trade prospers and the exchange of goods and ideas increases, prejudices tend to disappear.

Betty van Geldern's grandfather Lazarus had already discarded his levite, and wore German clothes ; he took part in everyday Christian life. In the whole of the Rhineland it was the Düsseldorf Jews who acclimatised themselves most rapidly. They were no longer content with a rabbinical education, for they found themselves attracted by modern civilisation, science and the arts. The eldest son of Lazarus, Gottschalk, after finishing his Jewish studies crossed into Holland and entered Leyden University, where he took his doctor's degree in medicine.

The German Jews were able to face modernity quite simply and serenely. Their religion isolated them more from the outside world than did the ghetto walls. Ideas of equality held no terrors for them : they knew themselves to be different from the Christians and were proud of the difference. Jehovah's people, scattered to the four corners of the earth remained strangers in the heart of any nation. The bond which held them, their " Land " wherein they had their roots, was a roll of parchment, the " Torah," the " transportable country " of the Jews—as Heine was later to call it. Against persecution, pogroms and hatred, they set up their faith in a God who chastised them because He loved them. The hope of a better future rendered them almost impervious to misfortune. They made not the least effort to disguise their origin and felt no vestige of inferiority ; even their pride showed no trace of unhealthy exaggeration.

The conscience of the persecuted nation gradually became troubled as it came in contact with the philosophy of the Encyclopedists. During their Calvary of eighteen centuries, they had known how to resist strange beliefs and to uphold their unique faith born of hope and suffering. But this race, disposed to calculation and reasoning, was not adequately equipped to resist the temptations of the Age of Reason. A new crisis burst forth among them, as serious and painful as that other revolution from which had been born the religion of universal salvation. The Jewish student in the Christian universities learnt not only new beliefs—which would have shaken his own to its foundation —but became a prey to Doubt. Previously, he had found the key to existence in a supernatural revelation. Now, he was forced to justify his faith and his life before a tribunal of sceptical intelligence. His individual destiny, hitherto so clear and bright, suddenly became highly problematical. The West had revealed to him a science far in advance of that laid down in the Talmud. His preoccupation with general Western ideas proved an attraction and a repulsion at the same time. In a world where Mohammedans, Protestants, Catholics and Heretics tore one another to pieces in the name of the truths revealed to them by God, the Jew, bearer of a truth of the same order though different to theirs, had not felt in the least out of place. To be alone, surrounded by foreigners in a world divided but of divine origin, was familiar to him. All this changed at the moment when Catholic, Calvinist, Lutheran and Anglican sunk their sectarian differences before the idea of Man. The Jew can oppose other religions, but Man . . .

Man, judge and creator of his own destiny ! What a splendid but tragic discovery. For the second time in history, the rigid framework of the Jewish religion, characterised by a conservatism and a rigidly exclusive nationalism, was thrown out of joint by the breath of universalism. The teaching of Christ had previously opened a large breach in the walls of the ancient edifice : now Reason poured through this same breach, which Jewish pride, strengthened by Christian ostracism, had laboriously repaired. The Jew, who had lived for centuries with God as sole companion, whom he had created in his own image, saw himself suddenly relegated to one of a species, one among many—often more beautiful, more dignified, more vigorous than himself. These species, shadowy and often evil-doing it is true, but previously without influence on his personal destiny, suddenly revealed themselves as beings full of good sense, beings who concerned himself, and who bore within themselves the whole of humanity. The Jew began to see himself with the eyes of others : *hic incipit tragoedia*. He became a stranger to himself. He discovered the incidence of other destinies upon his own, a grotesque affinity with their customs and the primitiveness of his own thoughts.

The men of the Middle Ages had only accused him of having crucified Jesus, the Crusaders of having spread the plague, the

Flagellants of having immolated Christian children to use their blood in midnight ceremonies. All these fanatics were perhaps less harmful than the modern philosophers who observed the Jews dispassionately and without prejudice, encouraging them to become what they virtually were—like other people. If God does not exist, if He does not represent the prerogatives of a race or a religion, the preservation of the Jewish community has no sense. As at the beginning of the Christian era—we repeat—the spirit of universality had splintered the rigid framework of their religion, but this time it was not an unknown God, but Reason (in the sense of the Age of Enlightenment) that tempted the Chosen People . . .

But would this new Almighty, the omnipotent Reason, provide a shelter or a fatherland for the Jews ? By sacrificing his ancient privileges would he be admitted by the others into the universal community ? Because of his foreign origin would not the Jew always be considered a stranger ? The professors of Leyden University, disciples of Spinoza and Descartes, will accord the accolade to Gottschalk van Geldern ; but for the ignorant Christian will not he and his brothers remain mysterious creatures, whose hands bear the invisible though very real stain of Christ's blood ? In 1818, the chaplain of Düsseldorf Cathedral will tell his parish children the story of the Jewish usurer who would only allow the Christian to redeem his pledged garments against the Sacred Host, which he needed for his unholy ceremonies.

The Jew, conquered by Reason, will lose the balance that his ancestors had maintained by virtue of their belief. A new type will emerge : the unbalanced Jew, a prey to metaphysical doubts, tortured by new nostalgias, seeking to become or at least to appear what he is not. " The times have changed, the ancient calumnies no longer produce the desired effect," as Moses Mendelssohn, the friend of Lessing and protagonist of the modern German Jews, wrote later. " They accuse us today of superstition, stupidity, lack of moral sense and education, incapacity for art, science and the useful professions, for military and national service, and an ineradicable propensity for fraud, usury and anarchy . . ." And he adds : " They continue to exclude us from all human activities, the arts, science, and all the useful vocations ; they close to us all the roads that could lead us to progress and at the same time justify that oppression of which we are victims by citing our lack of culture. They bind our hands and reproach us for not using them." The Jew who spoke thus had a new ideal, the ideal of an enlightened century— Universal Progress. He asked to be admitted to the human community.

Heine's grandfather, Doctor Gottschalk, was an "enlightened" Jew, entirely absorbed in his learned profession. He had succeeded admirably in reconciling his ancestral cult with modern rationalism. But his brother Simeon was of an entirely different temperament. Heinrich Heine looked upon the latter— not without reason—as his spiritual ancestor. The young Simeon, maturing early, did not consider his place to be in the narrow family circle in Düsseldorf. He had hardly finished his studies when he set out in search of adventure. A strange restlessness and an insatiable curiosity spurred him on from one country to another : from Holland to England, from Austria to Italy. His travels had no specific goal ; he was in search of himself, in search of a solution to life, based on a fundamental truth which he hoped to meet by chance in the course of his wanderings.

He was a handsome and elegant man, a brilliant conversationalist with an untarnished wit ; he loved music and dancing. Continually without resources, he nevertheless managed to travel like an aristocrat by giving lessons in languages. The van Gelderns had relations everywhere and the wandering Jew was received with open arms. Women and young girls adored him, and brilliant offers of marriage and remunerative positions were proposed to him time after time. Simeon would hesitate, accept, and finally, terrified of security and stability, would pack his bags and disappear overnight.

One day he found his journeys to be senseless and his existence completely futile. Only God could quench his thirst for the absolute. Perhaps the God of his ancestors could disclose the significance of his torment ? And yet Simeon was obsessed by a name that he had always sought in books and on the lips of women, in the harmonies of Glück and in learned conversations with enlightened Rabbis—Jerusalem, the name of the Holy City. There he would hear the voice of the Omnipotent, there God dwells in His glory.

Simeon embarked at Leghorn. During the voyage his boat was attacked by Corsairs, and next we find the prisoner discoursing to the sea pirates of the mystic meaning of the revelation and the truth of eternal life . . .

Simeon's hopes had not been in vain. He saw a vision on Mount Moria. God appeared and conversed with him—but neither in the shape of a cloud nor a man. God was the sun and His words were the sun's rays. God was the flower-strewn meadow, and His word the perfume of the flowers. God was the olive grove, and His word the rustle of the silvery leaves. God was the Arab steed and the choice fruits of the Orient, the twinkle of stars and the howling of jackals in the desert. God spoke and His Word was the world. Yes, the world was the Word of the Lord . . .

It was in this manner that God was revealed to Simeon van Geldern on Mount Moria. In joy and terror he prostrated himself : he wanted to pray but only an inarticulate groan issued from his lips. In his excitement he ran down the mountainside to bring the glad tidings to men. But when the Bedouins asked him what the Lord had said Simeon could only stammer incoherently. God was revealed in all His power and splendour, but had refrained from making any useful pronouncement. " He had nothing to say," murmured Simeon. " The man is out of his mind," the Bedouins declared mockingly. Simeon rode away and set sail for Europe ; his body was ravaged by malaria and hardship. He returned to Düsseldorf, and devoted the rest of his days to prayer and meditation. His co-religionists venerated him as a saint.

Many years after Simeon's death, little Heinrich, rummaging in the loft among the old chests full of well-thumbed prayer books, ledgers and worn-out hats, came upon the diary of Simeon's journeys written in German. No other book—with the exception of *Don Quixote de la Manche*—made such an impression on the child's mind as this incoherent manuscript of his wandering uncle. It was perhaps the enchanting and passionate recital of Simeon van

Geldern's adventures that awoke in him a taste for travel and a curiosity about the world.

Doctor Gottschalk van Geldern had given shelter to his brother, the prodigal son, and looked upon him as a maniac and a parasite. He did his best to immunise the three children, Juszpa, Betty and Simeon, against the temptations of an adventurous or a purely meditative life. He often quoted to them the words of peace and truth written by the wise Wessely, friend of Mendelssohn : " During our exile, the glory of Israel does not shine ; we must grasp with both hands anyone who can guarantee us an honourable existence, so that we need not have recourse to strangers . . ." Juszpa and Betty took the paternal advice to heart, but Simeon was more like the uncle whose name he bore. Bowing to the wishes of his father, he began the study of medicine, but never finished his studies. Simeon, wishing to exhaust the whole of science rarely left his library : *Ars longa vita brevis.* After his own fashion the poet's uncle was also an adventurer ; without leaving his study he wandered in spirit perpetually through the world of ideas. A quasi-Jewish Faust, he forced himself to learn everything. The young Heinrich often spent long hours talking and dreaming in the modest retreat of this amiable failure, where the bookshelves bent under the weight of massive dusty folios. Heine at a later date gives a picturesque description of this pale and serious uncle ; his nose had a classic straightness, although it was a third as long again as the Grecian prototype. He wore short breeches, silk stockings and buckled shoes ; his hair was looped up in a long pigtail, which flapped about from shoulder to shoulder as he trotted along on his short legs.

" Uncle Simeon, can I pull your pigtail ? "

The sight of this lock of hair always reminded the child of the bell-pull. The charming little old man would lift up his hands :

" Ah-là-là-là ! What are we coming to ? What degeneracy. The modern generation has no respect, it makes fun of the old. What will become of us ? "

When the child came to visit him, he would find the old man seated at his desk poring over some enormous tome, muttering strange and fascinating words. With one hand he held the book and with the other he stroked his Persian cat. Although his sight was failing he persisted in reading. He studied Hebrew, Latin, the Talmud and Paracelsus, the Bible and Aristotle ; he studied until he became almost blind, shut up in his Noah's ark— so-called because of the ark carved on the door by a Jewish work-man. Caressing his sleepy cat, he would read in undertones, occasionally giving vent to a deep sigh. The child, curled up in a chair, would listen to him for hours and then, his nose full of dust, he would fall asleep. The Latin and Hebrew words seemed like magic incantations, and conjured up strange images, a mixture of reality and legend, history and childish dreams. They were exquisite hours, and he always remembered them with a deep nostalgia.

CHAPTER THREE

SAMSON HEINE

FATHER and son are walking along a lime-fringed avenue in Düsseldorf. Father Heine has a graceful carriage ; and with a suave gesture he acknowledges the greetings of the passers-by. The small boy, now a pupil in the preparatory class of the Düsseldorf Lyceum, does his best to keep pace with him. His air is proud and detached like that of a grown-up person, and he often raises his cap with dignity. Suddenly he stops in the middle of his walk, like an old Jew does when struck with an idea. He catches hold of his father's sleeve.

" What is it ? "

" Tell me about grandfather, papa."

The child knows nothing of his father's father; nothing of Chaim—known as Heinemann Heine.

" Your grandfather," says Samson after a moment's reflection, with an air of making a wise pronouncement, " your grandfather was a little Jew with a large beard."

For some strange reason Heinrich finds this answer enchanting. On the following day, with a look of importance, he tells his classmates :

" Do you know who my grandfather was ? . . . *Ein kleiner Jid mit einem grossen Bart !* "

Much to his surprise, the whole class roared with laughter. A little urchin climbed up on to the rostrum :

" Do you know what Heinrich's grandfather was ? . . . *Ein kleiner Jid . . .* "

Oh, it was wildly amusing. They all began to dance round the boy like Red Indians : " Your grandfather was a little Jew with a large beard ! " Heinrich, who had not anticipated the effect of his words, was flabbergasted, but although his eyes were moist he did not flinch from the hurricane that he had unleashed.

Depressed and profoundly discouraged, he stumbled through the little winding streets to his home in the Bolkerstrasse. From that day on he made no attempt to learn more about his grand-father—and furthermore he never did learn anything about him. But to his dying day he carried the hurtful memory of that laughter. For the first time he had encountered the cruel fact that he never wished to recognise, against which he would have to protest and fight : that in the eyes of his neighbour the Jew is different from the rest of the world, and that his very aspect renders him ridiculous—if not repulsive. It requires very little to humiliate a man. Heinrich Heine had received a wound that would never heal. Would he not say at a later date : " ' Jew ' does not signify a religion, but a misfortune " ? " The misfortune of being a Jew " was to be the *leit-motiv* of Heine's art and poetry.

He told his parents nothing of the humiliation that he had just received. In any case, Samson Heine would not have been in the least disturbed ; it was impossible to humiliate him. He was one of those men who go through life as though in a dream, always smiling, always fascinated by the pleasant aspects of life, and who remain impervious to material worries as well as to spiritual torments. The young Heine admired his father enormously, and in his autobiographical passages always speaks of him with great tenderness. Across the pages of the poet's memoirs Samson Heine appears as a distinguished person with powdered hair held by a tortoiseshell clasp in a charming little queue ; he had long sensitive hands of remarkable whiteness, which the child loved to kiss.

A miniature on the sideboard made the greatest impression on Heinrich ; framed in silver, it portrayed an imposing Samson Heine in magnificent scarlet uniform, his face glowing with pride. His childish imagination wove a legend of heroism around this portrait ; actually, Samson had been elected by his fellow citizens in 1806 an officer of the municipal militia, *Bürgermiliz*. He must have enjoyed a certain popularity in Düsseldorf, as his nomination to Inspector of the Poor in his district proves. This duty, which fell upon the representatives of the greatest and oldest families, had never previously been entrusted to a Jew. The inhabitants of Düsseldorf were, furthermore, exceeding proud of their charitable " Institution," which did so much to combat the rising poverty.

Public benefactor and officer of the Militia, and a veritable charmer to boot, Samson Heine was especially doted upon by the dowagers, who appreciated his attentions and his compliments. " His assiduity and manners were worthy of the Seven Wise Men," his son wrote later with gentle irony. The wisdom of Samson Heine lay in a sort of *savoir-vivre* : simplicity, devotion, respect for self and others, an enjoyment of life, and refusal to recognise ill luck—to deny it vigorously if necessary—and to value every piece of good fortune that came along. Always in the clouds, only wishing to please, he naturally lived outside the bounds of reality . . .

In his hosiery in the Bolkerstrasse, he busied himself endlessly behind the counter. He would climb his little ladder with agility and sort the lengths of canvas, silk or velvet, and display them with the skill of a conjuror. He would unroll the fabrics with inimitable elegance.

" Here is the best, the most reasonable merchandise in Düsseldorf. It suits you admirably . . . I should never forgive myself if I deprived you of it ; I would prefer to let it go at a loss . . ."

What is even more touching, he would be speaking the truth. This blue-eyed hosier had no business acumen. He played at business, with the vanity and delight of a schoolboy. Instead of looking upon the silks, cloths and materials as wares, he knew how to extract from them sensuous tactile pleasure ; he loved to feel and caress them. He was inordinately proud of having discovered velveteen. This was a kind of English velvet, pleasant and lustrous, with no trace of coarseness—a material that he would have chosen life to be made of. Having been the first to import it into the country, velveteen became for him a positive maggot. He offered it to everyone and praised its qualities to the skies.

Samson Heine never lost his equanimity ; he was always good-humoured, and refused to be perturbed by either misfortune or success. Several times he was completely ruined and lived at the expense of his relations—chiefly on the good nature of his brother Salomon the Hamburg banker, that great man of business

—without being in the least disconcerted. On Saturdays he would go to the Synagogue and sing the psalms in his clear voice, returning home at midday to a well-laden table, when he would say grace and settle down to enjoy the food. His four children, Heinrich, Charlotte, Gustav and Max regarded him with unbounded admiration.

Samson felt entirely at home in the bosom of his Judaic religion. He observed the ancient customs with fervour, and profited by the feast days to display his love of good cheer and his taste for company. Heinrich has given us a moving description of Easter in his *Rabbi von Bacharach*, and how his family celebrated this marvellous feast. In this portrait of the Rabbi Abraham we can recognise the poet's father. The mistress of the house, who lights the candles at sunset in the old house, is none other than Betty van Geldern, his beloved mother. She lights the candles, lays the cloth and places three flat unleavened loaves called *azymes* on the centre of the table, covering them over with a napkin. Next, she brings six little dishes of symbolic victuals : an egg, a lettuce, horse-radish, a lamb bone, nuts and cinnamon and a paste of raisins. Everybody sits down to table. Samson Heine reads some passages from a curious book called the *Haggada*, a strange jumble of antiquated legends, miraculous stories of the Jewish sojourn in Egypt, controversies and feast-day canticles. Despite all this solemnity an enormous supper is eaten, and at certain predetermined moments during the reading the symbolic foods are tasted. " This ceremony," writes Heine, " is full of serene melancholy and grave though not unhappy tranquillity. There is something so poignant and intimate . . . that even those Jews who have long since renounced the faith of their fathers in the pursuit of the pleasures and rewards of an alien world, are moved to their very depths when they hear those ancient and familiar notes of the Easter ceremony . . . "

Father Samson empties his cup of red wine, takes an unleavened bread and raises it gaily aloft in salutation to Uncle Simeon, the van Geldern aunts, his wife Betty and Heinrich—the other children are not old enough to stay up to supper—and then he reads from the *Haggada* those words that will remain for ever in Heinrich's memory :

29

" Behold the food that our fathers ate in Egypt !
Let all who hunger come and eat !
Let all who are afflicted come and partake of our Paschal Joy ;
This year we celebrate this feast here, but next year
It will be in the land of Israel ! "

Samson Heine joyfully chants the old canticle of insensate and unconquerable hope.

" Thus did the Rabbi of Bacherach celebrate Easter among his own people, when the two strangers entered and demanded hospitality . . . " thought Heinrich. The boy shivered as he recalled the story that his old aunt Rebecca had told him one day . . . " Oh, that happened a long time ago," she had said to reassure him, " in a dark age when the Jews were entirely at the mercy of their enemies . . . an age which, as your father says, will never come again . . . "

However, the child hears the noise of footsteps at the door. " Was that a knock ? " He looked at the strangers who pretend to be members of their religion, but who have come to leave the bloody corpse of a child in the house . . .

" This year, we shall celebrate once more in slavery . . . "

Behind the feasting and the joyful singing Heinrich feels the hidden menace, the ever-present danger, the past and future horrors. Betty notices how pale her eldest son is. She frowns : the child is too sensitive. She puts her hand on the boy's shoulder and he gives her a little timid smile.

" Next year, we shall celebrate in liberty . . . "

CHAPTER FOUR

THE FRENCH ARRIVE

THE following year brought the soldiers of Liberty to Düsseldorf. The German Nationalists never forgave Heine those pages
full of warmth, gaiety and irony, which he dedicated to the
French troops that occupied his native town. But was it Heinrich's fault that, like most of his fellow citizens, he retained the
pleasantest memories of those invaders who in fact were the true
liberators of the Rhineland—as they had been of Italy ? Certain
chapters of the *Chartreuse de Parme* are most enlightening witnesses
to this.

What is more, Heine did not remain silent about " the heavy
stupefaction " that the brusque departure of the reigning Prince
at the enemy's arrival had caused in Düsseldorf : " Everyone
wore a funereal air, and silently made for the market-place where
a long declaration had been posted outside the town hall. The
weather was overcast . . . an old pensioner of the Palatinate
read the text aloud, and at each word a tear trickled down the
white moustaches that framed his loyal old face. I was at his
side, and I wept also, and asked him why we were weeping. He
replied as he went on reading : " The Elector thanks his subjects
for their loyalty to him " . . . and as he came to the phrase, " and
releases them from their oath of fidelity " . . . he began to sob . . . "

The people of Düsseldorf had a strong sense of fidelity towards
their Prince ; after his departure they felt as though a family had
suddenly been deprived of its well-loved head. To whom should
they now show allegiance ? Who would reign now in the castle ?
Who would watch over them by night and guard their coffers ?
To whom would they pay their taxes ? The period between the
Prince's flight and the entry of the invincible French army was
extremely wretched. Everyone was haunted by the memory of
pillage and rape of olden days, tortured by the agony of uncertainty. Even in the enlightened Heine family, they feared a
political upheaval . . .

But the clouds blew over very quickly. Heine tells us in his *Buch Le Grand* : " The following morning was gay and fine, the sun shone in all its splendour. In the streets there was a sound of drums, and when I entered my father's room to say good morning I found him with his wigmaker, who was telling him that that very morning the oath was to be sworn to the New Grand Duke Joachim in the Town Hall ; that he was of the best family and had married the Emperor Napoleon's sister . . . Fears vanished very quickly at the sight of the French troops, at the sight of those happy carefree soldiers who crossed the world singing and playing their music, at the sight of the bearskins, the tricoloured cockades, the gleaming bayonets . . . "

But that is lyricism ! Possibly. But will it ever be said that the entry of the Germans in field-grey between 1940 and 1942 into any continental town has left in the heart of some poetic child a memory so charming and so tenderly joyous ? If Heine was fascinated by the French it was because they really were enchanting. The reputation of their invincibility must have done the rest. However Rhenish the citizens of Düsseldorf may have been, they were Germans, whom the display of force and military pageantry has always impressed. Accustomed to masters, they now had new ones—but more just and humane ones. Historians of the French occupation of the Duchy of Berg recognise that for the two most oppressed social classes, the foreign conquest proved a deliverance. Joachim Murat, the Emperor's brother-in-law, distributed to the peasants the lands of the aristocrats who had fled. To the Jews he accorded the rights of man. Through the energies of the French administrator Beugnot—who, as Heine told later in his *Briefe aus Berlin* : " . . . despite a position created to excite hatred, gave to the inhabitants of the Grand Duchy of Berg so many proofs of his great and noble character . . . "—commerce expanded, industry revived, and a fresh breeze of French Liberalism sprang up. A new order appeared in the schools, and the old college of the Jesuits became a Lyceum into which entered a healthier and freer atmosphere. Young Heinrich struck up a friendship with a French drummer, a M. Legrand, who was billeted on his father. " He had a small vivacious face," he tells us, " with a fierce black moustache, beneath which one could see a pair of thick red lips ; his eyes sparkled like fire." M. Legrand--if one can trust Heine's description—gave him French lessons on the drums : " He knew how to make himself understood by that means. If I did not know the meaning of *Liberté* he would beat out the *Marseillaise*, and I understood. If I could not grasp the significance of the word *Egalité* he played me the march *Ça ira! ça ira! les aristocrates à la lanterne*, and I understood . . ."

Betty van Geldern also understood the significance of the word *Egalité*. It meant for her the crumbling of those artificial barriers which, until then, had barred to the sons of the lower orders and to the Jews the roads that led to high social position. " To each according to his capacity, to each according to his worth . . ." Napoleon—let us stress this—personified above all, in the eyes of his humble contemporaries, the possibility of bettering oneself by sheer force of intelligence and will-power. If, in a few years a little insignificant Corsican Officer could become Emperor of France and Master of Europe, anything was possible. The traditional concrete class barriers had become much more flexible. Frau Heine's ambition was awakened : she wanted her sons to emerge from the rank and file. This Jewess, who read Cicero, Tacitus and Caesar in the original, believed that the Roman eagle had risen again from its ashes. Her human ideal was entirely classic : she would have liked her son Heinrich to resemble her, to become a man of universal *esprit*, healthy and vigorous. She watched over his studies, tried to orientate him towards mathematics, geometry and natural science. She could already see Heinrich in the uniform of the Polytechnic . . . She taught him that there were neither angels, fairies nor goblins, and that the stories he loved to listen to were the inventions of superstitious peasants.

The child, however, found science—in all its branches, mathematics, systems and classifications—to be thoroughly repulsive. Sensitive, highly strung, a dreamer and slightly wild, he wrote verses rather in the manner of the pious Haller, or the fiery Klopstock—author of the *Messiah*. Nevertheless he took pains to satisfy his mother's wishes and to set a brake on his own temperament. The contradictions and schisms that showed themselves later in his character rose from the conflict between his tender and dreamy nature and the desire to adapt himself to his mother's practical arguments and rational admonitions. Frau Heine frequently mocked her eldest son for his sensitiveness. Could those famous thrusts, those deadly arrows which at times coldly pierce the poet's sentimental outbursts be the repercussions of the mocking remarks made by his mother? We carry in ourselves much of those whom we have loved; united in our hearts they form a small family, sometimes in harmony, but sometimes in conflict among themselves. We are not ourselves alone: we are also our fathers and mothers, our nurses and brothers, our friends and our enemies.

But if Betty Heine did not succeed in making a Polytechnician of her son, she certainly helped to develop his " Bonapartist religion." For Heinrich, as well as for his mother, Napoleon was and remained the symbol of power and earthly glory. It was all very well his hearing his Republican masters at a later date accuse Bonaparte of being a traitor to Liberty and Equality: in spite of himself—despite all reason—Heinrich loved the Emperor. Napoleon was for him the apotheosis of his burning youth, the hopes of his mother and his race; he remained in the poet's eyes the incarnation of the *Marseillaise*, of emancipation, of free trade and unfettered science. The cult which he had built up around the person of Napoleon prevented his staunch adherence to the Republican party. The Republic, to Heine, was a magnificent formula, a glorious idea, but nothing more; Napoleon was a living person, a reality. All his life Heine dreamed of a noble and universal democracy.

Between the 2nd and the 11th of November, 1811, Napoleon paid a short visit to Düsseldorf. In his *Buch Le Grand* Heine paints a grandiose fresco of those days, when with his own eyes he saw the Emperor in the flesh. " . . . Hosannah, the Emperor! . . . Napoleon with his retinue rode down the centre of the avenue, the very trees seeming to bow before his advance, the very sunrays to dart and tremble with an air of curiosity through the green foliage; in the blue sky one could clearly see a golden star. The Emperor was wearing his simple green uniform, and carried the small flag that has become historic . . . He rode on a small white charger; it carried its head proudly, and looked

very calm and distinguished . . . The Emperor sat at ease,
almost relaxed in the saddle, holding the reins in one hand while
with the other he patted the little horse's neck . . . It was a
marble white hand, that gleamed in the sun, a powerful hand—
one of those hands that had crushed anarchy . . . His face was
marble white too, the colour of Greek and Roman busts, with
well-chiselled features, like those old heads which seem to say :
" Thou shalt have none other God but me." A warm smile
played about his lips, which were outwardly quite calm, but which
one could feel had only to whistle and Prussia would be no more
. . . They had only to whistle and the entire Holy Roman
Empire would take fright . . . The drums died away : the
trumpets blared . . . and the German people of Düsseldorf
roared with a thousand voices : ' Long live the Emperor ! ' "

At the end of his unhappy life, a disillusioned witness of the
shabby adventure of the " Little Napoleon," Heine half-admitted
his repentance for having all his life been one of the high priests
of the Bonapartist religion. But so strong were those first impressions that he was never quite able to break with them . . .
with the faith of his youth. He has often been reproached for his
caprices, his inconsequential ideologies, his lack of character, and
his critics have not always been wrong. But what they often omit
to say, and what Nietzsche understood so loyally, is that throughout the peripatetics of his tortured career, Heine remained faithful
to his conception of the superhuman grandeur that Napoleon
stood for in his eyes. In his heart there had been no other God
than Napoleon.

CHAPTER FIVE

CHILDISH DIVERSIONS

IN the courtyard of the house in the Bolkerstrasse there was a huge chicken-coop, which up to a few years ago was still shown to visitors. This chicken-coop was the favourite hiding-place of the Heine children. Heinrich would scream " Co-co-ri-co ! " and Lotte would reply " Co-te-co-da ! " They would laugh, tussle with each other and roll about in the hay. Heinrich would pull his sister's hair, and Lotte would cry and scratch her brother's face. They would squabble, wrestle, and then, laughing, would continue their crowing and cackling.

When they had grown tired of this game, there were other wonderful attractions : the courtyard was full of great packing-cases—what an opportunity to scramble over them and to play hide-and-seek among them ! The largest of these cases served as their " apartment." They had arranged it well. From the attic they had dragged down old strips of threadbare carpet and broken-legged chairs. This was their own house, their very own. How delicious it was to crouch in ! They spent hours in it, chattering and playing. If anyone came near they made wild Red Indian whoops and invited the intruder to pay a visit. They had a regular visitor : the neighbour's cat. They received him with deferential bows, forcing him to take a place of honour, and engaging him in long conversations.

Or else, they would spend their time in imitating the grown-ups. Sitting opposite each other, they would complain gravely :

" Ah ! In our days it was very different," said Heinrich.

" Of course it is different," agreed Lotte.

" How expensive life is, eggs have gone up a penny."

" It is my turn to say that eggs have gone up a penny ! "

" Nonsense, I'm the woman."

They would get angry, and then make it up or sulk with each other.

They also played at heirs, but this was a game that was not confined to the children alone. The whole family played at it—

seriously and quite convincingly. Has there ever been a family of poor Jews that has not relied on a heritage turning up from some fabulously wealthy relation? The Jews, who have been dispersed to the four winds, continue to disperse. There are practically no families that have not, somewhere in foreign lands, an ancestor or a descendant who has made a fortune and who is perhaps without children. How many families suffer their miseries patiently in the hope that one day they will receive a windfall?

One day the postman brought Frau Heine a letter from Nymegen. It read: " Hannelchen, I have great news! You must pass it on to Pinchas of Sieburg. A great *yerouché* (heritage) should fall to the Bock family . . ." Betty read the letter several times. She yearned for the promised *yerouché* as a thirsty Bavarian yearns for a jug of Münich beer. Flinging a shawl around her shoulders she rushed into Samson's shop waving the letter in her hand and crying: " *Yerouché! Yerouché!* Thirteen million pounds—thirteen millions!" Samson's eyes opened wide. The excitement took hold of him in turn, and he echoed the sum incredulously: " Thirteen millions! Thirteen millions! A fortune!" What would his " mighty " brother Salomon, the Hamburg banker, say?

Moses Adolphus von Büren, the Jewish millionaire, had died without heirs in London, and the Bock family of Amsterdam were claimants to his fortune. However, wrote the relation from Nymegen, grandfather Gottschalk had married the daughter of Pinchas Bock of Sieburg. Therefore, if the Bocks had any claim to the inheritance, the van Gelderns must have equal rights. Samson shut up his shop, summoned uncle Simon, and finally called a family council.

Excitement was intense in Betty's homely dining-room. The old people discussed, gesticulated, leaped up from their seats only to sit down again. Samson walked up and down the room with his arms folded on his chest, his face transfigured by a smile of hope. " I always thought that we couldn't go on like this for ever. Something was sure to happen. Thirteen millions! If we only receive one, we can go and live in Hamburg, and perhaps I will go into partnership with Salomon . . ."

Uncle Simon, the scholarly failure, took a pencil and began to work out everybody's share. Looking up, he announced with a shake of his head :

" Well, none of you will be multi-millionaires : the family is too large."

" But, good Lord, even if each one receives only a million it will certainly be better than nothing ! "

" Of course, it wouldn't be bad to have a bit more," put in Samson. He stopped for a moment in front of Simon, arranged his tortoiseshell clasp, and then started walking about nervously once more.

" For goodness' sake sit down ! " said Betty who was becoming irritated.

" Me ? Why should I sit down ? Am I obliged to remain constantly seated ? " Samson replied in his sing-song voice.

In the meanwhile the children listened quietly in a corner, wide-eyed with astonishment. The game was most absorbing. The family council arrived at a conclusion : Simon must write to uncle Pinchas in Sieburg at once. " Although I do not write to you very often, you are often in my mind and I try to safeguard your interests to the best of my ability. As a proof of this I am sending you the news which I have just received, and am eager to pass on to you : you will learn from the enclosed letter that a great inheritance will revert to the family."

There followed a feverish exchange of letters. They made the unfortunate discovery that the world was positively teeming with Bocks. Büren, who had died without heirs, seemed to be suddenly surrounded by near or distant relatives. Samson took the affair so seriously that he travelled to Amsterdam with uncle Pinchas of Sieburg. There they engaged a lawyer, and day after day they planned and eagerly discussed their chances. They tried to persuade the Bocks of Amsterdam to recognise their claims, but the Bocks refused to co-operate. The lawyer encouraged his clients, and they returned home to nurse their hopes.

The case lasted for years. The lawyer had to be paid. Finally, the affair petered out and was forgotten. They had not received a penny of the thirteen millions. But it was marvellous to live like that, in hopes that lasted for weeks—years. It was marvellous to make plans. During the wait Samson had neglected his business ; why should he bother with such trifles when soon . . . However, his brother Salomon, the Hamburg banker, had incurred no such expenses : he went quietly on with his business, always making money, his riches increasing every day. Samson felt for his brother a mixture of admiration and jealousy.

*   *   *   *

One day Heinrich was playing with a little boy named Fritz Wissewsky on the banks of the Düssel near a monastery. Near by, a kitten had fallen into the stream. " Rescue the cat ! " ordered Heinrich, as the elder of the two, to his fair-haired companion. The boy obeyed. Throwing himself into the water, he swam towards the struggling kitten, and was just on the point of seizing it when he was caught in a current and disappeared from view. Heinrich, his feet glued to the ground with fright, wanted to call for help, but not a sound came from his lips. As the boy failed to reappear he started to run, shouting " Help, Help ! " But his little friend was past all aid : the current had thrown his body up, swollen and lifeless, several hundred yards downstream.

Heinrich kept his secret for a long time—the secret of his having urged little Fritz to jump into the water. This was the first time he had come face to face with death. He saw it seize the boy, who a few minutes previously had been sailing his small paper boats, and who now lay dead on the river bank. A fisher-man arrived and covered the body with a cloak ; they lifted it on to a cart and took it home to his unsuspecting mother. " It is I who was the cause of his death," thought Heinrich, horrified, but he said : " I told him not to jump in after the cat, but he wanted to save it at all costs, and wouldn't listen to me."

He was lying and he felt guilty. He had the desire to confess to someone. But he could not. If he should tell his father, what would he say ? Samson would be terribly afraid, and would immediately forbid him to tell anyone. What good would that do ? And his mother ? He must not speak to her either. To Lotte ? She would chatter. " It is I who am to blame for his death . . ."

His way of thinking about his act shows his realisation of the crime committed as well as a certain pride. A painful pride, of which he was ashamed, but pride all the same. He felt with agony that the death of little Fritz did not move him as much as it should have done. Had he been able to understand he would have seen that in the depths of his feeling there was an evil joy. The event began to assume lesser proportions. He did not think about it any more, and children forget quickly. He only recalled it many years later, when he wrote : " When they found his body it was wet and dead. The little cat lived for many years afterwards . . . "

CHAPTER SIX

THE AWKWARD AGE

HEINE, who was never reticent about his childhood, showed himself much more discreet about his adolescent years. For the ordinary individual—and more so for the poet—this period of change is both painful and fraught with pitfalls. The superior type of man develops his personality slower than the normal. Just as mothers force themselves to forget their painful travail, artists usually forget the circumstances which have moulded their characters. A great deal hinges on the manner in which they themselves have shaped their individuality ; on the effort they have made to break away from their environment and from their family ; on the canalisation of their passions, and on their choice of essentials.

We only know the dates and the general outlines of Heine's awkward age. He was a pupil in the Lyceum at Düsseldorf without interruption from 1800 until 1814. In his later works he speaks of two of his professors with affection. The first is old Schallmeyer, the rector, who had been one of Gottschalk van Geldern's classmates, and who had taken a personal interest in him from childhood and wanted to make him a priest. He is largely responsible for awakening in Heine an interest in Greek and modern philosophy. The second is Schramm, a dreamer of the type of Bernadin de Saint Pierre, who wrote a book on world peace. It was he who gave Heine his taste for Classic German literature and the fashionable writers of the day—Klopstock, Lessing and Wieland.

We have reason to suppose that young Heinrich read avidly, though rather unsystematically. He read poetry, romance, history and philosophy, politics and philology, modern and ancient writings, in conscientious preparation for his literary career. When he passed the residence of Pempelfort, where the learned Jacobi brothers had received Hamann, the " North German Mage," Herder—and even Goethe—he must have felt a certain secret pride : *Anch' io sono pittore !* It was during these years as a scholar in Düsseldorf that he discovered, in a German translation, the book that, apart from the works of Sterne, Byron and Goethe, made the most profound impression on him—*Don Quixote.* In the preface to an *édition de luxe* of the epic, which he wrote in 1837, he evokes a melancholy picture of summer afternoons spent reading the adventures of the tragi-comic knight of the rueful countenance, on the moss-covered benches of the " Walk of Sighs " in the Royal Park. Let us note, by the way, that the preface in question is one of the deepest and most mature of Heine's prose works, though written in a light and bantering vein. Unamuno, in a letter to Barrès, describes Heine's analysis as " definitive." The young man understood only too well the conflict depicted in Cervantes' romance : the drama between a sensitive soul brimming over with optimistic enthusiasm, and a realistic spirit, sober and distrustful of illusion. Few men have experienced this conflict to a greater degree than he did himself.

But it must not be thought that the young Heine was just a callow romantic, tormented, rebellious, and carried away by spasms of sadness and anger. The dramatic outlines of his later life slowly begin to appear, but the background has not yet become sombre. On the contrary, Heine appears at this stage to be rather tender, genial and attached to life. Ten years later he would seduce the German and foreign public with the naïve spontaneity of his Love Songs. This guileless mood is by no means artificial, nor an imitation of folk-lore, but fundamentally his natural mood and the real expression of his temperament. His personal conflict would not have been so tragic and heart-rending had his tenderness, his affinity with flowers, birds, murmuring streams and stars sprung only from a sense of artistry rather than from true sensibility. Heine was and remained naïve until his death, and never lost the ingenuousness of his childhood. Certain social circumstances only confirm in him that sympathy which—as Michelet remarked—artists rich in sensibility feel towards artistic manifestations of the people, and more particularly towards the people.

The doors of the patrician houses in Düsseldorf were closed to Jewish boys. Heine's first friends were classmates from un-

pretentious families. In their company he took part in the life
of the people of Düsseldorf, in their cares and rejoicings. He
listened to his companions in the cabarets on the Düssel with a jug
of beer in front of them, singing old songs, alternately malicious,
mysterious or sentimental. He accompanied the singers. The
language of the popular songs became his mother tongue.

His first loves evolved in a whirl of gaiety and colour . . .
" I loved . . . to sit under a window arch near the girls, to laugh
at them and at their laughter, to make them throw their flowers in
my face, and to feign anger until they confided their secrets and other
important stories to me." The names of these gentle, blonde
and blue-eyed maidens do not matter. Whether it were Kather-
ine, Gertrude, Hedwig, Veronica or Joanna, the boy caught his
breath when he saw her, cast longing glances after her or at her
windows during his evening strolls. He fell in love easily and
forgot just as quickly. It was Sephen (Josepha) who made the
greatest impression on him. She was the widow of the Düsseldorf
executioner, and she lived outside the city confines with her sister
—as though ostracised by the law-abiding citizens. This pale, red-
haired girl with enormous eyes taught him strange songs, and
read him macabre stories which frightened her much more than
him, and sought refuge from the spectres she had evoked in the
arms of this stripling with his beardless cheeks.

Or is the auburn Sephen but the invention of the poet who
wrote *Buch Le Grand*? Imagination plays as great a part in even
the most corporeal love as the object itself. *Wenn ich dich liebe,
was geht's dich an*? Heine would write later, rather bitterly.
" The true Amélie," the projection of Heine's unhappy *grand
amour*, had little in common with the real passion inspired by his
cousin Molly. At this time, Molly—it was her nickname in the
family—who was only fourteen years old, had arrived with her
father Salomon to pay a visit to the house in the Bolkerstrasse,
where they were received with the deference due to their rank and
wealth. Salomon, a massive man with broad shoulders, although
in his fiftieth year, was still very erect ; his features were energetic,
his eyes lively and full of irony. Heinrich felt hurt by his uncle's
malicious and condescending remarks and humiliated by his
manner. But he was well aware that he had to control himself,

as his parents had already impressed upon him that Uncle Salomon must be treated with respect ; the family hoped that if their eldest son found favour with the millionaire he would be given a position in the bank at Hamburg, and would thus assure his fortune.

It was 1815, the year of Waterloo. The mirage of the Polytechnic as well as the grandiose projects of the Emperor vanished at the same time. However, the early illusions were replaced by others as soon as the French garrison had left the city. The people of Düsseldorf had long since lost their faith in the Emperor. The French fashion was out of date ; the youth enthused over nationalistic poets, the verses of Arndt and Körner, the revolutionary philosophy of Fichte, the frenzied sermons of " Turnvater Jahn." In the schools they tried to decline the noun *Liberté* with the adjective " German." German Liberty . . . it sounded unfamiliar but enticing. The occupation was no longer a popular feast. To be free of the Napoleonic yoke, whose weight, through the interminable wars, followed by taxes, prestations and requisitions, had only served to increase and to create, thanks to Prussian and Liberal statesmen like the Steins, Mantteuffels, Scharnhorsts and Hardenbergs, a great independent and progressive Germany, to the glory of the human race : this was the ideal of the best Germans in 1810.

Prussian diplomacy had done everything in its power to make the State appear as continental trustee of English Liberalism. The population of Düsseldorf, like that of the other Rhenish towns, lent itself to the Prussian game. The pupil Heine, too, was carried away by the revolutionary current, and would have let himself be enrolled in the popular army had his mother not curbed his enthusiasm. Betty considered—and the future confirmed her judgment—that the cause of Jahn and the Steins was not the cause of her son. Salomon agreed and thought that Heinrich, instead of hankering after military laurels, would do better to start on a commercial career in Frankfurt. " We shall see about the future," said the important uncle with a knowing air.

We must note that Heinrich, towards the end of the visit, had more respect for Uncle Salomon than at the beginning, when he had had great difficulty in controlling his revolt against the banker's tyrannical manners, his pretension to superior knowledge and his business concepts. This change of heart was chiefly due, however, to the tender passion—sometimes frivolous, sometimes " deathly serious "—which he bore the little Amélie, Salomon's daughter. " Molly," in the unanimous opinion of the family, resembled Heinrich very closely. Slim, fair-haired and blue-eyed, this delicate maiden brought an atmosphere of luxury and of the great city into the provincial home of Samson. Her thin proud lips, superior carriage, and long straight nose : all these made her appear to Heinrich the incarnation of a better world—a world in which he realised he would like to have been brought up. Heinrich's sentiment towards his rich cousin was not yet what may be called love, but simply wounded vanity. It is only a short step from hurt pride to love. He wanted to make Molly understand that he, too, in his own fashion, with his ambitions and imagination, was rich and brilliant. He confided to her the secret of his essays in poetry. Blushing and with clumsy compliments, he paid court to the little girl.

One day, Salomon and Molly climbed into the post-chaise, the horn rang out and the coachman cracked his whip. Heinrich stood miserably and waved his handkerchief as the coach disappeared in a cloud of dust. Then he took out his pocket-book, in which he kept a lock of Molly's hair—the pledge of hope. They had never spoken of love ; the kisses they had exchanged were purely fraternal, at least so Molly had thought. But for Heinrich the world had taken on new colours. The buds were beginning to blossom, the sky was brightening, Spring was at hand.

> *Im wunderschönen Monat Mai*
> *Als alle Knospen sprangen*
> *Da ist in meinem Herzen,*
> *Die Liebe aufgegangen . . .*

he wrote some years later, in poignant memory of his first taste of love.

The family, with Salomon's approval, decided that once Heinrich's schooling was over, he should perfect his English in the commercial school at Düsseldorf and then go to Frankfurt, where the banker Rindkopf had promised to initiate him into the mysteries of accountancy and professional practice. Heinrich, although saying very little, bowed to their decision, but without renouncing for a moment his intention of becoming a poet and a writer. But he admitted that Uncle Salomon was right when he announced in his Jewish accent " To be a poet, my lad, is not a profession." Heinrich would have welcomed permission to take a University course in literature, philosophy and law, but Salomon was of the opinion that, under the new régime, Jews would have no chance in a career that these studies opened up. Merchant, banker possibly—or starve : a Jew had no other choice in the Europe of the Holy Alliance . . . And in view of the straightened circumstances of the Düsseldorf family, it would be out of the question for him to go to the University without the help of Uncle Salomon.

The political changes and the interruption of communications with France had brought about a major economic crisis in the Rhineland. The chief traders and industrialists wrote in their memorial to the Prussian Governor Sack : " Thanks to the political changes which have arisen, our country has been freed from the domination of the foreigner, but our business and our manufactures have foundered in the most deplorable manner. Patriotic enthusiasm gave way to general lamentation. Frederick William III had not fulfilled the hopes that had been expected of his reign and victory. The word Liberty was very soon put on the Index ; the activities of commoners and Jews— who had been employed under the Napoleonic regime—were curbed. This was the period when Börne lost his position as Police officer in Frankfurt, and at the same time his faith in the possibility of Prussian Liberalism. This was the period when the plaintive verses of *Die Grenadiere* were born—the poem in which Heine mourns the Emperor :

> *Der Kaiser, der Kaiser gefangen . . .*

France had capitulated, and young Heine was obliged to lay down his arms before necessity. But he was determined that if he were obliged to take up a commercial career, so incompatible with his literary ambitions, it must be in Hamburg where he could see Molly. Since her visit she had never been out of his thoughts.

His stay in Frankfurt lasted only a few months. The banker Rindkopf advised him to leave his house after three weeks, for reasons we do not know. Next, Samson apprenticed him to a wholesale grocer. Heinrich was not long in informing his new employer that the last thing in the world that aroused any interest in him was grocery.

" I will become a merchant if you like. I am quite agreeable. But on one condition : it must be in Hamburg ! " the young man repeated obstinately. At last Samson decided to put his son's request before his brother. " All right, we'll try it out," was Salomon's laconic reply.

CHAPTER SEVEN

OUT INTO THE WORLD

Heinrich lived with the Widow Robertus in a row of old houses in the Grosse Bleiche quarter. He worked all day in Salomon's bank. His superiors treated him with a certain amount of deference, for although he was a "poor relation" the name of Heine impressed them. He did his work quietly and with dignity, like the hero in the fable who, to win the hand of his beloved, tended her father's sheep. In the evening, dressed in a yellow frock-coat, he would stroll, hands in pockets, in the Alster Park or along the *Jungfersteg*—"The Virgin's Walk." This pale adolescent, with his delicate air and boyish figure, his chestnut hair and small moustache which he had cultivated to look more manly, caught the eye of the girls . . . Often, when he had finished work, he crossed the busy streets and made for the harbour "where the golden sunrays played on the tarred ships' sides . . ." He would sit on a bench and listen eagerly to the jolly "Heave-Ho" of the sailors . . . He wrote later : "Such a harbour in the Spring greatly resembles the heart of a young man who is going out into the world, and plunges for the first time into the stormy sea of life. His thoughts are still beflagged with multi-coloured bunting, rashness fills the sails of his desires. Heave-Ho ! — but soon the storms spring up, the horizon darkens."

The horizon was still far from becoming dark. Heine remembered all his life those years passed in the great northern port as a lost and ever regretted paradise. When he arrived in Hamburg, Molly, whom he had not seen for two years, was away on a visit to her mother's family. It was a real test to wait four weeks for her after such a long separation. Finally Amélie arrived, having developed during those two years into a splendid, haughty and coquettish young lady. The garden of the *Château de Rainville* was filled with a noisy band of laughing youth. The young debutantes were surrounded by young clerks, tradesmen and employees of the bank. Over all this fascinating, singing, dancing youth sat Salomon, bearded and severe, intransigent as Jehovah on his throne. Everyone tried to win his favour . . . Heinrich plunged into the whirlpool of activity, taking part in their daily life, their outings and their holidays. He was one of the young people who centred round Molly and the leading lights of Hamburg society, who were all old friends of the house. He captivated them all with his witty sallies, original ideas and bold jokes. It was in Hamburg that Heine became the brilliant conversationalist who, in Berlin and Paris in later years charmed everyone he met. After all, by what means could a poor relation hope to draw attention to himself except by his elegance and witty talent.

Certain malicious biographers of Heine have insinuated that in his love for Amélie, his desire to become one of the millionaire's family played a large if not exclusive part. This theory can be upheld by several telling arguments : one can quote the fact that after the marriage of the " faithless " girl, Heine—as soon as he had recovered from the first shock—had immediately begun to pay attention to Thérèse, the youngest sister. It seems, suggest the biographers, that the young poet's love was inspired more by the size of his uncle's purse and the estimated dowry, than by the persons of Amélie or Thérèse. But perhaps they were forgetting the little masterpieces, the simplest and sincerest in the whole of German if not world literature—the *Lieder*, which were inspired by Heine's love for his two cousins. *Aus meinen grossen Schmerzen mach' ich die kleinen Lieder.* And furthermore, is it so rare that a man who has had an unhappy love affair, or having lost his mistress, seeks to console himself with a sister or a near relative ? No, it is unfair to drag the romantic and spellbound love of the young Heine down by such suspicions. On the other hand, it must not be supposed that his love—or if you wish, his loves— were as simple as his poems suggest, his poems which were as light as a breeze :

> *Ein Jüngling liebt ein Mädchen,*
> *Die hat einen andern erwählt;*
> *Der andre liebt eine andre,*
> *Und hat sich mit dieser vermählt . . .*

It is certain that Heine's love was more complex than this. Love as a rule is always more complicated than we think. There are always underlying problems of which we are unaware ; our relations to the world and our destiny are interwoven with our loves. His uncle, family and social conditions might have played an important part in the development of his sentiments—we are prepared to admit it—but objectively and outside all moral considerations.

His contemporaries had already noticed the ambivalence of feeling that Heinrich displayed towards the banker. At the beginning of their acquaintance he had admired and at the same time detested his uncle. Salomon was, in fact, a curious person : he was brutal and tyrannical, a kind of Jewish condottiere, extremely vain, choleric, capricious and intolerant of any contradiction. " He is one of the men whom I esteem most," Heinrich confided some years later to a friend. " He has an innate nobility and force ; the last of these two traits is for me the essential one." Heine, like Balzac, in whom he found a kindred spirit, was susceptible to forceful and energetic personalities, who inspired in both of them an almost religious devotion. They both liked meeting the heroes of "authentic novels" in the flesh. Above and beyond moral assessments, they appreciated men for their real temperament. Heine's democratic belief and the Royalist concepts of Balzac were based upon the conviction that nobility and aristocracy are not inherited : to be a distinguished nobleman, just as to be a poet, one must be gifted. By this feeling of his innate nobility Heine was the mortal enemy of all privileges of birth ; Balzac deduced from the same feeling the vital necessity for a hierarchic society.

Salomon was a great natural seigneur in his nephew's eyes, while representing at the same time the antithesis of his own temperament and tastes. He wrote to Frederica Roberta, the poetess and sister-in-law of Rahel Varnhagen, in 1825 : " He is a redoubtable man who despite great faults also has great qualities. It is true that we live in constant dispute, but I love him tremendously—perhaps more than I love myself. By nature and in character we are much alike : the same obstinate tenacity, the same boundless tenderness of soul, the same unpredictable folly :

only Fortune has made of him a millionaire and of me a pauper, that is to say, a poet, and for this reason our views on life and our modes of living are very different . . . "

Salomon had but one God—money ; one cult—commerce ; one passion—profit. In the hierarchy of his values gold reigned supreme. All the rest : happiness, renown, women, power . . . these could be bought with money. Rothschild had conquered Napoleon with it. Salomon's whole attitude, his opinions and judgments toward the naïve spirituality of the young poet, were in the nature of a challenge. Heine's pride as a man and as a writer was wounded by his uncle's insulting remarks on the subject of clerks, intellectuals and Talmudists who, according to him, lived—or rather vegetated—outside their period.

Salomon sensed the danger to the stability of his family and to his own convictions in his nephew's wit and growing opinions. He was far too imperious and autocratic to tolerate anyone in his immediate vicinity who contested the faith to which he had devoted himself without reservation. On the other hand, Heinrich's persiflage, intelligence and genial arrogance attracted him. Even the most materialistic Jews cannot resist irony and wit. In his person Heinrich was pleasant and attractive and quite different from Carl, Salomon's own son, whose insignificance was a continual source of shame to the banker. Salomon would have given anything to convert Heinrich to his own ways of thinking, and in fact tried all his life to achieve this end, using every means at his disposal, ranging from generosity to pettiness in all its most irritating forms. On his side, Heinrich strove to bring his uncle to admit the superiority of his own aims, concepts and ambitions. For years he importuned him for money with threats, supplications and cajolery, with humility or violence. In actual fact, it was not so much the money he wanted, for he could have made a living on his own account, but the recognition that this money was his due, not merely as a relative but as a distinguished member of the family, a tribute to the poet who dispensed inestimable wealth to his contemporaries and to future generations, and deserved on this account to be treated by those who had the means with the greatest generosity.

Some years later, after a visit to Hamburg, Heine wrote on the subject of his relations with Salomon to his friend Moses Moser : " My uncle . . . is generosity itself ; but I am firmly resolved to free myself as soon as possible from his bounty." These lines were written in 1823, but in spite of them Heine let himself be financed by Salomon until the old man's death—and even, one might say, beyond the grave. He quarrelled hundreds of times, and frequently broke with the banker—but there was always a reconciliation. Sometimes he felt as though they had arrived at the degree of friendship to which, after so many deceptions, he had always aspired. But invariably Salomon, with an almost sadistic pleasure, would wound Heinrich's pride with one of his insulting and humiliating remarks.

We shall follow later the course of this interminable conflict. For the moment we wish only to cast a glimpse at the relationship which constituted one of the main factors in Heine's life, and without a knowledge of which it would be impossible to obtain a true picture of his love for Amélie and Thérèse. These two loves—or rather, this Janus-headed love, with all its heights and depths, idyllic calms and storms, only represents a secondary episode in the great struggle that broke out at intervals for more than a generation between uncle and nephew, between banker and poet. There were victories on both sides, but the issue remained undecided. The means employed by Heine were not always above-board, but we must not forget that it was for both of them a question of pitiless warfare, which brooked no delicate choice of weapons. Heine cared little for the money—which he needed to continue with his studies, to pay his expenses in Paris and to safeguard his health—no, what he exacted from Salomon had to be a symbol of esteem from the " good, noble, generous, miserly, charming, detestable " banker.

It would obviously have been easier for the poet had he abandoned this incessant and thankless war and been prepared to sacrifice his bourgeois standard of living for poverty, as so many other poets have done, with the approval of posterity as reward. But even during those periods of his life which were most dominated by spiritual aspirations, Heine was a bitter enemy of renunciation and asceticism, and loathed poverty. Although he did not love money for its own sake as his uncle did, he could not give up the comfort, certain refined pleasures requiring immediate satisfaction, and all sorts of desires which money could procure him. He was a proud individual who would admit no one his superior, and with a rooted conviction that he was entitled to preferential treatment in exchange for the gifts that he bestowed on the world in the shape of his genius. He refused to allow that a creative genius—as he quite rightly considered himself to be—should be deprived of his share in the goods of society, such as are enjoyed by any great courtesan or banker.

But let us return to Amélie. "If, by a single word or a single look, I have ever been lacking in respect for you or for your family, which I have loved only too well, then you would have the right to be annoyed," he wrote to his uncle twelve years later from Italy. Heine perhaps never dreamed how true his words were. In and through Amélie, he was devoted to the family and the Hamburg house, of which she was the gayest and most enchanting member. For a long while neither Salomon nor his wife, who incidentally never had much sympathy for Heinrich, noticed his attachment to Amélie. Perhaps the child herself did not really perceive in the beginning that the shy compliments of her cousin, his alternately embarrassed and proud attitude, amounted to anything more than the affection of an impressionable young man. And when Heinrich declared his love, she did not attach undue importance to it. But since she was young, coquettish and vain, and found Heinrich amusing and charming, the game seemed to her desirable, and she yielded to his furtive kisses, his melancholy dreamings, his looks full of significance and the tender pressure of his hands. She thought of the troubadours she had read of in her school-books, and was flattered to receive verses from this young poet whom all the girls stared at and whispered about behind his back—verses that told of exotic flowers, of nightingale song and murmuring streams, of messages from distant stars. She was often sweet and gracious to Heinrich, and made him happy by the wave of a hand, a smile, a flower placed in his buttonhole, or a meaning look. At other times she applied herself with all the age-old cruelty of her sex to make him jealous, by showing some mark of favour to a rival, or to

torture him by her indifference. This apparent coldness naturally only made him the more attached.

Love, poems, good society, excellent food—there was nothing
lacking to render the young Heine happy in Hamburg, or to make
it appear at a later date as the lost Atlantis of his youth and
happiness. He quickly overcame his diffidence, and sent some of
his verses—not under his own name but under the pseudonym
Freudbold Riesenharf—to the *Hamburger Wächter*, where they
were immediately published. He proudly related his success to
an old classmate of Düsseldorf days, Christian Sethe, whose only
comment was : " If the editor of that anti-semitic rag had known
you were a Jew, he would have flung your poems into the waste-
paper basket."

Young Heinrich, during his stay in Hamburg, gave a great
deal of thought to the Jewish question in general, and to his own
case in particular. Certain incidents in the town also attracted
his attention. One day he witnessed a strange demonstration : in
the evening, after the shops had shut, a procession of workmen,
young men and pot-bellied burghers, marched through the town
yelling and decrying the Jews. " Out with them ! Out with
the foreign rabble ! " they roared, breaking several Jewish shop
windows as they passed. It was a miserable sight and a humiliating one for Heine. More so—and here we have the key to his
Jewish complex—because he himself had so little sympathy for
the shopkeepers and profiteers, who were mostly Hamburg Jews.
He himself, a probationer in a Bank, who only that day had
discussed with Salomon the possibility of opening with his help a
warehouse of English cloth to rehabilitate his father's business,
was to become a merchant among the merchants. But no Junker's
son, no son of a patrician official, could have been so revolted by
the thought of a commercial career as Heine. Years later, when
the Saint-Simonist French wished to draw his attention to the
" glory " to be found in economic activity, he declared regretfully
to his friend Varnhagen von Ense that with the best intention
in the world he could not discover a vestige of romance or
poetry in commerce and industry. It was more of an aesthetic
than a moral sense, due to his classical and romantic upbringing,
that made him protest against these practices. And if the word

" Jew " signified a special occupation, he despised both it and the Jew—and himself as much as the Jew. He saw more and more clearly the crux of the Jewish problem : how could one erase the historical legacy of the Jews, when envy of their commercial acumen was revived in every social class, and became an ever-renewed source of anti-semitism ?

At this period, throughout the whole of Germany, the Jews were agitating. Discussions in the Hamburg community were extremely heated between the partisans of " modernism " and Orthodoxy. Heine took no part in these ; liturgical reform did not interest him. He dreamed of deeper and more general reforms, but naturally at the same time deplored the Jewish mentality, by which he felt himself surrounded. He hoped to tear himself away from this spiritually sterile environment. The violence of the German rabble, self-styled Christian, offended his conscience both as a Jew and as a human being. It would perhaps suffice to say only his human conscience, for he had the feeling that if he had not been born a Jew he would have revolted equally strongly against the persecutions unjustly carried out by the authorities and the mob—despite the propaganda of the Encyclopedists—against the sons of Israel. However great the faults of individual Jews, or even the majority of them, faults to which the Christian peoples of Europe are equally prone, they could not possibly justify violence and cruelty. It was at this time that Heine studied the writings of the Encyclopedists and French revolutionaries on Jewish questions, those brilliant and humane texts such as the correspondence of Lessing and Mendelssohn.

If he had hitherto felt his predestination only as a poet, he was now convinced that he had other and more important tasks ahead of him than the writing of sonorous verses or idylls upon Love and Springtime. But to succeed in this task, to continue the noble work of Lessing and Mendelssohn, he would have to learn a great deal, study, and above all break away from his present environment which fettered his spirit like a bird in a cage.

He became more and more constrained and sulky in the shop that Salomon had opened for him, until finally the banker realised that his nephew was utterly unsuited to a commercial career. Perhaps the legal profession would suit him better . . . After discussions, quarrels and entreaties which lasted many months, Salomon generously agreed that Heinrich should enter the Faculty of Law newly founded at Bonn University, the intellectual centre of the Rhineland, and he promised to help towards the expenses. This occurred about the middle of 1819.

Heinrich was not wholly pleased with his victory. It was not so easy to leave Hamburg and Amélie, who latterly had listened with a greater understanding to his woes, cares and projects. The parents still did not suspect—or pretended not to notice—the young couple's attachment. Heine thought later that Salomon had only raised oppositions to his departure as a blind, and that in reality he had been delighted to separate the lovers. It is possible that there was a certain amount of truth in this suggestion.

Before going to Bonn, Heinrich paid a visit to his home in Düsseldorf. He found that his father had aged considerably and was thinking of closing his store. His mother was still very lively—she sold a few of her jewels in secret to give him pocket-money. His sister had grown up, and he confided his secret to her. With regard to his younger brothers, he discovered that Max wrote poetry which he thought superior to Heinrich's. " Better write prose, my dear Max, one poet is trouble enough in the family," Heinrich advised him. He did not feel unduly alarmed, because, in addition to writing verses, Max was an enthusiastic dissector of frogs ; he wanted to become a doctor like his uncle. As for Gustav, greatly influenced by his Virgil studies, he was convinced that the sanest and most beautiful life was to be found in the country, and had decided to go to an agricultural school and become either steward or bailiff of an estate.

After a few weeks' rest in Düsseldorf, Heine took the post diligence for Bonn.

CHAPTER EIGHT

BARON VON SCHLEGEL

THE vast amphitheatre is crammed with students. There is a hum of chatter and bursts of laughter. Someone whistles in the back rows, and then all of a sudden complete silence reigns. A door opens and a little man, slim and elegant, enters the hall. With rapid steps he makes his way to the rostrum. The students stand up, and the professor acknowledges their greeting with a slight nod of his greying head.

Heinrich rises with the others. A feeling of " awe and trepidation " overcomes him. So this is the great Augustus Wilhelm Schlegel, the legendary travelling companion of Madame de Staël on her travels ! Heinrich follows his smallest gestures and hangs on every word that falls from his thin lips. The professor is dressed according to the latest Paris fashion, and the students seated in the front rows can just smell the delicate perfume that he affects. His long gloved hands illustrate certain of his expressions with graceful gestures ; his sentences are rounded and witty. There is a certain worldliness under the pedantic cloak of the professor ; his caustic remarks are accompanied by a " sceptical smile " and in his eyes there is a weariness that is mannered and significant. He speaks in low tones as though he were addressing a circle of intimate friends in a drawing-room rather than giving a lecture. He discusses the history of German literature and language in almost frivolous tones : he might be telling the latest racy Parisian story. The young men with their pale faces, coarsely dressed and reeking of beer, listen spellbound. A liveried footman stands at the professor's side, and when one of the candles in the silver candlesticks begins to gutter he hastens to replace it. Shadows play across the diaphanous, almost feminine face of the professor. His soft, well-modulated voice rises and falls in dithyrambic cadences as he discourses on human harmony and the psychic unity of the Middle Ages. " Awe and trepidation " give place to fascination and enthusiasm : Heinrich, freed from his commercial *milieu*, feels in the outer shadows of this hall as though he were in a hothouse ; he would like to weep and cry with delight.

"The world of make-believe," the professor is saying, "the twitter of birds and the sorrow in our hearts become indistinguishable ; the blue of the sky, our cherished memories and the sweet scents of the meadows unite in ethereal and beautiful arabesques."

He would like to weep, to run up to the Master and kiss his hand. Fortunately no one has noticed his flushed face, his trembling hands.

The "Baron of Literature" is propounding romantic philosophy—for which the poet has a natural bent. Schlegel has awakened in the twenty-year-old adolescent the highest spiritual aspirations. Heine is conquered by the play of irony and sensuality of German romanticism, with its faery atmosphere . . . that half lunary world where monsters dwell. Everything becomes possible, frontiers disappear between the real and the marvellous . . . any idea can materialise . . . the laws of morality and reason no longer apply. The freedom of dreams is the dominant factor for Heine in this world whose principles Schlegel has revealed.

He has not yet realised that he is destined to be at one and the same time the champion and stern enemy of these flights into the infinite, these heavy mists of sensibility, and that the clear-sightedness and cold criticism defined by Schlegel as the evil heritage of French eighteenth-century wit will be revived in him, and he will destroy with his own hands the azure blossoms of romantic illusion . . .

He was taking Law, but attended few of the lectures given by Mackeldey and Welcker. Apart from Schlegel's lectures on Aesthetics he only attended a few History classes. He haunted the University Library, and simply devoured the *Minnesinger*. He studied the songs of the great Walther von der Vogelweide, and the works of the romantic poets. While walking through the little winding streets under the leafless trees he would declaim the *Lieder*. Dressed in a woollen overcoat, his hands thrust deep in his pockets or joined behind his back, he would stroll with the uncertainty of a convalescent—one could say with Baudelaire

" like an albatross that planes majestically and surely through
the air, but once on the ground he feels clumsy and feeble
. . ." A shy, almost childlike smile played constantly about
his lips. Was he a prey to his mad thoughts, to his sorrow, to
his ungratified desires, or to his loneliness ?

*   *   *   *

In Hamburg he had never been entirely alone ; the " family "
had always been there to comfort and protect him from the unknown. Invitations had been a distraction that annoyed him
but kept him busy. Now the family was far away—and so was
Molly. So was the musical club in Düsseldorf where, clumsy and
shy, he had learned to dance. He missed his sister Lotte ;
sometimes he fancied he heard her clear open laugh. He was
alone, even though he had found again his great childhood
friend Christian Sethe. Christian had changed ; he seemed to
avoid him and to be more at ease with his new friends. When
they met they embraced as brothers, but they were both ill at
ease. Christian felt it most : he was hiding something. Was it
that he feared to be compromised by associating with a Jew ?

Heinrich became sceptical of friendship. Hitherto he had
looked upon it as a defensive and offensive alliance to last a
lifetime, and perhaps even beyond life—a perpetual exchange of
confidences and a source of mutual consolation. He had imagined
it as a bond impervious to mere vanity, above any social or racial
prejudice, beyond all personal interest, jealousy or intrigue.

One day he called upon Christian and accused him directly :
" You don't love me any more, and you haven't the courage to
tell me so. You're not a man ! " Christian's eyes moistened and,
throwing himself into Heine's arms, he cried : " How can you
think such a thing ? You are mad ! " They sat down on the
yellow-covered bed and embraced and wept for a long time.
Reassured, Heine left him, but as he was crossing the courtyard
he felt that tears had not solved the problem. He retraced his
steps to his friend's room.

" By the way, I forgot to ask you whether you had read Rühs'
book ? "

" Who ? " replied Christian hesitatingly.

" Rühs' book on Jewish claims to citizenship in Germany. What is your opinion ? " He looked hard at his friend.

" I think . . . "

" What do you think ? "

" Oh, he exaggerates a lot . . . I know it's true there are a lot of Jews who've almost entirely lost their nationality, like Neunzig, like you, or many others—"

" He doesn't only exaggerate ! " screamed Heinrich, his eyes blazing. " No, my friend, he vilifies and lies outrageously— and it's you who ought to say it, not me. You are a pitiless and appalling race ! " Heine was livid with rage. " I detest everything German," he yelled, " and you as well, for you are a German. Everything German makes me vomit—the word German offends my ear like the caterwauling of lecherous tomcats at night. I loathe my poems too, because they are written in German. I would never have thought that these animals who are called Germans could be such a stupid and wicked race . . . and I am going to leave Germany and go to Arabia . . . I hate you ! "

Christian listened to this diatribe without interruption. Heinrich leaned against the door and sobbed ; his whole body was trembling.

" You are not being just, Heinrich," the fair-haired German said gently.

" You are not qualified to speak of justice ! " replied Heinrich, slamming the door behind him with a note of contempt in his voice. On the following day he apologised and asked forgiveness in a long letter . . .

He was now alone, quite alone. He felt an exile, a stranger among these students who sauntered through the town and swilled their beer. He could not mingle with them and enjoy their company. *Ich tanz' nicht mit.* He could neither carry liquor nor smoke a pipe, and in his desire to remain inconspicuous did not join in their clandestine orgies with the buxom wenches of Bonn. He felt like a beggar, and could almost have begged at street corners for a little love, warmth and understanding. Sometimes a kind word would move him deeply, at other times he would adopt his haughty air and play the proud genius : he would clown and make a mockery of everyone, and alienate even those who were well disposed towards him. More and more often his companions heard his fine shrill laugh—*das schöne gelle Lachen*—which sounded strangely like a sob. It was a bitter, sardonic laughter which disfigured his whole face, fearful and provoking, insolent and suppliant, sorrowful and cruel ; the laughter of defeat, neurotic, unhealthily gay ; a laughter that protested against his loneliness, weakness and impotence ; funereal and mourning laughter which bantered and railed against his own destiny.

Sometimes a desire for vengeance seized him. He would unexpectedly swing from the defensive to the attack, and mercilessly lay bare the foibles of his companions ; a fusillade of savage laughter would follow. Unlucky the victim singled out for his attack : to his dying day those diabolical phrases would ring in his ears. It was a hostile and ill-starred music to a German ear.

*   *   *   *

The young poet was castigating himself, wallowing in his suffering, tearing at his own wounds, and finding therein a strange, sensual delight. The echo of his fine shrill laugh remains.

Occasionally there were moments of respite, moments almost of happiness . . . of harmony. The spirit wearied of anger and self-conflict, of banter and ridicule against the world. Sometimes, lying with a girl on a river bank, a calm lassitude would envelop him, a far-away look would come into his eyes, and an unattainable happiness seemed within his grasp.

One day he was reading the poetry of a certain gentle and charming poet called " Riesenharf " to a class-mate, J. B. Rousseau, and began to tear some of the poems to pieces. How terrified he was lest Rousseau should agree with him ! But his friend, suspecting nothing, passionately defended this unknown poet's lyrics : " Those verses are the best of any new German poetry ; Riesenharf is one of the best modern German poets." Amidst tears of pleasure Heine cried : " I am Riesenharf ! " They embraced each other and became inseparable friends.

Heinrich then made a bold move : one afternoon he took his verses to Schlegel. The professor received him kindly, and read the poems. His heart beating fast, and holding his breath, the young aspirant to Parnassus waited for his verdict. It was favourable. " It is good poetry, but you will have to work very hard . . . There are too many rococo mannerisms and too much artificiality in the verses . . ." Schlegel was a very severe critic. " Your Muse, my young friend, still wears a hooped skirt and a flowered bodice, her face is made up with beauty spots, she has a wasp waist and her hair is tired to a monstrous height—" Heine protested timidly, but the professor went on : " I know, I know . . . the poems show your first deception : you do not love her any more, you are already unfaithful to her in your heart. But you have not yet met—you are looking for, and certainly on the right road to finding—your new love. In the North, in the arbour of some secular manor, the radiant lady sleeps an enchanted sleep. She is the real German Muse. Pale, dolorous Knights, spurred on by their nostalgia, fervidly seek her. Perhaps you, my friend, will find the magic word to awaken her from her long sleep. Then the bells will ring out, the trees begin to sing, and nature will wake from *her* sleep. The ruins will be transformed into a fine palace, and the Gods of Greece will reappear in all their pristine splendour . . . May Apollo guide your footsteps."

No wine had ever intoxicated young Heine more than the words of this great aesthete who had crowned him poet.

CHAPTER NINE

THE BYRON OF GÖTTINGEN

At Bonn Heinrich had studied poetry assiduously, but sadly neglected Law. At the wish of his parents and Uncle Salomon, who was financing his studies, he entered the ancient university of Göttingen in October, 1820. He had the firm intention of immersing himself in jurisprudence and devoting only his leisure hours to the Muse. " I am horribly bored," he wrote of his first days in Göttingen. " It is celebrated for its sausages and its university ; it has nine hundred and ninety-nine lights, several churches, a madhouse, an observatory, a prison, a good library and a municipal tavern where the beer is excellent." The only course that interested him was High German poetry, given by a professor named Beneke. He felt completely lost among his new companions, these " Burschen " who boasted of descent from " Vandals, Frisians, Swabians, Teutons, Saxons and Thuringians . . . " whom he saw in hordes, distinguishable only by the colours of their student caps and their pipe trimmings, strolling down the Weenderstrasse, duelling daily amongst themselves on the training fields of Rasenmühle, Ritschenburg and Bowden . . . " Races who have retained the usages and manners of the time of the great folk migrations, and who are governed partly by their dukes, whom they call *cocks*, and partly by their Gothic code which they call *comment*, and which deserves a place *in legibus Barbarorum*."

He found the students even more gullible and narrow-minded than the philistines, whom he despised, except that they were more boisterous, more pretentious, and more insolent. The Hanoverian aristocracy sent its sons to Göttingen. Heine's bourgeois blood always boiled when he recalled those noble youths who spoke of nothing but their dogs, their horses and their family escutcheons. They seldom graced the modern History class, and then only because they were fascinated by the " Counts' Table," at which they were assured a place. This table was reserved exclusively for students of high birth ; it characterised to perfection the servile spirit of the Göttingen university.

It was here, in this old town, that Heine saw for the first time the rudiments of the feudal system, which had almost completely disappeared in the more commercial and populous Rhineland. Here in Göttingen he made the acquaintance of "the old Germany" about which the old romantic poets spoke so delightfully. And he, who recognised no authority or privilege outside that of the spirit, conceived a hatred of the aristocracy represented by the Hanoverian Junkers in the university. Among the leading minds in Europe there were few more bitter enemies of this class than Heine.

* * * *

The clock in the adjacent dining-room strikes midnight. It is the moment of phantoms, spirits and lovers. Sublime and perfect hallucination ! Fine and wondrous chords surge and murmur in his ears. O ecstasy of the poet ! Sweet reveries. There is a knock at the door, already the Exquisite glides into the room. There is a scent of roses. Her dress is a thin veil. " Oh, Molly . . ." murmurs the poet, " you are slender as a Gothic tower, your hair is a spray of flowers ruffled by the wind. You are sweet, tender as a roe in the Tiergarten, and I am as savage as a wolf. My blood is on fire, the anguish of possession is upon me and I will tear the delicate flesh of your frail body . . . How magnificent is the aura that surrounds you ! How it shines as for a celebration ! Palace of crystal, faery music ! You have the intoxicating scent of musk roses . . ."

And suddenly the light vanishes, the crystal breaks and the music dies ; the vision of fragrant muslin has disappeared. The unhappy poet is alone in his bare student's room. Nothing remain but a few trite verses and the agony in his heart. Eternal refrains of his existence . . . an icy shower on his fevered body . . . eternal disenchantment, eternal deception . . . unfulfilment . . . " I kissed her mouth and breathed the heady zephyr of her soul, and felt the sweet trembling of her charming lips . . ." But in an instant the darkness descends, and all is confused in a

Rachel Varnhagen

[To face p. 64

Charlotte Embden, Heine's sister

[*To face p.* 65

wild and angry sea. How sad that his dreams should always finish so unhappily.

* * * *

It was probably the dramatic lyrics of Byron, which he read at this period, that influenced Heine to set his broken passions in dramatic form. The majestic personality and indomitable temperament of Byron and the sombre ardour of his verse had a liberating influence upon young Heine. " He is the only man with whom I feel an affinity," he admitted several years later, when he heard of the death of the author of *Manfred*. He found in Byron all that he had sought in vain in German romanticism, which was effeminate and at the same time tinged with feudalism : promethean revolt, fever of modernity, cult of the renaissance, contempt for normal morality and hypocrisy and a virile affirmation of the sovereign rights of poetry.

Almansor, which he began to write in 1820 at Göttingen, is a lyric drama like *Manfred* or *Cain*. The Moorish intrigue of an old Castilian tale served as a pretext for Heine to open his heart. "I have put into it the whole of myself : my paradoxes, my wisdom, my love, hatred and all my folly . . ." he wrote on the subject of his work in progress to Steinmann, a colleague at Bonn University.

The hero of the poem is Almansor, an Arab troubadour of proud and noble character, who escapes from the Spanish Conquistadors and returns to his own country to see his Zuleima once more and to carry her off. No sooner have we read the first few lines than we can recognise in the hero Heine of Düsseldorf. The chief theme of *Almansor* is the burning hatred of the outraged Moor for his Christian conquerors. The Arab troubadour returns to Castille disguised as a Spaniard, but his humiliated spirit soon produces this fiery admission :

> *Trotz Hut und Mantel bin ich doch ein Moslem,*
> *Denn in der Brust hier trag' ich meinen Turban.*

He burns to take vengeance on the Christians, who have forced the surviving Moors to accept their barbarous and insensate laws and to submit to a hypocritical farce.

Heine freed himself of many a choking and sombre fixation once he had expressed in these stormy verses all his Jewish hate and misery. But *Almansor* is not only a drama of suffering and hatred, it is also a testament of tender love. If Almansor represents Heine, Zuleima is the incarnation of Amélie who, in her father's fortress, faithfully awaits the return of her lover . . . But is she really faithful? The doubts that tortured Heine during his sleepless nights come to life in the drama. Zuleima's father, Ali—who in spite of his national costume is an unmistakable portrait of Salomon Heine — forgetting his promises, forces his daughter to marry an insignificant young man, a young Spaniard whose only interest is her dowry. Perhaps Heinrich had learned in the meantime that his uncle had already chosen a husband for Amélie. In the play, Almansor learns with horror on his arrival that his fiancée, who loved him, is to be led that very day to the altar. Drawing his gleaming sword, he rushes with his companions among the wedding guests and abducts Zuleima at the height of the feast; he carries her off into the mountains where, in a paroxysm of love and hate, he plunges with her into an abyss.

While writing this piece Heine felt that he was offering to the world a work of undying glory. Some months later his enthusiasm waned. "There are scenes and passages of staggering beauty, its originality is very striking throughout; sparkling images and thoughts of surprising lyricism follow in quick succession . . . but the dramatic critics, ruthless and perfidious, declare that it is only a fine piece of mechanical brassware . . . Is it possible that I have no dramatic talent?" The chief requirement of a dramatist is a capacity to slough his individual limitations : this was lacking in Heine. The worth of his play was only to be found in the lyrical rhapsodies and tirades, but his language often degenerates pathetically into hollow rhetoric. The plot is ludicrous, childish and primitive. But we must not forget that *Almansor* is the work of a twenty-three year old student, and that it showed a real poetic feeling far in advance of the romantic plays then being shown on the German stage.

Three years later the Director of the Brunswick Theatre offered a production of *Almansor* to the public. There was an uproar on the first night. The hisses were not directed against the dramatic shortcomings, but against Heine the Jew—or, if you prefer, Almansor the Moor—who would not accept defeat but rebelled against the injustices of the Christian order. It was useless Heine's protesting " that they wished to interpret the spirit of his verses by the history of their author." The plot was far too obvious, its tone far too lyrical for the public not to identify it with the author's private life. Nor was Salomon Heine particularly pleased with his portrait as his nephew had drawn it. He was on the point of breaking off all relations with the ungrateful young man and withdrawing his material support. However, already Zuleima—Amélie . . .

CHAPTER TEN

BERLIN 1821

ONCE he had finished *Almansor* Heine did not stay long at Göttingen. One evening in a cabaret he had a quarrel with a fellow student named Wilhelm Wiebel who, while in a state of drunkenness, had probably accused Heine of lying. Heine refused to accept the insult and challenged him to a duel with pistols. The University authorities intervened and the duel did not take place, but Heine received the *consilium abeundi*, that is to say, an order to leave Göttingen for six months.

He was not unduly alarmed by this interruption of his stay at Göttingen and asked the permission of his parents and his uncle to continue his studies in the Berlin University, because the best teachers in Germany were to be found there, in particular Hegel, the greatest philosopher since Kant, who had revived the philosophy of law, and Hasse, Schmaltz, Bopp and Raumer. Some weeks later, after a flying visit to Lüneburg where his parents now lived, Heine arrived in "Athens on the Spree."

The University windows looked out on to the street. By craning one's neck a little, one could see the Opera House. "For the poor student it is like sitting on live coals," wrote Heine ; " the feeble jokes the professors make fall on deaf ears, and his eyes wander ceaselessly out into the street where he may delight in the gay scene of smart coaches, marching soldiers and nymphs sporting . . ."

After lectures the students, with high Bolivar hats after the English fashion, or wearing the traditional red cap and beaver, would wander nonchalantly towards *Unter den Linden*. Heine, too, preferred the fresh air of the lime-bordered avenue to the white-washed walls of the university. He had had several new suits made by the best tailor, bought an ivory-topped cane and tied up his hair which he had been accustomed to wearing down to his shoulders. He would spend one evening at young Felix Mendelssohn's concert, and the next at the Opera.

The music-crazy Berlin public was divided into two camps : just as in the Paris of Marie Antoinette there was rivalry between the admirers of Glück and Piccini, so now in the " new musical capital " there were the devotees of Weber and Spontini. The aristocracy swore by Spontini while the bourgeoisie hummed the arias of Weber's *Der Freischütz*.

The works of Sir Walter Scott were in great demand in the libraries—whose catalogues were constantly under police supervision. The sentimental Berlin ladies wept copious tears over *Waverley*. When the novelist's son passed through Berlin and attended a great masked ball in national costume, everyone affected costumes representing his father's characters. The political police arrested thirty students on charges of demagogic agitation. Heine felt in his element in the midst of this whirlpool of activity in the rising capital.

No sooner had he arrived than he called on Gubitz, the editor of the fashionable review *Gesellschafter*. " Would you care to publish my poems ? " Gubitz looked a trifle surprised at the stranger. " I'm sure I am quite unknown to you, but I should like you to get to know me," continued Heine proudly. His self-assurance succeeded.

" Willingly, if it is possible," replied Gubitz, recovering his calm. The poet left his first sentimental and ironical *Lieder* with the publisher. A few days later he received a letter . . . Very slowly he opened the envelope : his poems would appear in the following numbers of the review.

He became popular overnight. Since the appearance of the young Goethe, no one had written such pure verses in German, so fresh in their charm. The best critics in Berlin were amazed by this new star and wished to make his acquaintance.

At the Café Royal Gubitz introduced Heine to his friends and collaborators, to Cosmeli the celebrated globe-trotter who had just returned from his journey to Turkey and Russia, to Doctor Koreff, Spontini's librettist, and to the philologist Wolf. Among the habitués of the Café was E. T. W. Hoffmann, the author of *Kater Murr und Meister Floh*, who attracted Heine the most. Hoffmann, as judge and member of the " Research Commission into Demagogic Activity," explained laughingly to him that he ought certainly to condemn himself to death on account of the subversive ideas that obsessed him . . . Heine read his manuscripts of the fantastic tales with unbounded pleasure, with their calm and idyllic background which changed suddenly into a world of exotic characters and phantoms, where monsters groaned and all the mysteries of the night took shape.

He discussed at length with Hoffmann the reasons for the difference between the German, French and English novel. The English novelists displayed a realistic conception of the world, while the French *romanciers* expressed the psychology of worldly heroes with Gallic elegance. Hoffmann attributed the peculiarities of the German novel and its unreality to the poverty and social conditions of the German writer, who was looked upon as an " original " ; shut up in his attic, he was obliged to create from his imagination a world peopled with imaginary figures instead of with real people, because these he had never known. " Thus, this type of romantic novel has greatly influenced the character of the people," pronounced Hoffmann, " and this is why, of all the nations in the world, we Germans are the most susceptible to mysticism, secret societies, natural philosophy, demagogy, to absurdities and—" with a knowing wink to Heine—" to poetry."

It was probably Gubitz who introduced the young poet to Varnhagen von Ense, whose salon had for some years been the meeting-place of the boldest and most cultured spirits. At first he had felt a little embarrassed among these men, who were all older and more mature than himself—Hegel, Schleiermacher, Baron de la Motte-Fouqué, Humboldt and Chamisso—but Varnhagen's wife Rahel very soon put him at his ease by her maternal sweetness and tender friendship. This woman, who was nearly forty, was one of the outstanding personalities of the period. She was a refined and quick-witted Jewess ; her most likeable trait was the cult she had made of the greatest of German poets, Goethe. It must not be forgotten that the contemporaries of the genial Minister of Weimar treated his artistic achievements with great reserve. His works like *Werther, Iphigenie,* and the *Elective Affinities* were popular enough, but neither the poet himself, his tendencies nor the significance of his art were really understood.

The German youth had turned its back on the Master since the Napoleonic war, because the patriotic authors then in vogue had accused him of treason, indifference and coldness. Rahel felt instinctively what a superhuman and important work the patrician of Frankfurt had undertaken. Just as she had previously done with her husband, Hegel, Humboldt and the other intimates of her Berlin salon, she now undertook Heine's initiation into the Goethe cult. As she filled his cup with golden aromatic China tea she would whisper her modest and passionate reverence for Herr von Goethe.

The first time she had seen Goethe in Frankfurt—the Weimar Councillor was in his carriage—she had nearly fainted with sheer joy. She ran after the carriage crying: "It's Goethe! It's Goethe!" Goethe looked round and, flattered by the enthusiasm of the young woman, smiled amiably at her. Shortly after this episode he paid her a visit.

"Oh, my dear friend," she told Heine, blushing a little at the vivid recollection of this meeting, "everything was against me that morning. I had risen late; at nine o'clock I was still seated at my mirror. A servant came in and announced that a gentleman wished to speak to me. Who could this visitor be? I sent Dora to find out, and she returned at once with Goethe's visiting card: 'The gentleman said he would wait . . .' Show him in at once! I told her. I hastily flung on a black peignoir, and that is how I went down to meet him . . . Even today I still feel ashamed, but I preferred to risk his disfavour than to keep him waiting. One does not keep a Goethe waiting! I was most embarrassed. "Thank you for coming," I said to him, quite forgetting to apologise for my attire. We spoke of trivialities—of course there were a thousand things I would have liked to ask him, but it is often thus when, after years of hopeless love, one meets the object of one's adoration and very reason for existence face to face . . ."

Rahel had devoted herself ardently to her cult, and she defended and spread it with fervour. Heine listened to her eulogies with impatience and jealousy. It was hard for him to bow to the superiority of Goethe, whom he considered Rahel over-estimated, and he was bold enough to disagree with her.

" Heinrich is not old enough yet for Goethe," she affirmed, unshakable in her faith. " One must mature, become polished, and educate oneself to be able to appreciate the wisdom of the Weimar poet—to appreciate that Goethean harmony which, with all its contradictions embraces the entire universe." It was not the poet that Rahel admired most in Goethe, but the pedagogue : this greatest exponent of humanity, who by his pagan and hellenic pantheism, by his life which seemed at times amoral, had created a superior morality and a code of ethics for a spiritual élite. Heine admitted at this period to having been " ill, soured, sulky, temperamental and insupportable." He might almost have been Rahel's son, so kindly and graciously did she treat him. After all, had he not also a right to a revolutionary period, to a stage of *Sturm und Drang* ? Revolt and discontent are certainly not Goethean : the man imbued with the Goethean spirit revolts against nothing, for his spirit contains that which he would revolt against. But a young man can plunge into the vortex of passion and chaos, from which at length he will derive balance and harmony.

Rahel and her husband, an aristocrat with Liberal leanings, watched the unrest and intransigence of their protégé with patience and indulgence. Something about him, his seductive naïveté, his impulsiveness, reminded them of the young Goethe—of Werther.

" Oh, Youth ! " cried Varnhagen one day with great feeling, when Heine had confided to him his boundless ambitions. They knew and felt that he was a real poet. They recognised the force, the savour and perfume, the originality of his writing. " A ne'er-do-well favoured by the Graces," Rahel often proclaimed.

The electric atmosphere of the Varnhagen salon gave free play to the young man's love for polemic ; he discussed heatedly and with verve. His intimacy with the Varnhagens was a decisive factor in his development as a poet and thinker. The least praise from Rahel was enough to make him forget the poisoned jibes of his critics, and make him happy ; he was filled with gratitude and admiration for her. " I shall tie a ribbon round my neck on which will be inscribed : ' I belong to Rahel Varnhagen ' . . ."

It was in a corner of this drawing-room in the Französische Strasse that he listened to Hegel expounding the ultimate objectives of his system ; there before his eyes he saw unroll the new pattern of human history. Varnhagen first called his attention to the activities of the French Saint-Simonists, to the *Globe*, to Michael Chevalier and his companions. Thanks to them his ideas found a new outlet, and he turned his attention to the particular social questions and problems of the nineteenth century. And if sometimes his intractable character and susceptibility made him suspicious of hidden motives in the advice given by the Varnhagens, sometimes to a point where he would retire in a sulk, he always came back in the end. He was faithful to them, just as Varnhagen, for the rest of his lifetime, remained his faithful friend and protector. In Heine's life, so full of misunderstandings, struggles and intrigues, his relationship with this couple represents one of the most human and sunny episodes.

Soon after Heinrich's *Lieder*—which had formerly been published individually in the *Gesellschafter*—appeared in a single volume, and overnight made him famous throughout Germany, he felt urgently in need of the protection and support of the Varnhagens. If his talent, his original and lively verse, made him many friends—Immermann of Düsseldorf, a much older man than himself, hailed him in the *Anzeiger* as the most brilliant young man of his generation, and the *Almanach* of the Rheno-Westphalian Arts sought permission to publish his poems—the number of his enemies also increased.

No sooner does an original nonconformist talent arise, in whatever age or country, than a conspiracy against it is automatically born. Historians have hitherto perhaps paid insufficient attention to this phenomenon, whose importance in the life of an artist cannot be over-estimated. Men normally well disposed, worthy people and loyal friends, immediately begin to vociferate when, with their amazing intuition, they sense a superior talent and originality which might prove a challenge to their mediocrity. Even when they harness themselves to his chariot, it is only the better to quench their hatred and malice. The attentions they shower upon him are only to hasten his downfall. They play on the vanity of his genius, swear eternal friendship, sing his praises ... but insidiously poison his moments of happiness, sow doubts in his heart, watch for his weaknesses and his vulnerable points. The conspiracy forms against him with all the powerful organisation of the sterile. They smother him with their hypocritical friendship—he who is athirst for love and understanding. They claim the right of superiority by virtue of their greater numbers, which is never valid in the realms of creation and the spirit. They take pleasure in persecuting the artist, who is already a martyr to his own sensibility and suffering. These mediocrities fight slyly among themselves for the places of honour—but they are always united against the common enemy. They set themselves up as judges and critics, as intermediaries and founders of schools ; they defend sacred " tradition " if the poet steps beyond it, and extol the *avant-garde* if he adopts the traditional medium. Under the pretext of giving encouraging advice to the artist they incite him to useless endeavour. They cleverly place him in some category, and it takes a tough customer indeed to escape from the coffin in which he finds himself. Obviously, they follow his work closely as it evolves—as needy relations with an eye to a legacy will watch the health of a rich old uncle—and they throw out glances of undisguised joy when they learn that inspiration has dried up and he is brought to a halt. They would give everything they possess to desiccate, in some miraculous fashion, the artist's very heart. They harry him unceasingly and without mercy, like the waves assaulting a proud and solitary cliff.

Heine, who was suspicious by nature, would soon have seen through his enemies, but at first he was discouraged, repelled and disgusted. How unworthy to struggle against these dwarfs, who hungered after immortality and deserved no more than a short-lived span ! What a sordid occupation to have to justify oneself day by day to aggressive mediocrity ! Furthermore, what defence was possible against vindictive senseless poetry-lacking oafs, these Fres' and Rühs, who in the city and provincial papers proclaimed him Jewish poet and not German, reproached him for imitating Goethe and accused him of the immorality which he was to hear so much about in later life. These inferior minds, with which the German literary world was teeming, discouraged him and occupied his mind far more than the half-crazy, half-genius Grabbe, who also hated him, because he sensed a dangerous competitor.

Grabbe, the son of a drunken gaoler, haggard-eyed, dishevelled and reeking of beer, was at least merely coarse. One day he burst into Heine's room bringing with him a wild and ill-balanced tragedy. "Professor Gubitz told me to show you my play, for he says you are as mad as I." He hurled the manuscript down on the table and stamped out, banging the door behind him.

The play smacked so much of talent that Madame Varnhagen, whose spirit was intimidated and warped by her classic standards, and to whom Heine had entrusted the manuscript, summoned him urgently. "Come and fetch this drama immediately, Heinrich, for I cannot sleep while it is in the house."

Heinrich tried to help the savage and barbarous poet. "He is no fool, he is a genius," he said to Gubitz; and he could not be angered when he learnt that Grabbe too—that drunken Shakespeare, as he called him later—had turned against him. When, after some months of acquaintance, Heine refrained from publishing anything new, Grabbe announced triumphantly to his clique in the tavern: "It is all up with the divine inspiration of Heine: the Christian Muse has left him for ever, this hideous and insignificant little Jew, this Jewish poetaster from Düsseldorf. Their hybrid marriage was dissolved—and it is not surprising," he added with a burst of laughter, "since our little friend has never known how to satisfy a woman." This tirade was immediately repeated to Heine.

Heine was not seriously offended, for he knew well the susceptibility of this bewildered and misunderstood being who drowned his visions and suffering in alcoholic stupor. He understood Grabbe's jealousy of himself, for he had, despite everything, achieved a success with his graceful and mannered *Lieder*. He understood and pitied him, and had far more sympathy for him than for the intriguers with their Judas smiles.

Heine forestalled Nietzsche in his clear perception of the "resentment" felt by the ineffectuals, those Lilliputian though powerfully organised minds who waged a pitiless war with every weapon at their disposal, but chiefly under the pretexts of morality, patriotism and race, against the creative lone wolves. But after a short spell of disappointment he pulled himself together. He would show them! If they wanted ruthlessness they should have it! If they spun webs of intrigue he would counter with other meshes. If they chose to make literature a question of power politics, and set themselves up between the author and the public, he would beat them at their own game.

He looked around for allies. He tamed his attackers by compliments or with threats; he played their shady game, which he despised and ridiculed. But he had to play it in order to protect himself, to be assured of success—of immortality. So, like some Richard III who elects to be evil, Heine decided to become a " politic " writer. As such he wished to build up his artistic success and authority by employing factors auxiliary to the intrinsic value of his art. It was not enough to conceive a work, to produce a masterpiece : one must launch it on its way, protect it like a helpless child and make friends for it, or otherwise it will remain alone and will die. Success must be " organised " minutely; it requires publicity—like any commercial merchandise. In the face of natural and organised enemies of the spirit of creative poetry one must enjoin support, and this end justifies all means—cajolery, hypocrisy, mutual assistance, implacable revenge. When later in life he was reproached for the viciousness of certain of his attacks, he replied with a shrug : " What would you ? It is war." For him it was a necessity to defend his work, his honour and his ideas, and he believed in the right to identify them with his person. Because of this many misunderstandings arose. But if others have made war with more tact and moderation, no one has made it with more wit and vigour than Heine. Others preferred to poison or ambush their enemies. Heine executed them.

CHAPTER ELEVEN

THE GREAT JEWISH SORROW

AT the Berlin University, during the Course of Philosophy and Law, Heine met a student of his own age called Eduard Gans— Hegel's most brilliant and loyal pupil. This young man, also of Jewish origin, was destined later to become one of Germany's most distinguished jurists and champion of liberal principles. He extended his sympathy towards the turbulent ambitious poet, and very soon considered him worthy of entry into the circle of intellectual Jews with whom he had founded " The Society for the Propagation of Culture and Judaic Knowledge."

Certain historians, like Max Brod, look upon this organisation—founded by the young Berlin scholar towards 1820—as the forerunner of the modern Zionist Movement. We do not think that this is historically accurate. The object of the Zionists is to enable dispersed, persecuted and homeless Jews to found a new national State. Gans, Moser, David, Zunz, Marcus, Wohlwill and the other young men who came together in the Berlin Society, had no dreams of founding a new fatherland. Their movement was of a more cultural than political nature. The rules of the Society were framed " to put the Jews, by a process of inner cultural evolution, in harmony with the State in which they lived." Like his new friends, Heine was saturated with science and modern German philosophy. Their native language was German and not Hebrew or Yiddish, and they felt and considered themselves Germans. But at the same time they all agreed that it would be unworthy of them to deny their ties with the race of their origin, and to dissolve the solidarity with their co-religionists, among whom were mingled Hebrew, Yiddish and German elements in such an inextricable confusion that there seemed no possible solution.

We must not forget that we are concerned with an age whose philosphers were baffled by the many phenomena that accompanied the commercial and industrial revolution, and who sought in the past the answers to the agonising questions of the present. It was Hegel who had formulated the dominant idea of the century under the term *Werden !* (to become), that is to say, Evolution. Everything being in constant transformation and full flux, we can only discover the direction and goal of evolution by exploring its origins. Gans and his companions chose this method—which one may call Hegelian—of finding their path.

They knew that the Ghetto Jews of the Middle Ages represented an historical anachronism, but they felt—and they had the proof of their own unhappy experiences—that the transformation, the adaptation of the Jews to modern European culture —in a word, the assimilation of the Jews—was not being accomplished without hard knocks. The conservative Jews, like their Christian counterparts, never ceased to raise obstacles. Equally repugnant to their moral and aesthetic sense was the transitional type of Jew who was to be met with everywhere, and who imagined he had individually solved the Jewish problem by changing his religion and giving himself a certain cultural veneer.

The members of the Society were true intellectuals. They wished to *know* in the fullest sense of the word : whence they came, the nature of the community they had abandoned, what was to be the basis of the new and more general community to which they desired to become attached. The only thing they had in common with Zionism was the tendency not to identify the Jewish problem with the problem of the Jewish religion. They considered the religion as one of the manifestations, and not even the most important, of the social and cultural Jewish community. They were not in the least interested in the reformation and modernisation of this religion, from which the Jews of certain large German cities expected such miracles. Purging it of certain ancient rites, changing the word Synagogue into Temple, preaching sermons in the language of Goethe and Lessing instead of in Yiddish, led absolutely nowhere.

To be a Jew is not to belong to a particular religion, but is a destiny—or as Heine expressed it " a suffering." To delve into the causes of this destiny of pain, to cure themselves and their co-religionists of their sense of inferiority and seclusion which oppressed them more and more, to put their tendencies towards emancipation on a philosophic and scientific basis : these were the aims of the Society for the propagation of Culture and Judaic knowledge, whose programme consisted of the publication of a *Review*, meetings, and the foundation of branches throughout Germany.

Knowing Heine's development, it is not surprising that he jumped at Gans' invitation to join the Society. Of all the members Moses Moser appealed to him most, and they soon struck up a deep friendship. Moser was in fact one of the most important figures in German-Jewish cultural life. He was a man of wide culture whose spirit of curiosity wrestled with everything : the humanities, mathematics, sinology, philosophy ; he had mastered both ancient Hebrew and the old Scandinavian languages. Although he himself had never written a line—his friends were constantly but unsuccessfully urging him to do so—he was the real giant of the Society and of the *Review* ; the editor was David Zunz. He gave advice to his friends while himself remaining modestly in the background, but without losing his position of " grey eminence " to the Society. Entirely devoid of personal ambition, he placed all his gifts and knowledge at the disposal of the cause to which he was so passionately devoted. Heine found in him a friend to whom he could confide his innermost thoughts, who would never betray his confidence, and whom he could treat as a kind of father confessor. Although Moser was not rich—he worked in a private Berlin bank until his death—he made several long-term loans to the poet, and they were in actual fact never paid back.

Heine's ambition was to interpret Moser's ideas in the domain of literature as Gans' had done in Law and Philosophy and Zunz in History—but he never dreamed of becoming a " national Jewish poet." He wished to remain a German poet, but a German poet who would openly ally himself with his ancestors and his " compatriots " in the most restricted sense of the word, a German poet who, without shutting his eyes to the failings and faults of the Jews, would awaken the German conscience to the injustices practised upon them—who were at least their spiritual equals. No one could say that these new ideas had made him particularly partial to them : when he was at Lüneburg several years later he wrote to his friend Moser : " The Jews here are the

same as everywhere else, quite insupportable . . . filthy merchants," and again from Hamburg, "They live in miserable
cliques . . . if one wishes to take an interest in them one must
never see them at too close quarters." Although finding them all
repugnant, from the dealers to Rothschild, and although des-
pising them for their business spirit and lack of culture—one
could compose a vicious anti-semitic pamphlet from his writings
—he never lost sight of the essential realisation that throughout
history and right down to modern times the Jews had been subjected to persecutions far in excess of their mistakes and shortcomings, and that they were not persecuted and hated for these
alone. The Society accepted neither the theological explanation
nor that given by the Jews themselves—according to whom
Jehovah would continue to heap punishments on them for centuries because they had not kept His laws—nor the Christian
viewpoint that the cause of their persecution and humiliation was
because they had ignored the message of Jesus and had crucified Him.

Moser lent Heine the work of a French priest, Basnage, who
had fled from Switzerland during the persecution of the Hugue-
nots. This book was based on authentic documents and had been
published in 1699 ; it dealt with the history of the Jews from
the birth of Jesus Christ to his own epoch. Heine thought of
writing a novel, set in the Rhineland of the Middle Ages, with
the fate of the Jews in the ghettos as subject. It was for this
reason that he studied Basnage. In the light of Jewish history he
tried to interpret the mystery that Börne had called "The Great
Jewish Sorrow."

Night after night he read this learned history by the flickering
light of his candle. He shuddered at the fantastic story of an
unequal duel that had continued for so many centuries. In
the margin of the book he wrote those verses full of revolt and
bitterness addressed to Edom—who personified in his eyes the
German spirit of persecution :

> *Ein Jahrtausend schon und länger*
> *Dulden wir uns brüderlich,*
> *Du, du duldest, dass ich atme,*
> *Dass du rasest, dulde ich.*

Buch der Lieder

von

H. Heine.

Hamburg
bei Hoffmann und Campe.
1827.

The first edition of the Buch der Lieder
published in 1827

[To face p. 80

Heine in the year 1827.   *A portrait by Grimm*

[To face p. 8

Manchmal nur, in dunkeln Zeiten,
Ward dir wunderlich zu Mut,
Und die liebefrommen Tätzchen
Färbtest du mit meinem Blut.

Now a thousand years and longer
In brotherly love each each has borne ;
That I may breathe, thou ever bearest,
I thy frenzies e'er have borne.

Many a time in darkened moments
Strangeness did inform thy eye ;
Then thy love's inspirèd talons
In my blood themselves did dye.

The mood changes to sadness and he adds :

Jetzt wird unsre Freundschaft fester,
Und noch täglich nimmt sie zu ;
Denn ich selbst begann zu rasen,
Und ich werde fast wie du !

Now e'en closer grows our friendship,
Daily it doth shine more true ;
And I myself do fall in frenzies—
Almost I become like you !

The abyss of the Jewish destiny opened in all its terrible
depths before his eyes. However, his reason refused to see in
this abyss the result of an original and irreparable sin. He alternately laughed and wept with rage, and threw his books about
the room. He would have liked to flee, but there was no escape.
His place, too, was here—he, too, was damned. Would not
collective suicide have been the answer . . . ?

" How can this scapegoat race dare to procreate ? " he cried.
" After each disaster its people begin all over again untiringly. It is
a miracle that they have survived, that they have managed to drag
out their wretched existence even behind ghetto walls, that they

have not spat in the very face of their Jehovah—that shameless and sadistic creator."

He loathed the patience of the Jews, abhorred their humility ; they allowed themselves to be slaughtered like sheep, enduring every inhuman violence with an equally inhuman patience. In their synagogues, stained with the blood of innumerable victims of pogroms, they continued to worship Jehovah, to prostrate themselves before this most infamous of all gods, this Sadist-God, who knew only how to punish, and doubtless rejoiced in the shedding of blood, who laughed at their humility . . .

In his small student's room he brandished his fists in the air. Then all of a sudden his anger and revolt dissolved in tears, and he intoned the Song of the Martyrs, the *De Profundis* of the eternal Jewish sorrow.

Brich aus in lauten Klagen,
Du düstres Martyrerlied,
Das ich so lang' getragen
Im flammenstillen Gemüt !

Es dringt in alle Ohren,
Und durch die Ohren ins Herz ;
Ich habe gewaltig beschworen
Den tausendjährigen Schmerz.

Es weinen die Grossen und Kleinen,
Sogar die kalten Herrn,
Die Frauen und Blumen weinen,
Es weinen am Himmel die Stern'.

Und alle die Tränen fliessen
Nach Süden im stillen Verein,
Sie fliessen und ergiessen
Sich all' in den Jordan hinein.

Break out in loud-tongued lamentation,
Thou mournful martyr-song,
That I so long in desolation
In flame-quiet bore along !

Through every ear it presses urgent,
Into the heart through the ears ;
Oft have I affirmed resurgent
The wound of a thousand years.

Both great and small are sadly weeping,
Even the cold men cry ;
The women and the flowers are weeping,
The stars weep to the sky.

And all the tears flow swiftly southwards,
In silent company,
To the Jordan overflowing downwards
Beside the inland sea.

The invocations of the old psalms mingle with the childish, almost rococo images of Heine. We consider them among the most sublime and poignant of all his verses.

The novel he was working upon at this time, for which he had been studying the history of the Jews for several years, was never finished, and only fragments remain. Heine had not the technique of the novelist—or rather he lacked the necessary patience in construction and composition. He lacked also the discipline indispensable in erecting the scaffolding of a plot ; his lyrical temperament was only successful in prose when he wrote pamphlets, travel descriptions, philosophical and political articles, in which he could dispense with systems and forms. But the story of the Rabbi of Bacharach remains a masterpiece of German descriptive prose, and can be compared favourably with Kohlhaus and Kleist. The indignation and despair which burst out in the two verses we have quoted, soften in the Rabbi into detailed description in the Walter Scott manner ; the sharp cry becomes a melancholy plaint.

Although the idea of the Rabbi of Bacharach was conceived during Heine's stormy "Judaising" period, the character who serves as a cloak for the poet is not the Rabbi who escaped in the time of the Pogroms, but one of his old university comrades of Toledo who had become a convert and a Spaniard—the pretentious Don Isaac whom the Rabbi had met in the Frankfurt ghetto. Let us see what this worldling replies to the Rabbi, who has reproached him for never having been sincerely attached to the Jewish faith :

"Actually, I prefer your cooking to your faith . . . I have never been able to stomach you Jews. Even at your best periods, even under the rule of David, our ancestor, I cannot envisage myself as one of you ; I should have slipped away from the Citadel of Zion and emigrated to Phoenicia or perhaps Babylon, where the vial of earthly pleasures foamed in the time of the Gods . . ."

And when the Rabbi mutters with a dark look : "Isaac, you blaspheme against the Only God ; you are a hundred times worse than a Christian, you are a pagan, an idolater," Heine, alias Don Isaac, replies with this atheist credo : "Yes, I am a pagan, I feel just as much respect for Christ the Nazarene, burning for self-immolation, as for the gloomy bigoted spirit of the Hebrews. May our Lady of Sidon, Saint Astarte, forgive me if I kneel in prayer at the feet of Our Lady of Sorrows, Mother of the Crucified ; my knees and my lips pay homage to Death, but my heart remains faithful to Life."

This Renaissance Paganism and hedonist cult manifested by Don Isaac already give an indication of Heine's later spiritual development. Under the influence of the French materialists and the German rationalist philosophers, Heine was violently opposed to the religious spirit and to Judeo-Christian morality which, according to him (and this was continued later by both Marx and Nietzsche, whom he had influenced) were based on a negation of life, recompensing humanity for its suffering and renunciation here on earth by the promise of heavenly wealth and a hypothetical immortality. Heine was in search of a new morality which would be an affirmation of life—the will to pursue happiness—which would justify the revolt of the suffering, the oppressed and the exploited against the privileged. "The natural enemy of all positive religions will never become champion of the religion which first introduced that human brokerage from which we are still suffering so grievously today," he wrote to Moser in the summer of 1823.

At the height of his Judaic period he dreamed of a new religious ideal, of a moral attitude surpassing both Jewish and Christian outlooks, which should be a rational and practical synthesis of the teachings of history as well as of the deepest and most general of human desires.

It occurred to him that the suffering and persecution of the Jews was only an episode in the universal system inherited from the past, and whose law rests on inequality and the abuse of man by man. Anti-semitism was only an element of a more general anti-humanism, which persecutes the lower orders, the poor and the coloured races and which is sanctified and justified by the positive religions as " The Will of God."

His reflections led him to the conclusion that the cure for anti-semitism did not lie in the consolidation of semitism—that would be to adapt it to an anti-humanism behind a Christian mask—but in the synthesis of semitism and Christianity in a humanism which would affirm, instead of the so-called Divine Will, the will of man. If at the start he had toyed with the idea of founding somewhere a national home for the Jews, for example, in America on the banks of the Mississippi, or as Noah Mardochee, sheriff of New York and spiritual forefather of Zionism, had proposed, at the foot of Niagara, in Grand Island—a fatherland where, as he jokingly wrote in a letter, " a happier generation would inhale *loulef* and nibble at the unleavened bread, and where a new Jewish literature would blossom "—he would soon have abandoned it as unrealisable and also unnecessary.

He accepted the dispersal of the Jews, " the diaspora ", as a fact that could but should not be altered. He envisaged their emancipation within the framework of the general evolution of humanity, and acted towards this end. He had once retorted to his sister's fiancé, Moritz Rab Embden, who thought him tainted with youthful religious mania : " No, I am not an ardent believer, I am a hardened indifferent. But I admit that I am an ardent believer in equality of rights, and in civic equality for the Jews. And in the difficult times ahead the German rabble will most certainly hear my voice . . . "

Equality for the Jews as a corollary of the equality for all men : this was the idea for which the young Heine was prepared to sacrifice his life and talents. Without ever denying his origin, and without dissociating himself from the suffering of the Jews, he was by no means disposed to devote himself entirely to their redemption alone. " May my right hand wither if I forget thee, Jerusalem," he said, quoting from the psalm. The lament of all suffering, persecuted and oppressed humanity found an echo in his heart ; and, feeling himself predestined, in the conflict against inequality—unleashed by the French Revolution—to become the champion of the oppressed, he drew a clear distinction between the baited Jews and those who participated in the maintenance of inequality and inhuman treatment. He considered that the Jew would gain the right to claim liberty and equality for himself when he renounced his material privileges—acquired by his acumen and mediterranean cunning, even in times of persecution—when the parasite would become a useful member of society, a worker among workers, a fighter among fighters. Karl Marx, following in the footsteps of Heine, his master and friend, wrote twenty years later in the Franco-German annals : " Jews, you are egotists when you claim for yourselves a special Jewish emancipation. You should, like Germans, work for the emancipation of Germany, and, like men, for the human race."

*   *   *   *

When, at this moment, we consider their cruel experiences, their shame and their mourning in the light of Heine's conception of the Jewish destiny ; when, in the course of a few years, they have been reduced to ashes, and the whole of Europe has lost that which all the fighters for humanity have built up for more than a century ; must we condemn and reject them ? Must they abandon the road they had taken, and which the Germanic tempest has almost swept away ? Must the survivors of this race, who had based their hopes in vain upon assimilation, follow another road ?

Have you seen them, Heine, crouching in their holes like hunted wild beasts, or wandering miserably, chased along all the roads of Europe? Have you seen them embark, tenacious and incorrigible, for other continents to start their lives anew? Do you know what happened at Auschwitz and Belsen and in the camps of Poland, Hungary and Rumania? They believed in human equality, in progress and reason, and were convinced that men could not indefinitely remain strangers among their fellows. And behold! They find themselves more humiliated than the cats and dogs which their murderers caress.

What would Heine's reply have been? Should these men, covered with lice, contemptuously spat upon, forced to eat excrement, these branded ghosts from concentration camps, continue to believe in equality and the social contract—in human friendship and a place in the sun?

"Yes," says Heine, wrapping himself more closely in his dark shroud to ward off the cold November air. "Yes. Let them believe still and for ever. What matter if their belief is mad and irrational—let them believe until only one man remains. Let them believe, for their blind, pitiable and ridiculous faith is the very essence of their eclecticism; this faith in the honesty and friendship of man, this absurd dream, this eternal illusion is their very crown of glory. Let them believe, though a thousand times the facts belie their faith, for it is thus that their cause identifies itself with the cause of humanity; it is thus that their misfortune waxes into a symbol of the wickedness and folly of man, and their imperishable hope becomes the symbol of reason and generosity.

"Comrades in exile, nomads, my unhappy friends," Heine cries, "wretched Jews, chased, robbed and persecuted, never admit that you are strangers, never submit to your persecutors. Do not identify sane peoples with the midden spawn and rabble that are to be found among them. Do not believe for one instant that they strike you because of your crimes and weakness, for they are using you as a scapegoat for their own weaknesses and lack of faith. Do not, moreover, think that they cause you suffering because of your superiority or because of your kindness, for it is against the best of their own people that they rebel when they are torturing you. You will not suffer alone when they throw filth in your faces, when they fling you into gas chambers and burn you alive, for they are torturing the human spirit at the same time. Universal liberty pales in the prison as well as your own . . ."

* * * *

" I only like the Jew," said Heine, " when he meets misfortune with imprecations and rebellion like Job ; he only moves me to compassion when he commences rebuilding as soon as his house has been brought to ruin, when he continues to build his home in a world that refuses him shelter, and does not sigh in resignation or repent of uncommitted crimes ; when he does not go mad and lose his faith, and refuses to accept eternal injustice—accepts nothing as eternal and irrevocable."

CHAPTER TWELVE

LOVE PASSETH

Die Jahre kommen und gehen
Geschlechter steigen ins Grab
Doch nimmer vergeht die Liebe
Die ich im Herzen hab'.

HEINE received the news between a lecture on Hegel and a Jewish reunion that his cousin Amélie had become engaged to Johann Friedländer, a rich young Hamburg Jew. During his last stay in Hamburg, while on his way to Lüneburg a few months previously, Salomon's family had received him with the greatest cordiality, and Amélie had even encouraged his hopes during the few moments that he was able to spend alone with her. This news, therefore, was a serious blow to him, for it took him quite off his guard.

He obeyed his first impulses. He packed his trunks and set out for Hamburg to verify the truth of the news. We do not know exactly what happened during this visit. In a letter dated one year later to his friend Moser, he speaks of those few weeks as the most critical and unhappy in his life. " My inner life was plunged in the sombre depths of the world of dreams, lit only by fantastic lurid flashes : my outer life was mad, disordered and cynical."

His soul was filled alternately with despair, anger and a desire for vengeance. We can easily understand his state of mind if we read his drama *Ratcliff*. This work played the same role in re-establishing the psychic equilibrium of the young poet as *Werther* had done in the life of Goethe ; the latter was saved from suicide by writing this heartrending love story, while the idea of *Ratcliff* prevented Heine from challenging Johann Friedländer to a duel or from burning down Salomon's house. Shutting himself up in his student's room he worked like a maniac for three days and nights on this work. It has been described by Immermann as a general confession. He says : " Either it is all true, or I myself am nothing but a lie."

The poem is " true ", but in this probably lies its fault : we must take into account the fact that Heine wrote it while the storm still raged within him. This is roughly the plot : A young Scots student named Ratcliff is inflamed by the beauty and coquetry of Marie, the daughter of an old nobleman, MacGregor, and on being turned down by her swears that if he cannot possess her no one else shall. He keeps his word and kills all her betrothed one after another. At the end of the play Heine stages a veritable hecatomb : everyone is killed, the fanatical lover, Marie, the father—only Duncan, her last fiancé, survives. It is a terrifying picture of what might have happened if Heine, instead of using his pen had used a sword or a pistol.

What troubled him was not so much the faithlessness of Amélie or the perfidy of his uncle, but the idea of his having been the victim of his own illusions. Many years later when he came across a gracious letter from Amélie his passion flared up again, and he was forced to admit : " You have been completely absolved before the Tribunal of Reason. The verdict is contained in these words : ' The little one broke her promise neither by word nor deed.' " Amélie had not expressly promised to wait for him until he had finished his studies—possibly two years—but Heine had lived as though this promise had been given. In his poems, his dreams, and in his burning looks he had so often declared his love and begged for her hand ; in his dreams she had so often sworn fidelity that he had never bothered to ask for real pledges. Powerless, as though pilloried before his shattered illusions, he was consumed by his own fire, and despised himself : " You threw no fuel upon the fire and said no word to me but, notwithstanding, my heart is obliged to condemn you."

His work on *Ratcliff* only acted as a passing anodyne. Apart from his intimate friend Moser and his sister Lotte, nobody knew the extent of his upheaval, but everyone noticed his changed manner. He became more irritable, more capricious and madder than ever ; he lost control of his nerves and often in Rahel's drawing-room he would burst into tears and flee from the room. He would be seen in the streets with prostitutes, and would wander about aimlessly, his eyes dark-shadowed and vicious. " Chill Death gave me a kiss . . ."

He never completely recovered from this deception. When he ventured to Hamburg a year later, he wrote to Moser : " My old passion burst out anew with all its pristine violence. I ought never to have come to Hamburg ; a dark anger like a band of burning metal lies on my soul. I long for eternal night . . ." From this intense suffering were born verses of great beauty and melancholy. But the joy of writing them did not suffice to fill the void she had left in his soul. He wept, above all, for his lost illusions. He refused Amélie's invitation to the wedding on the pretext of his studies, and remained in Berlin.

But in his imagination he was present at the ceremony in Hamburg. He watched it sorrowfully as though through a glass window against which he pressed his burning forehead.

> *Der Bräutigam füllt den Becher sein*
> *Und trinkt daraus, und reicht gar fein*
> *Der Braut ihn hin ; sie lächelt Dank,—*
> *O weh ! mein rotes Blut sie trank.*

> *Die Braut ein hübsches Apflein nahm,*
> *Und reicht es hin dem Bräutigam.*
> *Der nahm sein Messer, schnitt hinein,—*
> *O weh ! Das war das Herze mein.*

> The Bridegroom fills his brimming glass
> And drinketh deep, and then doth pass
> It to the Bride ; she smiles her thanks,—
> Alas ! My own red blood she drank.

> The Bride a lovely apple took
> And gave it him with loving look,
> He took his knife, cut it apart,—
> Alas ! That apple was my heart !

It mattered little where he went, to Lüneburg, his home, or to the island of Nordeney where he passed the mild summer in a peacefully rocking fishing-boat, the image of " the faithless one " rose constantly before his eyes. He discovered a Dutch town at the bottom of the sea, where ". . . old men in black cloaks, with white ruffs and chains of office, with long swords and long faces, walked near the Town Hall whose façade resembled finely carved lace. Not far away at the outskirts of the town stood a large old house, where at a low window a young girl sat with her head on her arms . . ."

> *Und ich kenne dich, armes, vergessenes Kind!*
>
> *So tief, meertief also*
> *Verstecktest du dich vor mir*
> *Aus kindischer Laune . . .*
> *Und sassest fremd unter fremden Leuten . . .*
> *Derweilen ich, die Seele voll Gram,*
> *Auf der ganzen Erde dich suchte,*
> *Und immer dich suchte,*
> *Du Immergeliebte . . .*

> And thee I know, thou poor, forgotten child!
>
> So deep, so ocean deep,
> Thyself thou hiddest from me
> Out of a childish mood . . .
> And strange didst sit amid strange folk . . .
> While I, with grieving heart,
> Sought thee throughout the earth,
> And always sought I thee,
> Thou ever well belovèd . . .

One after another songs of sadness and grief welled up in his soul, and the pages of his poetry note-books were filled with comments of his new chagrin, torments and meditations. Each time he thought himself cured of his passion it would break out again in some new form. In June 1823, on the occasion of his sister Lotte's marriage to Maurice Embden, he learnt that Salomon, his wife and daughter Thérèse were to be present. Heine did not relish this meeting, knowing that Salomon was furious with him

for the uncomplimentary allusions to his family, which could not
slip by unnoticed in the recent publications of *Almansor* and *Ratcliff*. But to his astonishment his uncle was most cordial towards
him, and even congratulated him on his literary achievements
before the whole assembled family. Here is the enchanting poem
that was inspired by this family reunion :

> *Ich fragte nach Muhmen und Basen*
> *Nach manchem langweil'gen Gesell'n,*
> *Und nach dem kleinen Hündchen*
> *Mit seinem sanften Bell'n.*

> *Auch nach der vermählten Geliebten*
> *Fragte ich nebenbei ;*
> *Und freundlich gab man zur Antwort,*
> *Dass sie in den Wochen sei.*

> *Und freundlich gratuliert' ich,*
> *Und lispelte liebevoll :*
> *Dass man sie von mir recht herzlich,*
> *Viel tausendmal grüssen soll.*

> *Schwesterchen rief dazwischen :*
> *Das Hündchen, sanft und klein,*
> *Ist gross und toll geworden,*
> *Und ward ertränkt im Rhein.*

> I asked after aunts and maiden cousins
> And many a comrade wont to bore,
> And, after, the tiny little puppy
> That used to bark beside the door.

> And after my own espoused belovèd
> Did I enquire, while I was there ;
> And friendly did they give me answer—
> She was confined a child to beàr.

> And friendly then was my rejoicing,
> And I murmured, filled with love ;
> That men should so right heartily
> Give myriad greetings for my love.

Mid this my little sister called out : —
The puppy, once a gentle hound,
Grew big and madder with his aging,
And in the river Rhine was drowned . . .

And the last verse :

Die Kleine gleicht der Geliebten,
Besonders wenn sie lacht ;
Sie hat dieselben Augen,
Die mich so elend gemacht.

The little girl's like my belovèd,
Excepting when she laughs at me ;
She has the selfsame eyes and glances
That e'er so wretched made me be.

After the marriage Heine left for Hamburg, and in August he informed Moser : " The magic of the place had a formidable effect upon my soul ; a new principle grew up little by little in my mind, which will doubtless be my guide for many years to come." However, the new principle was only an ancient air with a new refrain. Heine could not exist for long without illusion and without an all-absorbing love. No matter that he struggled against the chimeras whose stupidity he realised in his more lucid moments, his instincts swept him away in spite of the better judgment of his intellect. Love is a madness and a sickness and has nothing to do with reason. Thérèse's clear laugh and innocent charms inspired his passionate verses anew ; Nature, which had been dormant, blossomed again. " The stars weep like unhappy children, their tears hail me with compassion ; the jasmines ring out hope and the roses whisper their scented promises . . . " Sweet and gracious eyes looked out at him from every cranny of this enchanted world.

Gérard de Nerval asserts that in the sublime verses—the best perhaps of all the poems in the *Buch der Lieder*—which were written at this period : " . . . there reigns a secret terror.

The roses are too pungent, the turf too green and the song of the nightingales too mellifluous. All this is fatal, the perfume over-powers, the green grass hides a ditch and the bird expires on her last trill. The magic charm is broken by the hiss of a serpent, the appetising russet apples are poisoned as in the fairy tale . . ."

The Baron de la Motte-Fouqué, author of *Undine*, who had met the young poet at the Varnhagen's, addressed a fraternal poem to him :

Beloved poet, singer of the bleeding heart ; Oh ! I have understood too well thy mournful chant ; but stay the echo of thy hapless tones . . . thy dull and vengeful cries of anger . . .

But the image of Thérèse vanished very quickly and the spell was broken. One cold morning in Hamburg the poet found himself once more alone and disconsolate. Thérèse played as little part in his deception—if it were indeed a deception—as in his hopes and love. " *Wenn ich dich liebe, was geht's dich an ?* " he wrote with bitter irony. Thérèse was only a pretext to develop his inner tragedy, with its langours, illusions, joys and sorrows. As Nerval remarked, Heine was not in love with a woman but a chimera—an image created from many parts, which the poet had forgotten to endow with a heart, a brain, flesh and blood. We may add here that the love poetry of Heine and his subsequent love life always retained this chimeric quality. He wavered between the. two feminine poles—*Loreley* and *The Dark Lady*. *Loreley* is the incarnation of seductive beauty, who only dazzles the better to elude her prey. The *Dark Lady*, to whom towards the end of his life Heine wrote one of his most striking sonnets, disintegrates her lover by her sepulchral attachment :

Es hatte mein Haupt die schwarze Frau
Zärtlich ans Herz geschlossen ;
Ach ! meine Haare wurden grau,
Wo ihre Tränen geflossen.

Sie küsste mich lahm, sie küsste mich krank,
Sie küsste mir blind die Augen ;
Das Mark aus meinem Rückgrat trank
Ihr Mund mit wildem Saugen . . .

She held my head, the lady black,
To her heart with close embrace ;
But then my hair went grey, alack !
Where'er her tears their course did trace.

She kissed till I was lame and ill,
She kissed me till I could not see ;
Her mouth sucked in and drank its fill
Of my inmost marrow savagely . . .

Loreley is the celestial love : the *Dark Lady* the terrestrial. Both, equally tragic, spell shipwreck and disaster to the man. There is no trace in Heine's poetry of the woman who is a human being with hopes and fears, who experiences deceptions that make her unhappy. He believed, either by conviction or from experience, that if to herself woman was human, to men she would remain of necessity inhuman and impenetrable. An oft-recurring image in his poetry is the woman as statue. " Thou who in the desert of my life stand there silent as a statue, beautiful as marble and as cold . . . " he hurled at Amélie. Another image appears even more frequently : it is the game of hide-and-seek played by two lovers through the woods and fields. " And we knew how to hide ourselves so well that we shall never find each other again . . . "

Heine's " break " with Thérèse coincided with his new ideological orientation. He had grown tired of sentimentality and illusions, of chimeras, tears and melancholy. He had the impression that the years passed in hopes and torments of love had been wasted. He wished to build his future on more solid foundations ; the old methods only led to disillusionment. He decided to change both his way of living and his philosophy, and the end of 1823 saw not only a revision of his poems and his conceptions about the world, but also of his friends. He erased from his list his Bonn colleague Rousseau who, in his Rhenish newspaper, had tolerated the attacks against the anti-Christian passages in *Almansor*, and he quarrelled with Varnhagen—but luckily was quick to realise that his judgment had been both hasty and unjust. He began to study Goethe, the great Weimar pagan, in earnest, in order to learn from him a harmonious way of life. After a long rest at Lüneburg, feeling a firmer control over his destiny, he decided to return to Göttingen, where he believed society and literature would not distract him from his legal studies—which it was really now time to bring to an end. He needed only some eighteen months of hard work to sit for his doctorate, and at the moment he felt disposed to work.

And after ? Heine thought that later he would look for a professorship or some other official appointment in Prussia. In the *élan* of his new-found energy after a long rest he wished at all costs to free himself from the spasmodic but humiliating support of Uncle Salomon—even more so as Salomon, to whom he had outlined his plans, approved them whole-heartedly. But to become a Prussian functionary he would be obliged to renounce his Jewish faith. " The problem of baptism arises," he explained to Moses Moser ; " none of the family is opposed to it except myself. You must understand that with my way of thinking baptism is an act of complete indifference ; it would possibly result in my having to make greater sacrifices in the struggle for the rights of my unfortunate co-religionists." Useless his trying to reconcile himself with the idea of conversion, for he constantly felt that he was committing treachery, that he was betraying not only his co-religionists but himself as well. " I find it beneath my dignity and prejudicial to my honour to be baptised in order to obtain employment in Prussia—in this *dear* Prussia." He had enough time at his disposal to weigh up the pros and cons, and to prove to himself—and incidentally to Moser—that his project of eventually abandoning the Jewish faith did not necessitate his estrangement from the Judaic ideals of his friends. He zealously renewed his studies of Basnage and continued work on *The Rabbi of Bacharach*. In each of his letters to Moser he evinced a warm interest in the work of the Society.

At the end of January 1823 he arrived at Göttingen, and threw himself heart and soul into the study of *Corpus Juris*. The Muse never once crossed the threshold of his student's room. The poet, with cold determination, remained constant to his ascetic vows— but by an oversight his door must one day have remained ajar, for at this time he wrote the enchanting series of sonnets, *Con*

Amore. They were addressed to Rahel Varnhagen's stepsister, Frederica Roberta. Here is a charming example :

> *Verlass Berlin, mit seinem dicken Sande,*
> *Und dünnen Tee, und überwitz' gen Leuten,*
> *Die Gott und Welt, und sie selbst bedeuten,*
> *Begriffen längst mit Hegelschem Verstande.*

> *Komm mit nach Indien, nach dem Sonnenlände,*
> *Wo Ambrablüten ihren Duft verbreiten,*
> *Die Pilgerscharen nach dem Ganges schreiten,*
> *Andächtig und im weissen Festgewande.*

> *Dort, wo die Palmen wehn, die Wellen blinken,*
> *Am heil'gen Ufer Lotosblumen ragen*
> *Empor zu Indras Burg, der ewig blauen ;*

> *Dort will ich gläubig vor dir niedersinken,*
> *Und deine Füsse drücken, und dir sagen :*
> *Madame ! Sie sind die schönste aller Frauen !*

Forsake Berlin with all its dust and sand,
Its watery rea, and men who pompously
Discourse of God, the world, continually,
And all of Hegel's theories understand.

Come now to India, the sunsteeped land,
Where amber blossoms flower fragrantly,
And pilgrims near the Ganges endlessly,
In holy raiment white, a pious band.

There, where the palm trees wave beside the stream,
And lotus lilies reach up to the sky,
To Indra's citadel, the endless blue ;

There will I faithfully kneel down to thee,
And kiss thy feet, and truly to thee cry !
Madam ! The fairest of all women is you !

CHAPTER THIRTEEN

AT WEIMAR THE BEER IS GOOD

At Göttingen Heine made the acquaintance of Eckermann—later to become the confidant of Goethe—whose " conversations " have survived. During his student years at Göttingen Eckermann had already become an ardent admirer of Goethe. To the generation of Heine and Eckermann must be given the credit, largely thanks to the influence of Varnhagen and Humboldt, of having really understood the poet of Weimar.

We have tried to portray the effect that Heine made on his ingenuous, pedantic and thoroughly German colleague, and we have filched a few pages from his unpublished diary in which he meticulously recorded his conversations with Heine and the reflections they inspired.

This reconstruction is based principally upon Heine's letters and upon his documentary writings relating to this period.

February 12th, 1824.—I have just met Heinrich Heine. A very curious type. He has somewhat Schillerian features—pure German. To the casual observer he does not betray the Jew at all. But when he laughs (he has a detestable laugh) his face becomes distorted, his glance becomes aggressive and scowling and he is changed into some Jewish Schiller, the living image of one of those anti-semitic caricatures of the Jew.

I do not feel that he is a stable and harmonious character. Sometimes he remains obstinately silent, almost morose ; at other times he is boisterous in the extreme, a great mocker with a love of playing jokes. He likes to give the appearance of a man to whom nothing is sacred ; he does not mince words, but at times manifests a rare sensitiveness. In a flow of words he will pass from irony to effusion, and thence to the most sincere confessions.

We have met only twice and already he has offered me his friendship. " How can we possibly be friends—we hardly know each other ? " I asked him. He replied with a laugh : " Councillor Bauer's chambermaid put exactly the same question to me the other night when I asked her if I could pay her a nocturnal visit. I had only met *her* twice," and he burst out laughing. "Like love, friendship is based on elective affinities . . ."

It is impossible to take him quite seriously. Hearing him speak so coarsely about love, it is difficult to conceive that this is the man who has written those delicate love songs woven in a gossamer web of dream and gentle breeze.

"I am not a monotheist in love," he replied to my question. "I love the Medici Venus *and* the Bauer's chambermaid ; and alas, both of them without hope of realisation!"

February 24th.—Spitta, the "Pietist," Peters, the mathematician, Heine and myself went a week ago to the *Landwehr Biergarten*. It is an hour's journey from the town. Heine was in excellent spirits. He must just have received some money from his uncle. He gave full reign to his gaiety and embraced the charming little Lotte as she brought the beer to our table. But Lotte, as we knew by experience, was by no means a girl of easy virtue. Her little face with its charming tip-tilted nose reddened with anger, her eyes danced with rage, and she began to struggle and scream so loudly that we had to put our hands to our ears. At first Heine took the episode as a joke, but a little later became embarrassed and silent, not knowing what to do. This was a week ago. Yesterday he did not wish to come with us again, and we were almost obliged to carry him there by force ; once he was seated he hardly dared to raise his head and look at the girl. But what a surprise when Lotte came over to the table and, smiling sweetly, put her hand on Heine's shoulder. We looked at her with astonishment.

"Don't be angry with me, Sir," she said. "You are different from the other students, and I have seen your poems. How beautiful they are! You may embrace me in front of all these gentlemen if you wish—but you must go on writing those lovely verses." She offered her cheek, and Heine—who would have thought it possible?—blushed and gave her a kiss. Spitta, I noticed, was white with jealousy.

"This is the happiest moment of my life," murmured Heine, with moist eyes. "For the first time I realise that it is worth while to be a poet."

February 28th.—Spitta has just made a portrait of Heine in verse : " The Devil went wandering. One day he came to a flowery arbour where Love was lying sick. Sad-faced angels ministered to him. The Devil sat himself down nearby, and ever since the passers-by have heard his sinister laugh amidst the angelic voices, and have seen the satanic mask in the midst of divine roses."

Spitta showed him his poem, but Heine was not in the least bit angry, and even admitted that it was a clever caricature. " I cannot speak of my sufferings without at the same time laughing at them," he admitted. It must be hard for him to live in such a manner ; his sufferings are increased tenfold by his bitter irony towards himself. It is not surprising that this continual secret struggle exhausts him. " I am at war with myself," he said the other day, and I believe this was more than a mere witticism. Actually, he is much more friendly and gentle towards us than he is towards himself. I often think of him.

What can be the meaning of this combat of the spirit ? Is it the struggle between Good and Evil ? The Angel at grips with the Demon ? The German with the Jew . . . the Christian with the Pagan ? Our harmony seems to me suddenly to be trivial and mean—philistine in fact—compared with his self-torture. However, I do not know whether he deserves to be considered as a " great man." It is not because I reserve this epithet for Goethe alone, but it seems to me as if true tragedy is lacking in his conflicts, and that he falls short of the sublime. Furthermore, I could not prevent myself from saying to him : " You are not deep enough."

He looked at me with his inquisitorial eyes, and after a moment's reflection answered disconcertedly : " I fear depth as I fear death." He seems to know himself well enough. " I love life," he continued, " more than poetry."

March 5th.—Heine affirms that the story which he told in his famous *Donna Clara* actually happened to him one day on the Unter den Linden. He was walking with a Baroness whom he had met at the Hohenhausen's. She had no idea that he was a Jew, and never ceased from blackguarding his race. He listened without saying a word, neither approving nor disapproving.

Finally, when on the point of leaving her, he observed : " Madame, Heine the German has much appreciated your company, although the same cannot be said for Heine the Jew." The Baroness nearly collapsed in the street.

May 25th.—Heine has returned from Berlin, where he spent his holidays. He looks much better, and his headaches are less frequent. He has shown me his poem *Edom*—which is far from flattering to the Christian.

He told me that he has no confidence in the German Radicals. " In England I should be a Radical, yes. In Italy I should be a Carbonaro, and in France a Jacobin. But I keep myself aloof from the German demagogue for a very simple reason : because I know that in the event of their victory, several thousands of Jewish heads—and naturally the best (mine, for example)—would fall into the basket."

June 28th.—Yesterday Heine appeared wearing a black armlet. We were embarrassed, for we thought that he must have lost a near relation. " The only man whom I considered as a real parent has just died," he said, and he drew from his pocket a newspaper announcing the death of Byron. " Don't smile," he added, with a seriousness we were not quite sure was sincere, " I bear a great resemblance to him—in so far as a poor and miserable German poet can resemble an English lord. I might have said what he wrote of himself in *Don Juan*." He quoted the following lines :

> " ' But this I must say in my own applause.
> Of all the Muses that I recollect,
> Whate'er may be her follies or her flaws,
> In some things, mine's beyond all contradiction
> The most sincere that ever dealt in fiction.' "

July 15th.—Heine is back from the Harz Mountains. His journey, he said, had been very pleasant, and his note-book is full of observations. As he walked, he read Sterne's *Sentimental Journey.* " This is a French book, written in English," he assured us. He, too, wants to write a French book—but in German. He has lent me the Sterne and I have read it. He is a really remarkable writer, and I can quite understand how he must have appealed to Heine. This miscellany of caprice and lyricism, impressions of a wanderer, of dreams and philosophy, this happy contrast between the serious and the frivolous, this clear and free humour, is very close in style to that of Heine.

" This is an essay," wrote Sterne, " that I am making on human nature, which costs me only my work, and this is enough, for it gives me pleasure : it stimulates the circulation of my blood and drives away the black humours, and clarifies my judgment and my reason. Is it not too frivolous, I ask myself, is it not prostituting art to derive from it only a physical refreshment as one does from a fine walk ? But there is at the same time, I admit, in these disquisitions a childish pleasure and a joy of life that carries one away . . . "

August 2nd, 1824.—Heine is taking on mysterious airs. " I also went to Weimar," he said casually.

" Really," I replied. " And ? "

He pretended not to hear, and started talking of other things. Could it be true? Half an hour later he continued on the same theme.

" Then I wandered around Weimar. The beer there is really excellent."

" Only the beer ? " asked Spitta.

" No," he replied absent-mindedly, " the roast goose too."

His voice seemed to tremble. His face clouded over, and gently passing his hand over his forehead he continued to chat. He spoke of the beauty of Ilse—as though Ilse could have any interest for us !

" Come on," I demanded impatiently, " that's enough. *Have* you been to Weimar ? Yes or no ? "

" I told you I've been there."

" Well ? "

" I told you that the beer and the roast goose are excellent there."

" Now stop this fooling. Have you seen him—*him* ? "

He made no reply, and looked at us with a wan smile as though he did not see us.

" Now, really ! You *haven't* been there, and you are just making a mockery of us ! " shouted Peters furiously. Throwing his cloak over his shoulders he left the table.

A few moments later Heine left also, without having said anything more.

August 25th.—Heine has still not spoken of his visit to Weimar. Yesterday, when I asked him what he was working at, he replied :

" Oh, lots of things. I am writing my *Harzreise* and polishing up the *Rabbi*—and I'm toying with several new projects, including a *Faust*."

" A *Faust* ! What do you mean ? " I asked him, really astounded. " Do you propose to enter the field with Goethe ? "

" It's not a question of competition," he replied, and began to expound at length that Goethe's *Faust* " was not the happiest solution." He reproached the " great pagan " for not having paid sufficient respect to tradition, and for not having been sufficiently faithful to the legend—and above all, for having failed in his characterisation of Mephistopheles. " The true Mephistopheles is not a wretched vagrant from Hell," he said, " but a subtle Spirit, a Demon of the highest order—the incarnation of human and Promethean knowledge." I remarked that Goethe's *Faust* might have its weaknesses, and that it was easy to write another *version*, but hardly a better or a greater one.

" We shall see," he replied. " And in any case, everybody should write a *Faust*. One cannot take a monopoly on the drama of humanity. Euripides treated the same subject as Sophocles, which in its turn had been used by Aeschylus before him—and this was not in order to write it better, but differently."

He was very annoyed, and I hesitated to say more. What has he then against Goethe ? Is it possible that the Olympian refused to receive him ? It was useless to ply him with questions : he refused to reply.

October 28th.—This evening I spent with Heine. He showed me a few extracts from his *Harzreise*. The verses he read me are exquisitely tender and full of whimsy. He was flattered by my enthusiasm, but whenever one compliments him he tries to show indifference and pretends to belittle his own work. " I only write to make money and for fame," he said disdainfully. " This type of work pleases the public. I hope one day to make a serious business—"

" Business ? You talk like a huckster," I replied. " I do not like to hear creative poetry spoken of like that—even in jest."

" But I am a huckster," he replied to annoy me, " my father sells silks and I sell literature. And both of us at considerable loss," he added, complaining light-heartedly, but naturally his words were not meant to be taken seriously. He is inordinately proud of his work. " At the risk of my life I have hewn out a completely new path . . . "

His prose has no precedent in German literature. It recalls somewhat the style of Jean-Paul, but is more balanced, refined and graceful—far more graceful. When I told him that, he made no comment, but only embraced me. Then we spoke very intimately. He complained of the insulting way in which his uncle gave him money, and he spoke of the young girl he wanted to marry in Hamburg. I waited for him to speak also of his visit to Weimar, and this time I was not disappointed.

He produced a letter from his pocket and showed it to me, and at my request allowed me to take a copy—but made me promise to show it to nobody until he should give his permission. Here is the letter :

" Excellence,—I beg you to accord me the favour of a brief audience. I do not wish to be importunate, and desire only to kiss your hand and then depart. My name is Heinrich Heine, and I was born in the Rhineland. Until recently I lived in Göttingen, and later for several years in Berlin, where I was graced with the friendship of several of your old acquaintances and admirers—the late Wold, the Varnhagens, and others—and each day I learnt to love you more and more. I myself am a poet, and had the temerity three years ago to send you a tragedy, together with a volume entitled *Lyrisches Intermezzo*. Furthermore, I too am a sick man, and this is why I went for three weeks' rest to the Harz. It was there, upon the Brocken, that I was seized with an overwhelming desire to make a pilgrimage to Weimar to pay my respects to Goethe . . .

" I have made this pilgrimage in the true sense of the word : I came here on foot, and my clothes are white with the dust of the road. And now I beg you to grant my wishes and to receive me.

" I am your enthusiastic and most devoted admirer . . . "

The letter is undoubtedly very deferential, and as respectful as that of a son, although there is in it—as I observed to Heine—in the tone and certain phrases such as "I also am a poet" and "I too am a sick man" a certain impertinence, subtle and difficult to define.

"So you saw him?" I asked.

"Yes," he replied curtly.

"Well?"

He told me how terrified he had been when he saw him. "Goethe is no more than a shadow of his former self: his face is yellow like that of a mummy, and his toothless mouth twitches unceasingly."

"And his eyes?" I asked fearfully. It was so painful to realise that Goethe was already an old man, that a god—for I am certain that he is more than man—can grow old.

"His eyes are bright and penetrating," he replied. "He was most gracious—I should almost say condescending. But he can afford to be, for he is an aristocrat, an Excellency—while I, I am only a student and the son of a merchant. I shall never become an Excellency. No, I shall never be a servant of princes!" he cried, and his eyes blazed.

For some moments we continued our walk in silence along the broad avenue, and somewhat more calmly he continued: "With a touching solicitude he inquired about my health. Actually he is very kind, but . . . Listen," he went on, looking me straight in the eyes, "I had imagined this meeting quite differently. I had thought for months for something noble and brilliant to say to him when some day I should meet him—and when that moment finally arrived I found that the only thing I could say was ' the beer is excellent in Weimar.' But he, he might have declaimed some of his verses, but he said nothing—"

His voice broke, and at that moment I felt profoundly sorry for him.

"He was sweet, amiable and courteous—but certainly not human. And this was the man whom I had tried to adore despite my tastes and despite our differences! Oh, what a terrible disillusion, my friend! And then—" He stopped and leant against a lime tree.

" And then ? "

" He asked me what work I was engaged upon."

" And what did you tell him ? "

" I said that . . . "

" That ? "

" That I was working on a *Faust*," he burst out with angry despair.

What blasphemous presumption ! My blood froze. It was as though Adam had said to Jehovah that he was preparing to create a new universe, a more beautiful and greater universe. A *Faust* !

" And were you not struck by a thunderbolt ? " I asked him, appalled.

" No. His Excellency's face clouded. ' What keeps you in Weimar then, Herr Heine ? ' he asked me frigidly. ' Nothing— after this visit,' I replied, bowing, and took my leave."

(In his diary Goethe had made the entry : October 1st, Heinrich Heine of Göttingen.)

Well, if this really took place at their meeting . . . but no, I cannot believe it. This is my theory : Goethe must have been, in fact, very reserved with him—doubtless the insolent undertones of his letter had offended him, and the young man's unbalanced tragedies had probably also displeased him. Humiliated by Goethe's godlike indifference—he was certainly entitled to be disinterested in everyone—Heine had wished to avenge himself by spreading the report that a new *Faust* was in preparation. And this is why, immediately on his return, he confided to me that he was working on a *Faust*. Previously he had never referred to it. The idea must have come to him *between* Weimar and Göttingen, and it was only *afterwards* that he invented his account of the Weimar meeting.

November 7th.—Today Heine was extremely angry with his uncle. He received a letter from him urging him to hurry up and pass his examinations. " Well, if that is all he wants, he shall have it. I will work like a beast of burden, and I will look for my bread and butter in the scales of Themis, and not on the charitable platter of my uncle's table ! " He was almost in tears with sheer rage. Then he showed me some further passages from the *Harzreise*, which are exquisite.

November 20th.—The other day—I nearly forgot to make a note of it—Heine was very shocked by a trivial incident :

Some gay Hanoverian students conceived the idea that it would be amusing to make the Express Runner, who was already exhausted from a full day's work, run a little more . . . They bribed him with a few pieces of silver. The good fellow started out, and the healthy young sparks rode at his heels on their hunters, throwing up a cloud of dust and sometimes almost grazing the calves of the breathless runner. Heine clenched his fists. " But it's a man ! " he cried, and his voice trembled with all the emotionalism of the French Revolution. In vain I tried to explain to him that it was only a game, and that the *Courrier* was himself a willing party to it—and had, moreover, been well paid. " It is a *man*," he repeated obstinately, " one should not do such things—not even to animals." " What about hunting ? " I asked him, thinking of the excitement of the chase in my own country. " If I had my way I would forbid it for once and all ! " Seeing my surprise he went on resentfully : " Do not forget that my ancestors were never to be found among the hunters, but always among the hunted ! "

December 2nd.—Yesterday Heine stayed with me until midnight. Quite suddenly he began to speak of Goethe, with a passion that betrayed his preoccupation with the subject. He took pains to persuade me—and himself—that Goethe was now no more than a feeble and aged god, a god in retreat, soured and angry at no longer being able to lavish favours on the small fry, and fearful of the rise of the Titans. " I am sorry for him," he said.

" Goethe is above all a man of this world, for whom the enjoyment of life is the most important factor. Sometimes he had felt, and made others feel, that ideas are predominant—but he has never known how to live profoundly. I, on the contrary," he continued, " am of a passionate nature, ready to sacrifice all for ideas—even if I am completely overwhelmed in the flood.

" But I, too, understand the pleasure of life and take a joy in it, and there precisely lies the root of my great internal conflict. I resist Goethe as I do my own natural leanings. And I often ask myself whether the fanatic who offers his life for an idea does not accumulate more happiness and intensity in one instant than has the septuagenarian Herr von Goethe throughout the whole of his selfish and comfortable existence."

" Would you consider Schiller, then, a better poet and a greater man than Goethe ? " I asked him.

" Alas, no," he replied after a moment's hesitation. " I know only too well that the idealised images and the pompous monuments that Schiller raised are easier to construct than the little worldly and shabby sinners whom Goethe brings to life in his writings . . . "

" I am glad that you realise it," I answered, in all my adoration for Goethe. " Goethe is at the same time Epicurean and idealist, aware and sentimental, Prometheus and Zeus, Greek and German, bourgeois and aristocrat, poet and sage, man and god. He encompasses everything with an unsurpassed objectivity. Goethe is the Whole ! "

The lamp faded, and I fell silent. Heine, too, was worn out and did not speak.

" Yes, it's possible," he conceded at last rather wearily. " He is too great. A god certainly, but a stone god. Goethe is too powerful, and I do not love those who are too powerful—neither Shakespeare nor Dante nor Michelangelo. I love Voltaire and Lessing and Walther von der Vogelweide—less perfect, but nearer to myself."

CHAPTER FOURTEEN

AESTHETE AND REVOLUTIONARY

AT this period Goethe was being attacked from two sides : by the Pan-German Nationalists because of his cosmopolitan outlook and indifference towards German nationalism, and by the Pietist Catholics because of his atheistic, or rather Pantheistic, views. Heine admitted to Varnhagen that " narrow-minded German Nationalism and anaemic Catholic Pietism, the leading factors in the opposition to Goethe, are the two things that I detest most in all the world ; and in consequence I shall remain faithful to the great pagan.

And Heine did in fact remain faithful to Goethe, who, in *Art and Antiquity* and in his study of modern, Christian and patriotic German art, had condemned " the feudal romantics." Several years later, when at the request of his Saint-Simonist friends he composed a general study of German literature, he did not hesitate to attribute to Goethe the place he deserved—the first place. The pages he devotes to admiration of the great poet, who was then no longer alive, do him honour as an author. But here and there the bitterness of the unrecognised poet, softened to a gentle irony, peeps through the moving memories and deep exegesis. In one passage he calls Goethe the Louis XI of German thought, against whom " the feudal barons " of literature revolted because he had turned the *Tiers État* to their disadvantage. " Goethe was wary of any original writer on principle ; he only praised, and was only impressed by, small and insignificant spirits. He pushed this to such a point that to be praised by Goethe was tantamount to receiving a brief of mediocrity." Let us note in parenthesis that the charges were not without foundation. The ageing Goethe did not care for the talented young Parnassians ; he thought that he himself had said the last word in German literature.

No one, neither among his contemporaries nor in the generations that followed, has been able to assess Goethe as accurately as Heine—for whom this assessment was a personal affair.

" His impartiality," he wrote, " was the result of his Pantheistic conception of the universe : if God is in everything, it is a matter of complete indifference to pay more attention to one thing than to another—clouds or antiquities, popular songs or monkey skeletons, men or comedians . . . " Goethe approved the world such as it appeared to him, and as he was not un-acquainted with practical everyday activities he did not lack passion. But being an artist, his only duty was to understand, write, and portray reality. In his view art corresponded to the Aristotelian definition : " the limitation of nature." If an artist wished to portray the Whole, he must guard against succumbing to his own passions, mixing in human conflicts and accepting pre-judices—which Bacon called " the idols of the Forum," and among which Goethe included moral, religious and political convictions.

Thomas Mann has shown, in his brilliant study of Goethe, how much his Universalism and aestheticism were determined by his family and social conditions, by his Patrician development and by the privileged status which his Weimar protectors assured him. Everything in Goethe's destiny was exceptional : his outstanding good health and physical power were ideally suited to his Olym-pian serenity, and his long life enabled him to bring all his literary projects to fruition. What could Heine, struggling with the problems of existence, tortured with neurasthenia, humiliated by his Jewish and bourgeois status, oppose to this Jupiter of literature who, by stretching out his hand could believe that his finger directed the stars in their courses ? Nothing, except the Promethean principle—the principle of justice, in whose name man and his friends revolt against the gods. Heine opposed the Pantheistic naturalism and the general acceptance of Goethe with the revolt of the modern man, to whom everything is not " a matter of indifference," and for whom the world does not only represent a marvellous opportunity for developing the intelligence and artistic taste, but is above all a bondage of suffering, fear and constraint. To Goethe and his disciples art was the highest human activity : according to Heine, " the first place belongs to reality."

What exactly did Heine mean by " the real world " ? He meant the active participation in history, taking a stand in the vital questions of the century, and being for or against the Revolution.

Goethe, in accepting nature, approved the existing order. Heine felt that Goethe, in teaching Youth the " objective " representation of social and political reality instead of action, had exercised the most sinister influence on the political development of the German people. Had not Goethe himself said : " Action is the daughter of the Word " ? And Heine added : " . . . and the fine words of Goethe are childless."

Several years later Heine was walking through the lower galleries of the Louvre and looking at the statues of the ancient gods. " There they were, with their sightless eyes and marble smiles full of hidden melancholy . . . " The antique marbles reminded him of Goethe's poems. " They are complete, splendid and calm, and seem sorrowfully to regret that their cold immobility separates them from our warm pulsating life, that they cannot rejoice and mourn with us, that they are not human beings, but unfortunates—a mixture of divinity and stone."

In fact, after some hours spent in Goethe's company we long for the society of an artist who does not represent only a way of looking—the universal regard—but is like ourselves ; who does not merely listen with an objective curiosity to our confessions, but participates in our bitterness and our revolt. Heine is just such an artist : he sits at our table without pride, tells us his adventures, and confides in us his maddest and gayest ideas. " Whoever possesses science and art has a religion : he that is ignorant of them has need of one," was a famous Goethean aphorism. Heine did not put so much pride and distance between himself and the common man and his beliefs. When a peasant girl in the Harz Mountains once asked him : " Is it true that you believe in neither God the Father, God the Son nor in God the Holy Ghost?" the young poet replied that as a small child he had believed in God the Father, Creator of earth and heaven, but that later he had understood the Son to have been crucified by the people, and today :

> *Jetzo, da ich aufgewachsen,*
> *Viel gelesen, viel gereist,*
> *Schwillt mein Herz, und ganz von Herzen*
> *Glaub' ich an den heil'gen Geist.*

Dieser tat die grössten Wunder,
Und viel grössre tut er noch ;
Er zerbrach die Zwingherrnburgen,
Und zerbrach des Knechtes Joch.

Alte Todeswunden heilt er,
Und erneut das alte Recht ;
Alle Menschen, gleichgeboren,
Sind ein adliges Geschlecht.

Nun, so schau mich an, mein Kindchen,
Küsse mich, und schaue dreist ;
Denn ich selber bin ein solcher
Ritter von dem heil'gen Geist.

Now that I am quite grown up,
Have read a lot, seen more than most,
My heart swells out, and from my heart
Believe I in the Holy Ghost.

He achieved the greatest wonders,
And yet greater does He still ;
He destroyed the tyrants' towers,
And the slave's yoke, with His will.

Ancient mortal wounds He heals,
And renews the ancient right :
All men born as equals now
Are a noble race of might.

Now, look well on me, my childling,
Kiss me, heed me more than most,
For I myself am one of these—
Chevalier of the Holy Ghost.

In opposition to Goethe, who soared high above the heads of all parties, the young Heine defined himself as the champion of liberty and equality. Goethe concerned himself with the enduring, the general and the immutable; it was not his own period that preoccupied him but the laws that regulate the periodic changes of epochs. His orientation can be summed up in these words : " To raise oneself above human contingencies." Heine was a contemporary and disciple of Hegel, who in his philosophy had transposed every system and every law into a kind of *perpetuum mobile*. He had no wish to live above his period, but within it ; he wished to be in accord with the people, with the progressive bourgeoisie and the workers who in every part of the world were beginning to rebel against the political and ideological system of mediaeval feudalism. He was for the people against the Church and the aristocracy, for the right to happiness against resignation and oppression. It is thus that the young Heine summed up the result of his visit to Goethe.

The *Harzreise*, written after his visit to Weimar, was active and enthusiastic propaganda for democratic ideas, at a period when—as Heine wrote in the preface to the French edition of 1834—" political oppression in Germany had imposed a general silence, spirits had fallen into a despairing lethargy, and the man who still dared to speak had to express himself with as great a passion as was his despair of ever seeing liberty triumph." And he added : " At that period I was still living in the terminology of 1789."

Towards the end of 1820 his political ideology became more profound, and he outgrew his radical-bourgeois phase. The aged Goethe had also been following the efforts of the French Saint-Simonists with interest, and had studied the *Globe* sympathetically. Did not the end of *Faust*, Part II, deal with the apotheosis of industry and the grandiose expansion of public works ? Heine did not confine himself to meditating upon the ideas which fired the enthusiasm of the Paris polytechnicians, but adopted them with the zeal of a missionary, or—as he himself said—he allowed them to take possession of him. " I am a fanatic about nature . . ." Above the rustle of the pine forests of the Harz, the tocsin of the grand revolutionary fête of humanity rang in his ears.

CHAPTER FIFTEEN

HEINE'S CONVERSION

AFTER his return to Göttingen, refreshed from the mountains, Heine flung himself with renewed vigour into his legal studies. He estimated that by the following spring (1825) he would be able to sit for his doctorate. In the formal letter that accompanied his thesis on the Law of Succession (probably compiled by his jurist friends) he apologised in advance to Professor Hugo for his inadequate knowledge of the subject. " I cannot congratulate myself on a complete success, as I have neglected certain very necessary lectures—due to my predilection for philosophy, Oriental literature and the study of mediaeval and modern peoples. At Göttingen, it is true, I have devoted myself entirely to the study of the Law, but the obstinate headaches which have tormented me for the past two years have affected my work most disastrously . . ."

The Faculty showed great indulgence towards the author of *Lyrisches Intermezzo*. Perhaps they also feared the young writer's satirical pen. The examination was a great success, and as he handed Heinrich his diploma with due solemnity Hugo declared him a great Jurist but an even greater writer. " Hugo is a great man," the poet remarked with ironical generosity.

* * * *

One day in June Heine paid a visit to the little town of Heiligenstadt, near Göttingen, and introduced himself to the Protestant Pastor, Christian Grimm, with a request that he be baptised as soon as possible.

The Pastor received him graciously, but insisted that he would require the permission of the Consistory of Erfurt.

" An Israelite of Düsseldorf called Heinrich Heine," the Pastor wrote in his report, " son of a former tradesman and now a man of private means living in Lüneburg, requests to be baptised. He is studying Law at Göttingen, but does not wish to be baptised in the town, where he is too well known.   Here no one knows him. He wishes the baptism to take place in secret, in order that his Jewish origin shall not be divulged.   Already as a boy at school he suppressed this fact, and has always been taken for a Christian. Heine does not wish to be treated as a Jew once he has abandoned that religion.   He would also lose the support of a rich uncle if that relation learned that he had betrayed the religion of his ancestors . . . "

The Consistory gave permission on the condition that Heine passed an examination in the Catechism.   This examination took place on June 28.   At the close of the ordeal the Pastor was satisfied that " his conversion was not simply a matter of form, but the result of an imperious inner need."

The Pastor's words contradict Heine's statement to Moser soon after his conversion : " I assure you that if the laws had allowed me to steal silver spoons, I would never have been baptised."   Could Heine have deceived the Reverend Father Grimm ?   It is much more probable that he opened his heart frankly and honestly before him, and confided his opinion on the Jewish question and the contradictory sentiments this subject inspired in him.   He must have told him that, on the one hand, he had tried since early childhood to conceal his Jewish origin, not through shame and fear but in the desire to become part of a broader human community, and on the other hand that he would despise himself if he betrayed his own community.   Had Heine been of independent and comfortable means, and had the achievement of a Government post not entailed his conversion, he would probably never have asked to be admitted into the fold of a religion whose principles he did not approve.   It might be quoted, as apology for the author of *The Rabbi*, that in looking after his own interests he believed that he was serving the cause of tolerance and liberalism at the same time—the cause to which he had devoted his entire life.

This act, however, brought no positive advantage.   Employment in the State of Prussia remained closed to Heine, not on account of his Jewish origin but because of his political views. On the other hand, his conversion did not prevent his enemies from referring in public to his Semitic antecedents—a very efficacious argument. Heine soon realised that whatever he did the Germans would never recognise him as one of themselves. He became discouraged, and would have liked to attach himself to some other race—to some other country. " How incredibly true is the legend of the Wandering Jew ! " He recalled Moser's description, wherein the Wandering Jew was no other than " . . . a gigantic Christ with his crown of thorns journeying down the ages." He thought sadly of the lovely days in Berlin when he had discussed the redemption and emancipation of the Jews with Moser, Gans and Zunz. The Society had been dissolved in the meanwhile, Gans himself had become a convert and was launching intensive propaganda among the Jews, advocating a mass conversion. " If he is doing it by conviction," Heine wrote to Moser, " Gans is a fool : if it is hypocrisy, he is a scoundrel." The Hamburg branch of the Society had broken up, and each of its members had continued the struggle for the rights of his co-religionists according to his own lights.

Heine left Göttingen for Lüneburg to visit his parents, and then after a few months rest returned to the " accursed " Hamburg. Uncle Salomon rewarded him generously for having passed his examinations, and made it possible for him to realise at length a long-felt desire : to spend the summer on the Isle of Nordeney. To crown the poet's joy, his childhood friend from Düsseldorf, Christian Sethe, embarked with him at Cuxhaven for the island in the North Sea.

" I love the sea like my own soul." Today, every schoolboy knows that the Alps are magnificent, and that there is an affinity between the sea and the human soul. It is difficult to conceive that the beauty of tall mountains was only discovered in literature towards the end of the eighteenth century. It is to a German-Swiss writer that we owe the first poems singing the magnificence of the peaks. Heinrich Heine was the first German writer to discover the beauties of the North Sea, with its curious legends of spectral flying Dutchmen and mysterious refrains murmured by the waves.

" I ought to have been a fish," he said to his friend. He spent several days in a fishing barque, alone with the sea. The salt air, the languorous freshness and the physical exertion calmed and distracted him at the same time. In complete harmony he rose and fell, sparkled and roared with the sea. The sun appeared from behind the storm clouds. Beautiful bronzed women lounged on the beaches, but he ignored them—his renewed friendship with Christian sufficed. The two men tacitly agreed that a veil should be thrown over their estrangement and over the injuries they had inflicted on each other in the past. They exchanged ideas on every conceivable subject, and became fully reconciled. Seated on a stone bench by the water's edge, they watched the eternal assault of the waves against the cliffs.

Heine wrote poems, hymns to the sea and rhapsodic odes : *Sunset, The Gods of Greece, Song of the Oceanides* . . .

> *Sei mir gegrüsst, du ewiges Meer !*
> *Wie Sprache der Heimat rauscht mir dein Wasser* . . .

From what country did the sea breeze bring an echo to Heine ? We do not know. Probably he himself was quite unaware.

At evening he strolled on the quayside—behind him the plain of Hum with its rolling hills, before him the vast and restless sea, and above his head the sky like an immense cupola of crystal. " Then I felt no bigger than an ant, and yet my soul spread out and became as large as the world. The sublime simplicity of nature as she enfolds me here, tames and exalts me at the same time . . . "

CHAPTER SIXTEEN

THE BOOKSELLER CAMPE

Between the autumn of 1825 and the summer of 1826 Heine was once more in Hamburg, studying Livy and putting the final touches to his sea poems. " I am revising my old ideas," he wrote to Moser, " and at the same time forming new ones."

He waited impatiently for the fragments of the *Harzreise*, which he had sent to Gubitz, to appear in the *Gesellschafter*. But number after number appeared without the inclusion of his work.

Retiring into his shell, he did not stir from his room, where he alternately dreamed, sulked, toyed with the idea of suicide, and consoled himself with reading Roman History. He worked desultorily but was dissatisfied with the results. Thoroughly irritable, he felt that the whole world was his enemy. His brother-in-law, Maurice Embden, reported to Salomon that his nephew passed his days in idleness or in playing cards. Heinrich lost his temper, and Lotte—the adorable Lotte—took her husband's side. " I have lost my sister," he cried sorrowfully. His plans for a post in the University of Berlin also proved unrealisable. He wandered disconsolately round the great harbour. Hamburg was dreary ; a damp wind was blowing, which banged the doors and spread an abominable stench from the quays. The statue of Hammonia, with her opulent breasts bared to the raw climate, was black with soot. At last the trees burst into bud—suddenly and vigorously, as though to repair a delay of several months. *Es früblingt wieder in meinem Herzen* . . .

One afternoon he entered the bookshop of Hermann and Campe.

" Have you any of Heine's tragedies ? " he asked the portly and jovial Campe.

" Certainly," replied the bookseller eagerly, and from his shelf took down not only the tragedies but his collection of poems as well.

The young man, having glanced through them, returned the poems with a contemptuous curl of the lips : " They mean nothing to me ; I don't want verses like these, my dear Sir."

Did Campe realise the identity of his customer ? Had he been struck by the haunting melodies of Heine's early verse ?

" What do you mean ? " he asked indignantly. " I disagree with you profoundly." And with his hands on his hips he took up a truculent attitude before his young client.

" My dear Sir, I know them better than you do, for it is I who wrote them."

Campe showed his astonishment, and bowed deeply with a respect that was tinged with irony. " Well, my dear young Sir, if you ever happen to produce anything as bad as this, bring it to me and I shall do myself the honour of setting the stamp of our publishing house upon it."

Heine did not wait to be asked a second time. On the following day he called at the booksellers with a huge bundle of manuscripts, including the *Harzreise* and seventy-seven poems.

CHAPTER SEVENTEEN

THE BLARE OF A HORN

AT that time he was working on a book, a type of fantasia. *Das Buch Le Grand* was to be the bizarre title of this work. Legrand was the French drum major whose memory he extolled. It was a youthful and insolent *capriccio*. "Oh, women," he wrote, "hate me, laugh at me, baffle me—but let me live! Life is so insanely sweet, and the world so pleasantly topsy-turvy." It was the work of a desperate man who had now rediscovered the lure of the meadows, the trees and the sea, and who rejoiced in the sight of women, whom "with a single look he possessed more completely than other men do in reality throughout their whole lives." The sound of his flute was sometimes roguish, but this prettiness was all his own : "I speak as I feel . . ."

Heine had discovered his true self. Light and elegant, this Jew would show the Germans, with their invariably heavy wit, how they could evolve if only they would shed their ancestral bearskin. Heine somehow managed to make the German language dance, and at a wave from his wand to arise and pirouette in a whirling waltz, or a French quadrille. His compatriots never forgave him for this evanescent and smiling prose. Hitherto they had looked upon an "idea" as a personal thing, heavy as a rock, which needed the demonic force of the Niebelungs to displace. Heine, that Mozart of prose, blew upon the rock and it began to float, and (Nietzsche later used a similar technique) turn somersaults in the air and rise up into the sun's rays. In the midst of these magical metamorphoses, these naïve outbursts of *joie-de-vivre*, there rang out the blare of a horn.

*　　*　　*　　*

In his Nordeney diary Heine had already shown his great admiration for Napoleon, who had died at Saint Helena. In *Das Buch Le Grand*, without the slightest regard for the interdicts of the

Holy Alliance, he glorified the memory of the man for whom "the earth was too narrow" with a positively religious fervour. Napoleon was the war-cry with which Heine wished to incite the people against their oppressors.

"The Emperor is dead . . . He lies at peace under a miserable hillock. Five weeping willows with their long green hair watch over him. A pious brook runs by with plaintive murmur. There is no inscription to be seen on the gravestone, but Clio has engraved, in invisible characters, the words that will echo down the centuries for ever."

"England! The sea belongs to thee. But the sea has not waters enough to wash away the shame that this illustrious man has bequeathed to you in death. For centuries in the future the children of France will sing and tell of the abominable hospitality of the *Bellerophon*, and when those songs of bitterness and tears resound beyond the Channel the cheeks of every honest Englishman will blush for shame. But the day will come when this song will be heard, and England will be no more. This proud people will be lying in the dust, the tombs at Westminster will be in ruins and dispersed, and the royal dust they contain delivered to the four winds and forgotten. Saint Helena will be the Holy Sepulchre where the peoples of the East and West will come in pilgrimage in their beflagged ships, and their hearts will be fortified by the memory of this great temporal Christ who suffered under Hudson Lowe . . . as it is written in the gospel of Las Casas, O'Meara and Antommarchi."

Heine's prophecy was never realised. England still stands, and a man of the twentieth century is horrified by the idea that a German Liberal and democratic writer could in 1826 have compared Christ with that adventurer of genius who had shed the blood of thousands of Frenchmen for the chimera of an unrealisable hegemony. But it must not be forgotten that Napoleon, in the eyes of Heine and many of his contemporaries, represented the thrust from below, the chance to succeed by personal gifts and intelligence, and not by birth. The English Tories, the Prussian Junkers and the Russian Knyaz all hated the spirit of revolution in Napoleon, and the democracy of which, despite himself, he was to some extent the representative. There is no shadow of doubt that

Heine, in his acclamation of the dead Emperor's glory, exalted the idea of Equality for his contemporaries, and his cry resounded like a powerful horn in the midst of the profound silence where German reaction slumbered.

How would the Prussian censorship react to this challenge? Heine thought it more prudent not to wait on German soil for a reply to this question. On the very day his book appeared he took the boat for England. In the eighteen-twenties it was still Great Britain who offered the safest refuge for those who attacked her. The France of Polignac would without difficulty have granted a request by Prussia for his extradition. How long would he remain abroad . . . a few months, or for ever? Who could have answered this question? Perhaps it had been a little premature to trouble the German calm by a hornblast of such violence. Perhaps it would have been better both for the Cause and for himself to have spread the principles of Liberalism and Equality in whispers. Heine cast aside all his doubts. He could not resist a final seditious quip: "In this dull and servile age something *had* to be done."

CHAPTER EIGHTEEN

THE ENGLISH, FRENCH AND GERMANS

AFTER a stay of three and a half months in England Heine returned to Germany with " a rich intellectual booty."

" I saw there the most astonishing thing that the world could show to a wondering spirit. I saw it and I am still astonished. There arises always in my thoughts that fairy forest through which flows the Thames, swarming with living figures with their thousand different passions and their quivering desires of love and hatred . . . "

London and London life, and through it the grandiose and unhappy vision of modern existence, was revealed to this son of unawakened Germany. At a corner of Cheapside he saw that vision of London which appeared to him like " The crossing of the Beresina . . . where each, in a frenzy of unrest, wishes to hew out a passage for himself ; where the insolent horseman crushes the poor soldier, where he who falls is lost for ever, and men trample pitilessly over the corpses of their best friends ; where thousands, worn out and bleeding, try in vain to clutch onto the planks of the bridge or fall off into the icy ditch of death . . . " This prescient and cruel vision of the rising capitalist world caused an uproar in England ; the *Athenaeum*, in its number of September 10, 1828, published this piece of bravura in its entirety.

In the mind of Heine, imbued with German radicalism, the sight of this astonishing spectacle aroused one question : how to reconcile the almost unlimited political liberty enjoyed by the English with the terrible injustices of their social and economic order. Would the political liberty from which the German Radicals expected a renaissance of their country and an emancipation of their society not prove to be the panacea they had imagined ? The English Radicals with whom he associated enlightened him with bitter irony on the deep reasons for the insufficiences of English liberty. These faults, they explained to him, arose chiefly from the national character. "The English are a domestic people : they lead a narrow and peaceable family life. The Englishman is content with this liberty, which guarantees his personal rights, protects without restriction his person, his property, his married life, his beliefs and even his caprices . . . He tolerates patiently the sight of a privileged aristocracy, and consoles himself with the thought that the rights he possesses prevent that aristocracy from interfering with his pleasures and external comfort—and his way of living."

Heine had perceived that with the English—even with the Liberals—the fanatical attachment to liberty and the respect for historic laws were allied with a complete indifference to social inequality. What the rationalist thinker considers as " revolting contrasts," the majority of the English take as the natural order of life. In England the present is not built on the past, but exists conjointly with a living past. In this "so modern country" the Middle Ages are a living reality. "The concessions made there to liberal ideas have been torn with difficulty from the ever present Middle Ages, and all the modern improvements have been the result, not of a principle, but of a necessity." But while the French doctrinaires such as Guizot, Royer-Collard and other disciples of Montesquieu rightly cited as an example the English Constitution, by reason of its practical and organic character, Heine criticised the " duplicity " (*Fluch der Halbheit*) of English political life—not with the delight and detachment of an aesthete, but with the indignation of a humanist in sympathy with the fallen and suffering. This duplicity, he thought, produced of necessity new sufferings and mortal combats, and naturally a host of consequences.

The " Lie " of popular representation, the heavy taxes, the harshness of criminal procedure, the persecution of certain sects, the misery of the industrial population . . . all these sombre aspects of English life were due, according to Heine, to the fact that the English had never carried their revolution for liberty through to the end, and had not completely eradicated the vestiges of the Middle Ages, had not destroyed once and for all the material and spiritual power of the religious and laic aristocracy. As long as this power existed, and as long—and this was the case at the time of Heine's visit—as "the good fairies" of Great Britain, the Whigs, were compelled to give place to the "demons," the Tories, the Continental Liberals could only look upon England with suspicion, and she would virtually remain the stronghold of counter-revolution.

It is perhaps not without interest to note that some years after Heine's visit to England a young English author, Benjamin Disraeli, in his novel *Sybil* or *The Two Nations* also criticised most severely the duplicity of the English system and the reign of the oligarchy, which entailed the "humiliation of Her Royal Majesty and the degradation of the masses." While Heine postulated that "between the four bare whitewashed walls of the English Episcopal Church one felt less at ease than in the spacious, ornate and effeminate spiritual prison of Catholicism," Disraeli by way of reply affirmed that "the English people had always been religious and Catholic, and that their vivid imagination was unsuited to the hair shirt of hypocritical Puritanism." And Heine added that the English laws were like so many tentacles by means of which the monsters of the aristocracy seized their booty, and that "on the Continent there was no tyrant capable of arbitrarily imposing on his good people as many taxes as the English are obliged to pay to their kings."

According to Disraeli, the oligarchic classes allied to the House of Orange were responsible for the unbalanced system of taxation : it was they who had introduced the "Dutch financial methods." Heine only awaited the complete realisation of modern revolutionary principles in England in a rebellion of the people, whereas the English author dreamed of a revolution that would re-establish "the true realm"—that is to say, absolute monarchy, based on the attachment and interests of a people freed from the talons of the oligarchy.

These two young men, both of great talent, despite the difference of their outlook on the world, agreed on certain points—chiefly in that they both regarded politics with an almost religious fervour and loathed the compromise that characterised the English Constitution. The one was fundamentally a Monarchist and Tory, the other a Democrat.

Heine's experience in England only strengthened his almost

boundless admiration for revolutionary France. To the English, with their too personal interpretation of liberty, he opposed the French, who could if need be forgo individual liberty, "provided one gave them that portion of liberty that we call equality." Equality, in the eyes and hearts of Frenchmen, is not a portion but the very essence of liberty. Men are born equal : it was the gospel of the century, the new religion. The chosen people of this religion were the French, "for it is in their tongue that the first gospels and the first dogmas have been formulated—like the New Jerusalem and the Rhine . . ."

Yes, the Rhine . . . At the corner of Cheapside, leaning against the lowered shutters of a shop window—the business had gone into bankruptcy—Heine dreamed of the mission of great nations, and his thoughts turned towards the German countries. If the English stood for respect of the Middle Ages and the modern lure of profit, and if the French were the apostles of liberty and equality, what did Germany signify in the eyes of the world ? English private life was a fortress whose walls were guarded by inviolate laws ; the French waged an interminable war for absolute liberty ; "the Germans," he thought with bitterness and disgust, "have no need of either liberty or equality." The author of the *Harzreise* discovered at the corner of Cheapside not only the secret of French and English political life, but also the astonishing anachronism of the German variety, with its somnolent lack of dynamism.

"We are a race of poets and thinkers." Very true, he thought. While the English were conquering India and the French were demolishing the Bastille and hoisting their tricoloured flag in most of the European capitals, Germany was watching the rise of a Kant who refuted the theist arguments, of a Goethe who depicted the tragedy of man, and a Mozart who recorded the delights of Spring and the agonies of love. But those were only isolated instances of genius : what had the German people themselves contributed to the grand concourse of nations ? Of what great idea could the Germans be proud that could compare with the Jewish Laws, the English Magna Carta and the French Declaration of the Rights of Man ? The patriotism of the Jahns dressed in their Teuton doublets ? The hatred of the Jews, of the French

Babylon and of Roman and Mediterranean civilisations ? Their abominable servility, which enabled them to tolerate the rule of the Junkers ; Prussian militarism that refuted the thesis repeated a thousand times by every philosopher from Aristotle to Voltaire : " that every race possesses a natural instinct for liberty and equality " ? Must then the originality of the German people consist in the substitution of the herd instinct for the sentiment of individual liberty ?

In one of London's West End concert halls, " The Fashionable," he saw a performance by a troupe of Tyrolean dancers in national costume, who yodelled and danced and were a great success. " My heart was filled with bitterness," he wrote. " It was as though I had heard the purity of the German language grossly insulted." These honest Tyroleans who were selling their serene and smiling servility for a few shillings appeared to him the true symbol of German inferiority.

One day he went to the India Docks in the Port of London, and boarded a ship that had just put in from Bengal. " The figures and grotesque groups, the bizarre striped costumes, the enigmatic faces and astonishing postures, the strange and savage accents, the gaiety and the laughter . . . all this was for me a very kaleidoscope of enchantment. Somewhat sated with the heavy and monotonous life of the West and tired of Europe, this little section of Asia, displayed to me in all its vividness and serenity, brought me true solace, and I filled my lungs with this atmosphere of which I had often dreamed at nights in the fog of Hanover and Prussia."

This was neither the first nor the last time that Heine felt his country to be neither Germany nor indeed Europe, but the bright and burning East. One remembers his charming poem in which he tells of the nostalgia of the Northern Pine for the Lotus on the banks of the Ganges . . . However, his nostalgia passed. If he had no fatherland he would create one for himself ; he would try to arouse the conscience of the German people with the whip of irony, and revive in it the sentiment of human dignity. As a disciple of Rousseau he could not conceive it possible that there could exist a people utterly devoid of all sense of civic dignity, generosity and truth . . .

CHAPTER NINETEEN

SISYPHUS

AFTER his stay in London Heine spent a few weeks in Ramsgate. There he started a flirtation with an English lady, whom he called in his diary Mathilde, and which was continued at a later date at the Spa of Lucca. When Mathilde—whose pleasant smile fills the happy pages of the *Bains de Lucca*—asked him how he had occupied his time since their last meeting, he replied with some bitterness : " I have carried on with my own profession, Milady. I have been rolling the great rock unceasingly. Each time I arrived half way up the mountain, it suddenly fell to the bottom, and I was obliged to start all over again."

The rock that Heine-Sisyphus forced himself to push with such effort to the top of the mountain was his own destiny. When he learnt through his friends that the German Censorship, contrary to all expectations, had closed its eyes to the revolutionary tendencies of *Das Buch Le Grand*, and that he could safely return to Germany, new hope was aroused within him. Was this indulgence on the part of the censor exceptional, or did it augur a more liberal attitude on the part of the Prussian authorities ?

Immediately on his return to Hamburg he used his diplomatic relations in Berlin to sound the attitude in Government circles for his chances of obtaining a professorial chair in the Berlin University as *Privatdozent* (private lecturer or teacher). The first replies were encouraging, but months slipped by without his receiving a nomination. It is therefore quite understandable that he accepted with alacrity the offer made to him by old Baron Johann Friedrich Cotta—the publisher of Goethe, Schiller and Hegel—of the editorship of the *Politische Annalen*, the periodical issued by his branch in Münich.

Before arriving in Münich Heine prepared a single volume edition of his collected poems—*Das Buch der Lieder*. Julius Campe agreed after much difficulty to publish this collection, from which Heine himself hoped for a literary more than a financial success.

This explains the paltry sum of fifty louis that he received for the manuscript. It was one of the greatest mistakes of his life : the first edition was immediately sold out, and from that moment Campe reprinted the poems every two years, from which he gained considerable sums of money—without ever sharing the profits with the poet. After the appearance of the *Buch der Lieder*, Heine paid a visit to his parents in Lüneburg. The sight of his father, who had in recent years become an impotent old man, saddened him. Then he set out for Münich. At Cassel he called on the brothers Grimm, the scholarly philologists and specialists in folk-lore, who received him warmly. During this visit the third brother Grimm, the painter, made a portrait in charcoal of Heine in a Byronic attitude, his head leaning on his hand and a far-away look in his eyes. He also spent several days in Frankfurt, where he met Ludwig Börne, whose name was known throughout the whole of Germany as one of the leading figures of German Radicalism.

An old memory surged up within him. Twelve years previously he had found himself in Frankfurt with his father. While the old man carried out his commissions Heinrich would wander about the streets admiring the shop windows until it was time to rejoin his father. Then they would go together to the reading-room of the Masonic Lodge. One day a young business man who knew his father leant over towards him, and pointing out a tall, soberly dressed man in a dark cloak who walked through the hall without even noticing them, said to them in a respectful whisper : " That is Doctor Börne, who writes against the ' comedians '. . . "

Now he hardly recognised the silhouette of the dark cloak that had once assumed such enormous proportions in his imagination. Börne, the revolutionary, the chastiser of " comedians ", as he saw him now was a rather stocky little man with a rosy complexion and sleek black hair.

" I am Heine."

" Well—continue always to be," replied Börne, shaking him cordially by the hand.

The brothers in arms, soldiers of the same corps, descendants of the same race, Judeo-Germanic revolutionaries, took stock of each other with that friendly hostility that is almost inevitable between allied rivals. They exchanged compliments and mutual congratulations . . .

"I have just read the second volume of the *Reisebilder*," said Börne. "You speak of God with too little respect," he reproached, with a twinkle in his eye. "But," he added in an almost cutting tone, "what is more serious—with too much respect for Napoleon. How can you possibly describe him as 'immortal, eternally admired, eternally regretted'? You must allow me to point out that a revolutionary writer should never be led into such idolatry . . . nor has he any right to falsify history. You display too much regard for a figure who, after all, was only a human despot. Have you forgotten the eighteenth Brumaire? A revolutionary can only be a Republican!"

Heine received these doctrinaire remonstrances somewhat coldly.

"Napoleon is for me the Code Napoleon," he replied, knowing full well that he was wrong, and that his admiration was more lyrical than considered. He admitted Börne's criticisms from the logical standpoint, but they appeared less acceptable in the light of romance.

He did not dare to argue with this intransigent inquisitor or face the challenge of those piercing eyes, knowing that Börne would dismiss any myth, either ancient or modern, with rationalist brutality. He promised to revise his conceptions of Napoleon, and to rectify his mistake . . . Börne emptied his glass to their friendship without the least suspicion that he had humiliated his friend.

"We must weigh our every word, and show the world the whole unvarnished truth . . . tear off every mask, dispel every illusion. What a cruel and magnificent task!"

Heine the iconoclast and blasphemer felt a sudden desire to defend the rights of illusion and poetry. They spoke at length of Goethe, of Campe and Cotta, and raged against the terms of his editions and against the censorship. Like two statesmen from different countries who have just concluded a treaty of friendship, they passed in review all questions of mutual interest, but neglected any topic that might have given rise to misunderstanding. Outwardly they parted in complete accord, but subconsciously they felt an antipathy for each other which neither of them could for long suppress.

At Stuttgart he met another young writer, Menzel, who had just published a history of German literature in which he had severely criticised the classicism of Goethe. Menzel received Heine with profound respect—he held him as one of the masters of the new literary school. Some years later this same Menzel violently attacked " the Semitic frivolity and cosmopolitanism of Heine," and denounced his revolutionary concepts.

He was welcomed with great enthusiasm by his new Münich colleagues : Michael Beer, the playwright and brother of the composer Meyerbeer, Baron Schenk and Lindner, whom Cotta had made his co-editor and partner. The Russian Ambassador, Baron Tiutchev, a broadminded diplomat of the French school, and amateur poet, introduced him into the most exclusive circles. The newspaper gave him little work to do, and Lindner took most of the tiresome tasks on his own shoulders.

Heine wrote articles on liberty and equality, and prepared for the publication of his *English Journal*. It was all very well for the son of the Düsseldorf Jewish hosier to live the life of a lord and to attract " smiles from the most beautiful women in the world : the Müncheners are making a great mistake . . ." he wrote to Varnhagen in Berlin. " . . . They are deceiving themselves if they think that I shall no longer hurl balls of fire at the aristocracy : my love of equality and hatred of the hierarchy have never been stronger than they are today. . . ."

Although he had asked Baron Cotta to present his books to the King, and to assure His Majesty that the writer was much more serene and peaceful than his writings would indicate—and that perhaps he had changed a good deal since his earlier writings— we have good reason to doubt the sincerity of his proffered allegiance. Without considering Heine as a knight of honour ready for every sacrifice, we must presume that he had more ambition than to sacrifice his pretensions as a political writer for a modest professorship. It would be unjust to accuse Heine of having tried to sell his pen during his stay in Munich. Many times during his life he showed that it was possible, without being a hothead, to take risks for his ideas by means of caution

and strategy : he was prepared to accept certain compromises—
but not to betray. Naturally, it was extremely important for him
to feel solid ground under his feet : although nearing his thirtieth
year, and while all his old schoolfriends had obtained situations,
he remained a wanderer whose subsistence depended upon his
publishers, the censors and Uncle Salomon. He was still a Peter
Schlemihl careering down the highways of life in search of his
shadow, which he had sold to the Devil. He was greatly in need
of material security to enable him to continue his creative and
militant work in freedom.

Having heard the rumour that the Munich Radicals were
accusing him of treachery because of certain paradoxes and his
" friendship with the aristocrats," he complained irritably to
Varnhagen that one could sometimes by a jest—and even in the
interest of the Cause—be guilty of a few peccadilloes, provided
that these did not impair the main principles of one's life.

He had a great number of enemies in Munich, chiefly in the
Jesuit salons, who had far more influence over the King, with
his mystical leanings, than the Liberals. The longer his nomination was delayed the more uneasy he became in the Bavarian
capital, which the courtesan writers boasted of as the new Athens
by reason of the buildings the King had built in the Grecian
style, such as the Pinakothek and the Glyptothek. Heine found
this mixture of Bavarian good humour, bigotry, the odour of beer,
Greek temples and Romantico-Catholic demagogy quite insupportable. It was here that he first encountered Catholicism as
a political force. He felt that the clericalism of Southern Germany represented as powerful an obstacle to German emancipation
as the absolutism of the Prussian King and the Junkers. " Without
the State Religions, and without the privileges of cult and dogma,
Germany would be strong and united and her sons would be great
and free," he noted in his journal. " But our country is torn
with religious dissensions . . . everywhere there is nothing but
suspicion regarding Catholicism, crypto-Catholicism or crypto-
Protestantism ; everywhere there are accusations of heresy,
espionage, Pietism, mysticism, delation of ecclesiastical gazettes
and sectarian hatreds . . . and while we speculate about Heaven
we are lost on earth. Indifference in the matter of religion would

perhaps be the only way of salvation, and a weakening of faith might give Germany a greater political strength." Ten years later the young disciples of Hegel : Ludwig, Feuerbach, Bruno Bauer, David Strauss and Karl Marx, developed this theme. Heine was at the root of their principal thesis, which insisted that the criticism of religion should precede the criticism of social institutions, and that this was the prerequisite to all political action.

CHAPTER TWENTY

THE BATHS OF LUCCA

During the winter of 1828 Heine often went to Schlössel to visit Schumann the composer, who had already put several of his poems to music, as for example *Die zwei Grenadiere*. They would abuse the Philistines and the Jesuits, and the smell of beer that drowns all inspiration. From the terraced gardens of the Bockkeller they could see the snowy summits of the Alps gleaming in the winter sun.

And then overnight came a change in the weather. This is how Heine himself described the revolution of the seasons :

" The mountains trembled with joy, and their snowy tears fell abundantly. The icy crusts of the lake melted and cracked . . . All Nature smiled, and her smile was the Spring. And then for me too there began a new Spring ; new flowers blossomed in my heart. Thoughts of liberty like roses, tender desires like young violets . . . and doubtless too, among them, many a useless nettle . . ."

It seemed as though the wind had carried the scent of lemon and orange trees from over the mountains into the Bavarian valley. Heine felt an irresistible desire to go to Italy. He did not yet know that land where the orange blossoms under a cerulean sky and where the shadows are deeper than anywhere else in the world. He felt the need for light and gaiety, and smiling foreign landscapes.

He arranged with his friends to wait in Genoa or Lucca for his nomination to a professorship, and the diligence bore him across the Tyrol into Italy. His brother Max accompanied him as far as the frontier.

The itinerary of Heine's Italian journey was Trieste, Verona, Milan, Genoa, Leghorn, Florence, Bologna, Ferrara and Venice. As soon as he had set foot in the peninsula he felt as though he had escaped from prison. " Ti-ri-li ! Ti-ri-li ! I see ! . . . I feel all the joys and sufferings of the world ! . . . I suffer for the salvation of the human race, I expiate its sins—but I rejoice too because of them . . ."

The three books that he wrote during his stay in Italy were books of happiness and revenge.

While he was there he received a copy of *Eos*, the Journal of Joseph Göres, wherein the Jesuit Father, Döllinger, attacked him violently for his anti-religious writings, and called him " an impertinent and shameless Jew." There too he received a comedy by an aristocratic poet, Count Platen, entitled : " The Romantic Oedipus." In the manner of Aristophanes the author pilloried Heine and Immermann, accusing them of mutual admiration and aggrandisement. In this comedy Platen puts the following words into the mouth of Immermann—whom he called Nimmermann :

"Nimmermann :   Am I not a great man ? Berlin acclaims my art, and my art criticisms are published in Hegel's weekly as a token of their worth. In them I have explained why the convert *Heine*, my companion in arms, appears to me not only a Byron but a Petrarch . . . but I might also have called him the *Pindar of the little tribe of Benjamin*, since he has hailed me as the leading tragic author of our time.

Then, tearing her hair, *Reason* bursts out :

Reason :   Oh, Lessing, Lessing, turn in your grave !

Nimmermann :   Oh, Heine, offspring of Abraham, thus I sing of you ! . . .

Chorus :   He dies, and groaning calls upon his friend the Devil.

Public :   You are mistaken : it is not the Devil he is calling, he is invoking the *Petrarch of the Feast of Tabernacles*.

Nimmermann :   You are one of the greatest poets : you say so yourself.

Public :   It is true : he admits it himself in a little poem. Only no one believes him—as happens to every *Prophet*.

Nimmermann : How well you launched your career, *O Pride of the Synagogues*.

Public :   It is true. He is your closest friend . . . and the most insolent of mortals."

The Jesuit Döllinger and Platen—in whom Heine recognised only the aristocrat—had attacked him simultaneously, and as though they had formed an alliance had tried to discredit him in the eyes of the public by drawing attention to his Jewish origin. Still smarting from his setback in Münich, where he had really tried to acclimatise himself, Heine thought that the moment had come to strike back. If previously he had exercised a certain restraint he now gave free rein to his indignation. He made a review of all those who had offended him during the past years : the Göttingen professors, Savigny the reactionary lawyer, the clericals of Munich, his Uncle Salomon, the Rothschilds of Frankfurt who had received him with condescension, Goethe and Count Platen . . . the living and the dead. He was convinced that by making a cruel and ruthless example of them, by taking a literary vengeance on his personal enemies, he would in the long run be serving the principles that he stood for in Germany. He worked with an infernal joy on these articles, which were a fire-work display of dialectic, sparkling satire, biting jest, glowing narrative, passionate avowal and Voltairean aphorism. It was as though he had just discovered his true personality and goal ; for the first time he showed himself to the world divested of false shame and consideration. It was on the battlefield of Marengo that the meaning of his destiny became clear to him : " . . . at the very place where General Bonaparte had drunk the cup of victory to the dregs . . ." the task of nineteenth-century man was fully revealed to Heine. At Verona and in Milan he had several opportunities for discussion with Italian Carbonari, who informed him of the extent of the Italian revolutionary move-ment—they did not hide from him that they were in communication with the clandestine French clubs, with Hungarian and Polish patriots and Swiss and Belgian Radicals. In every country saps were being built which would lead to the downfall of the clerical and aristocratic monarchies. On the battlefield of Marengo he wrote in his diary that aphorism of historical importance that constitutes one of his greatest merits : " There are no more nations in Europe—only parties."

Kings and aristocrats can only rule nations while the latter have not yet recognised the fact that the true threat to their security comes from monarchist ambition and not from other nations. This truth, which was rapidly gaining ground in Europe, was breaking down nationalist barriers and the frontiers of language and politics. " There are no more nations : only parties . . ." Heine was so delighted with this axiom that he proposed it as epigraph to his new series of *Politische Annalen*. He formulated with simplicity and brilliant clarity the credo of the nineteenth century, for which thousands of men were to die on the barricades of every capital in Europe. That credo, that religion, was :

> " *Emancipation . . . not only of the Irish, the Greeks, the Frankfurt Jews, the negroes of America . . . but the emancipation of the whole world—and above all of Europe, who has achieved her majority . . .*"

To the French, as Heine the German fully realised, went the credit of having revealed this emancipation. The Milanese Carbonari took their instructions from France—from Paris. Liberals and Democrats all over the world turned to France as Mohammedans turn towards Mecca. The German Radicals would have to overcome and abandon their antipathy to the French, born of the " struggles for independence " of 1813. Heine profited by the occasion to rectify his previously professed conception of Napoleon : he warned his readers that he must not be considered a Bonapartist. " I pay my homage," he wrote, " to a man's genius—whoever he may be—and not to his actions, whether he be called Alexander, Caesar or Napoleon. I admire neither the act nor the fact, but only the human spirit."

It was in the course of these Italian reflections that Heine became the " good European," whom Nietzsche later placed in the same rank as Goethe, Stendhal, Beethoven and Napoleon. " All the uncouth idiosyncracies of peoples are smoothed away under the influence of European civilisation . . ." wrote Heine. At the same time, thinking he saw an increasing exchange of European literature, Goethe took up a similar stand for the unity of world literature. Political ideas have no more nationality than mathematics or natural science. The works of Shakespeare were appreciated as much in Germany as in England—and even the French, who were much more exclusive intellectually than the Germans, were beginning to enjoy Walter Scott, Cervantes, Byron, Goethe and Hoffmann. *Europe, my country!* exclaimed Heine during his wanderings, with the same joy as three and a half centuries before Christopher Columbus had evinced on first sighting the New World.

In the best European minds there sprang up with a fatal simultaneity a new international-cosmopolitan patriotism. This new internationalism, the European movement, the idea of which was conceived both by Heine and Stendhal on Italian soil, did not merely signify a theoretical unification of European culture ; the conflict waged by the patriots of Europe for the realisation of French revolutionary ideas gave it a concrete meaning. Because Heine so vigorously attacked Teuton nationalism he was obliged to disassociate himself from the privileged Jews, from the Rothschilds and the Salomon Heines. One of the most amusing passages in his Italian writings is the satirical portrait of Baron Gumpelino and his valet, Hyacinth Hirsch. Max Brod, one of the best biographers of Heine, is exaggerating in our opinion when he asserts that in the character of Gumpelino the author wished to hold up to ridicule the " assimilated Jew." Heine took as his target two types of Jew : firstly, the financial snob who, like the Baron, imitated the Christian aristocrat: " . . . . in Rome pretending to be a man of the Church, in England maintaining the best racing stable and in Paris keeping the most beautiful opera girl " ; and secondly, in the person of Hyacinth Hirsch, the Jew with the soul of a flunkey. He made no secret of the fact that to these two types who, by ambition and love of money, denied the faith of their ancestors without exchanging it for a more generous, human and universal belief, he preferred the poor rag and bone man in his levite : " . . . The ragged Moses of Hamburg who, with all his worldly belongings on his back, wheels his cart every day of the week in the wind and rain to gain a few marks, but who, when he returns on Friday evening, finds the five-branched candlestick lit and the table covered with a white cloth, and laying down his bundle and his cares, sits down at the table next to his neglected wife and even more neglected daughter, eats fish with them cooked in a savoury white garlic sauce, sings the most glorious psalms of King David, and rejoices once again with all his heart that the children of Israel have been delivered out of Egypt." The cosmopolitan Heine reserved all his sympathy for the poor Jew in rags, who was as pitiful and magnificent as the Catholic Silesian weaver or the Protestant serf of East Prussia.

On the battlefield of Marengo, leaning against a weeping willow, Heine reflected on his friends, his enemies, loves and hatreds, sorrows and hopes. Henceforward he was no longer alone and without a country on this earth, but a member of a party and an army, and at one with all those who struggle for liberty. Humanity was only just embarking upon this great world struggle ; in his clearer moments he saw the great suffering it would entail. Whoever wishes for emancipation must desire war with all its privation, suffering and horror. However terrible war may be it bears testimony to the intellectual grandeur of man—who can defy death. He thought of Hegel's words : " Only he is worthy to be called citizen who offers his life and death to the community . . ." Life and Death . . . was it too heavy a price to offer one's life for an idea, whose ultimate meaning was Life ?

Heine suppressed all these doubts that were unworthy of a fighter. He chased away the terrifying images of death, prison, torture and exile that lay in wait for the pioneers of emancipation. Hope of a time, " . . . when liberty and the sun shall warm the earth more joyously than all this aristocracy of nocturnal stars, is worthy of any sacrifice and suffering ; a new generation will be born of free embraces, uncontrolled by the ecclesiastical marshalsea. From these men born without fetters will arise a world of thoughts and sentiments of which we others who are slaves have not the least idea." However precious human life may be, and however painful the renunciation of physical and spiritual pleasures in the course of our single life, the risk must be taken—for the benefit of future generations. . . .

Heine now knew whither the road led that hitherto he had taken instinctively ; towards a tomb upon which his descendants would perhaps place wreaths of laurel. But these he did not covet. "When I am dead," he wrote, "place no laurels upon my tomb, but the sword—signifying that I have been a good soldier in the war for the deliverance of humanity . . ."

*　　*　　*　　*

Heine spent the happiest and perhaps the most productive period of his life at Lucca, where he shared his time between work and the beautiful Englishwoman whose name we do not know. Never had his pen flowed more freely . . . every line bubbles with gaiety. But suddenly the skies clouded over : he received a letter from his mother telling him of the grave state of his father's health. He became a prey to evil forebodings. His proposed visit to Rome was postponed and he packed his trunks ready to return home.

At Venice a second letter brought news that his father was worse. How slowly the diligence crawled along the dusty roads . . . At Würzburg he learned that his father was dead. He burst into tears in the tiny village post-office. "One only has one father—and he should live for ever!" Never again would he kiss Samson Heine's lemon-scented hand or see that dignified white head . . .

In Lucca he had felt a god among the gods, and now to punish his pride—having given him nectar to drink and garlands for his hair, and he had been intoxicated by the feast—they had hurled him down from Olympus into the mud. After the great vision of Marengo and the euphoria of Lucca, Heine, once more sober, discovered to his sorrow the frailty of human life.

CHAPTER TWENTY-ONE

THE GALLIC COCK CROWS A SECOND TIME

HEINE went direct to Lüneburg to see his father's tomb. He spent several weeks with his mother trying to console her as best he might, and finally persuaded her to move to Hamburg where she would be nearer to the family and to her daughter Lotte, and where she would not be so lonely. Then he set out for Berlin to finish his Italian writings.

In Berlin he quarrelled with Rahel Varnhagen, who had reproached him during a discussion—it was again on the subject of Goethe—for his excessive vanity. " The future will show that I am capable of sacrificing my personal vanity and any private considerations for a noble cause," the poet replied, stung to anger ; and it was many months before he was seen again in the Varnhagens' salon. He drowned his sorrow and impatience in his work, studying Sterne, Thiers and the first numbers of the *Globe*, and preparing himself scientifically and zealously for his career as a " political writer."

In the summer of 1829 he revisited Heligoland, and having finished his Italian articles returned to Hamburg to supervise the publication of the third volume of the *Reisebilder*, which was to appear in the following spring.

The book was received with a storm of vituperation. Even his best friends were indignant over the crudity of his attacks on his literary adversary Platen, whose alleged homosexuality he blatantly exposed. " The coarseness of this attack upon Platen," they told him, " unfortunately casts a shadow upon a book that is rich in philosophical ideas . . . " Heine protested in vain that in attacking Platen he had aimed at " the representative of a party " : those who knew the Count knew only too well that he was no more aristocratic than Lord Byron, no more clerical than Goethe, and that he read the French Liberal reviews with as much enthusiasm as did the poet. The duel between these two men was tragi-comic since, as it was learned later, Platen had belittled the *Buch der Lieder* because he had given credence to erroneous reports that Heine had deserted Liberalism during his stay in Münich. He had ridiculed the phantom of a " traitor Heine," while the poet had stabbed at the shade of a reactionary clerical poet who had nothing in common with the true Platen. It must be admitted in Heine's favour—and Immermann pointed this out to their mutual friends—that it was not he who had first brought the discussion down to a personal level, and that having realised his mistake in retaliating, he had had the offensive passages erased from subsequent editions, and apologised publicly to the Count.

* * * *

In June 1830 he returned—for the last time in his life—to Heligoland, in the hope of curing his neuralgia. He took long walks round the harbour and lazed on the red rocks watching the patient fisherfolk repairing their nets. But this summer not even the sea view could restore his nervous equilibrium. " . . . Just as birds foretell physical upheavals such as storms, earthquakes and floods, there are men who can scent social revolution, when they become strangely disturbed, paralysed and stupified . . . " he wrote to his friend Varnhagen. He was torn between doubt and hope. The lack of appreciation shown for his Italian book, even by his best friends, depressed him profoundly. He thought of abandoning politics and philosophy and devoting himself to art criticism and the observation of nature. " What is the use of tormenting myself," he wrote in his notebook, "I may well sacrifice myself for the general good ; but *what* good will it do the world ? . . . "

He did not sleep at night, and was haunted by nightmares in which he was arrested by Prussian Police, fettered and thrown into a gloomy prison. Outside he heard dogs barking furiously, steps approaching . . . He leaped from his bed and opened the shutters feverishly. No one ! But perhaps yonder . . . in the distance—hidden behind the shrubbery on the further side of the palisade . . . He could hardly wait for the dawn. Perhaps the sun would never rise again . . . perhaps time had come to a stop !

He lay full length on his bed, motionless ; he tried to cry out, but no sound would come from his throat.

One day he confided his nightly torments to Fräulein Siebert, the Berlin actress, as they waited for the weekly post in the little harbour. On the narrow quay the summer visitors chattered in their gay costumes ; children cried, mothers scolded and the Captain barked out embarkation orders in a harsh voice. Heine and Fräulein Siebert kept a little aloof and could not hear the Captain's words ; he seemed to be making an important announcement . . .

" What is he saying ? "

Heine forced his way through the crowd. " What news—revolution in France ? "

" The King has fled ! "

The Captain handed him a crumpled news-sheet. The poet's hand trembled as he took it : " *Revolution in France . . . Polignac régime at an end . . . citizens up in arms . . .* "

The people had taken up arms again to avenge fifteen years of lies, hypocrisy and humiliation.

Heine handed back the news-sheet, and forgetting Fräulein Siebert, pushed his way through the crowd who were excitedly discussing the news, and ran towards the hotel. He felt that he must be alone with his overwhelming happiness ; he rushed into his room, threw himself down on his bed and began to sob like a child. This was the day he had waited for, hoped for and summoned for many a long year.

Here was the proof. " . . . the great French Revolution was no hazard, no vagary in the course of history, but on the contrary a stage in an ineluctable historical evolution—an evolution that none could stop with impunity . . . "

The spirit of the Revolution had not been dead, it had only slumbered. Heine had the feeling of awakening along with the new-born world . . . he was living historic hours in the midst of armed comrades, surrounded by the Tricolour, smelling the powder, intoxicated with blood and liberty, intoning the *Marseillaise*. He thought with tenderness of the French, the sons of Tambour Legrand, the citizens of Paris, of whom he was as proud as though they were his own brothers. " *Yes, Frenchmen,*

you deserve to be free, for you carry liberty in your hearts . . ." He
blew kisses to the white head of Lafayette (he did not know that
the hero of the two worlds wore a white wig). Now begins a new
era for France . . .

The French people had not only overthrown the Polignac
regime, but had through the French Restoration struck a decisive
blow at the whole system of the Holy Alliance.

In 1815 the reigning princes had promised a Constitution not
only to the French but to the other European nations. The July
Revolution gave a healthy warning to monarchs, and showed them
what awaited them if they obstinately opposed the people's claims.

In one blow all Heine's doubts disappeared and he felt full of
renewed hope. " Now, once again, I know what I want and
what I should do. I, too, am a son of the Revolution. I am
all joy, all enthusiasm. I am the sword. I am the flame ! "

At the other end of Germany, at Sode, that other champion of
German Liberalism, Börne, had received the news of the July
Revolution with the same enthusiasm. He returned to Frankfurt
in great haste, and his friends hardly recognised him, so youthful
had the breath of revolution made him. The following day,
Heine, urged by the same desire for action, embarked for Cuxhaven, bound for Hamburg.

He found the free port in a turmoil. " . . . even here,
where the hatred of the French has taken such deep root, there
now reigns an unquestionable enthusiasm for France. Everything
has been forgotten : tricoloured flags waved at several windows ;
women strolled about with cockades pinned on their breasts ; the
cabarets, filled to overflowing, rang with the strains of the
Marseillaise. In the Masonic Lodges fiery speeches could be
heard ; in the cafés men who understood French translated from
the *Journal des Débats* . . ." Heine was acclaimed wherever he
went as the representative of victorious liberalism.

News of demonstrations arrived from the industrial towns of
the Rhineland, from Saxony and Bavaria. Order and calm
reigned in the Prussian capital.

It was whispered that in order to prevent an uprising the
Prussian Government, warned by events in France, were considering the introduction of a Liberal Constitution. If this proved

to be true, thought Heine, his place was in Berlin. However inadequate this new Constitution might be it would blaze the trail of liberty. He shared the conviction held by his contemporaries that where the Press is free the essential conditions of Democracy are evident.

He approached his friend Varnhagen again and asked him whether, in view of the proposed changes, he could count on a chair in the Berlin University. He quoted the example of the French Liberals on this subject who, while implacably opposed to Charles X, did not refuse their support to the Duke of Orléans. He himself was no more radical than Thiers or Lafayette, but, he warned Varnhagen, in the event of his failing this time he would take extreme measures. If he were not allowed to live in Germany as a free man and a free writer, nothing remained for him but to take refuge in France. A régime incapable of taking an object lesson from the misfortune of the Bourbons could not count on his indulgence.

Certain of Heine's biographers consider this letter to Varnhagen to be in the nature of an ultimatum, and that in exchange for a professorship he would have been disposed to abandon the struggle for his own convictions. This interpretation appears to us to be incorrect. As he had done in München, we think that Heine was ready to consider a compromise with the Government on condition that his intellectual liberty was guaranteed.

At this time no Liberal political organisation existed in Germany. Had one existed, its leaders would probably have proceeded in the name of their party in exactly the same way as Heine had done on his own initiative.[1]

On the other hand, Heine was led to revise his political ideas. He widened his historical conceptions and, paradoxical though it may seem, discovered in his new ideas a justification for a truce with the monarchy. The *Globe*, which in the autumn of 1830 had passed into the hands of the Saint-Simonists, now became Heine's main spiritual diet. As he read the articles by Enfantin,

---

[1] Twelve years later the young Marx, whom no one could easily accuse of being indulgent, took sides against the ultra-Radicals in defence of the Liberal and practical men who had undertaken the thankless task of fighting for liberty step by step, while remaining within the bounds of the Constitution.

Chevalier and Comte, the German writer familiarised himself with the doctrine that placed the " social question " foremost in the minds of all in Europe.

He saw at once the truth underlying the Saint-Simonist doctrine. The criticism of bourgeois liberalism that it contained appealed to and found a response in him. He hated plutocrats even more bitterly than the " privileged " by birth and of the Church. The moral and religious principles of the Saint-Simonists also struck a responsive chord in him, for theirs was the new evangile, the new revelation whose arrival he had so earnestly desired : " . . . the progress of industrial technique and political economy allows men to free themselves from their material misery, and to achieve happiness while they are still on earth." To achieve a high standard of life is possible for everyone. The Saint-Simonists were the first to announce this truth, which for us today has become a commonplace.

We shall return later to the Saint-Simonist activities of Heine—we have only alluded to them here to explain his political attitude in 1831. Once the intoxication of the July Revolution had abated he fully realised that a similar revolutionary movement of importance could not be expected in Germany. On the contrary, more and more symptoms appeared to show that governments were determined to prevent any uprising by paralysing the activities of agitators, Liberals and revolutionaries. Already heavily compromised in the eyes of the reactionaries by his recent publications, Heine seemed to be left with only two alternatives : either to remain in Germany, under the protection of certain guarantees, where he would have to refrain momentarily from playing an active political role and confine himself to poetry ; or to go to Paris for an indefinite period, openly break off relations with the Prussian Government, inform the outer world of conditions in Germany, and become— as he wrote to Varnhagen—one of the high priests of the new religion.

Varnhagen's reply decided the issue : he would go to Paris. Before leaving Germany he determined to flay the aristocracy and the Government in the eyes of the public. His opportunity was not long delayed. Graf von Moltke, an aristocrat with Whig leanings, had just published his book in Hamburg, *Über den Adel und dessen Verhältnis zum Bürgerstand* (Of the nobility and its relations to the bourgeoisie). In this book he had developed the thesis that the nobility, by virtue of their high culture, experience, tradition and aptitude for affairs, could play an important part in a democratic Germany. A Hamburg Radical lawyer replied with a violent pamphlet against Moltke and asked Heine to write the preface. Both the preface and the pamphlet were published anonymously, but no one could mistake the hand of Heine :

" The Gallic Cock has crowed a second time, and the dawn is rising in Germany too. The shadows and the mysterious ghosts take to flight," declared Heine with pathos. " The German people can expect nothing good from their lords, whose sole preoccupation is with the chase—the drive against the ideas of liberalism . . . "

In this extract it was not the voice of the Saint-Simonist Heine that was speaking, but the Heine saturated with the ideas of Rousseau :

" Men are born equal. The few renegade philosophers of liberty may at their leisure evolve the subtlest syllogisms to prove that millions of men are created to be beasts of burden, and some thousands to be privileged riders. They will never convince us until they can prove, as Voltaire said, that they were born with spurs on their heels and the others with saddles on their backs."

In this pamphlet Heine outlined for the first time the thesis that he was later to develop in his book on Germany. German philosophy had accomplished the revolution against the old régime in theory, while the French people had brought it about in practice. Robespierre had lopped off the King's head while Kant was dethroning God. Napoleon was crowned Emperor, but Fichte enthroned his *Ich* as sovereign and centre of the world. Louis Philippe introduced the just mean while Hegel achieved the synthesis of German philosophy. With Hegel the theory is consummated. Political action must follow. Hitherto the German people had only dreamed of revolution ; it was now time to emerge from their philosophical stupor and fight for their rights.

This trenchant pamphlet with its aggressive style, very reminiscent of the Communist Manifesto of 1847, greatly influenced some years later the Left Wing of the young Hegelian school, and in particular Karl Marx.

Heine invoked the German revolution, but was fearful of the issue. His apprehension first appeared in a note written a short while before this incendiary pamphlet, wherein he compared the German people to the Emperor Maximilian in captivity and himself to the emperor's jester—the legendary Kuntz von Rosen :

" Oh, German Fatherland ! Oh, dear German people ! I am your Kuntz von Rosen . . . the man who makes the time pass agreeably and diverts you in your good days, and who now visits you in prison in the days of your misfortune. Here beneath my cloak I bring you your fine sceptre and your beautiful crown. For you, my people, you are the true Emperor, the true master of your land . . . Your will is sovereign, and the sole legitimate source of all power . . ."

But the people do not trust the advice of buffoons, and do not believe that the hour of liberation is at hand. They ask the jester how they shall recompense him for his faithful services.

" Oh, my dear master, all I ask is that you will not have me killed . . ." replies Kuntz von Rosen, that is, Heine.

The poet feared and desired the revolution ; there was in his mind a curious contradiction between the idea of popular sovereignty and mistrust of the people. He considered popular sovereignty to be just and unquestionable, but he wondered whether the German people would use the power that the thinkers had placed in their hands with equity and honesty. The deplorable memories of 1813 constantly recurred to his mind. It was not the bourgeois in him that feared the reign of the people, for Heine had no more to lose than a peasant or a working man : he feared that, once freed from the control of their Princes and Priests, the people might fall into the hands of chauvinist demagogues like Jahn, or the bigoted fanatics of the *Burschenschaft*. Without political organisation and with no practical tradition of Liberalism, the servility of the masses would be reinforced by a brutality that was only kept in check by fear of the authorities. In the work on German philosophy which he published at a later date in Paris his fears were expressed even more vigorously and more prophetically : " . . . you wish to fight, not to destroy nor even to conquer, but solely for the joy of fighting . . . "

*　　*　　*　　*

Had the philosophers been wise in disturbing the Christian faith of the German people, Heine asked himself?

" . . . Christianity has to a certain extent softened the brutal and belligerent ardour of the Germans, but has never been able to destroy it ; and when the Cross, that talisman which holds them in fief, is broken, then once again the ferocity of the ancient warriors will be unleashed—that frenzied exaltation of Berserkers that the Nordic poets still sing today. Then, alas, will come the day when the old warlike divinities will rise from their legendary tombs, rub the secular dust from their eyes, and Thor will come with his monstrous hammer and destroy the Gothic cathedrals . . ."

And Heine, an exile in France, addressed a warning to his hosts :

" When you hear the noise and tumult, my gentle French neighbours, be on your guard and do not become embroiled in what is taking place in Germany . . . it could roast you to a cinder. Beware of adding fuel to the fire or of putting out the flames, for you could very easily burn your fingers. Do not scorn my counsel, although it is given you by a dreamer who cautions you against the Kantists and Fichteans and the natural philosophers ; do not laugh at the fantastic poet who is waiting to see a revolution that has already taken place in the spirit translated into action. Thought precedes action as the lightning precedes the thunder, and the thunder in Germany resembles somewhat Teuton thought : it does not travel very fast, and arrives in a sequence of rumblings . . . but it does arrive ! And when you hear an ominous clap louder than any that has ever occurred before in the history of the world, you will know that the German thunderbolt has struck. At the sound of it the eagles will fall dead from the skies and the lions in the remotest African deserts will slink away to other lairs with their tails between their legs. A drama will be played in Germany compared to which the

French Revolution will be but a benign incident. Beware then ! You have more to fear from Germany than from the entire Holy Alliance together with all the Croats and Cossacks . . . Furthermore, you French are not at all loved in Germany—with what exactly they reproach you I have never discovered. One day in a beer garden in Göttingen a young man of the old Germany cried out that the death of Conrad von Hohenstaufen, whom you beheaded in Naples, must be avenged by French blood . . . You must certainly have forgotten that a long time ago, but we forget nothing, we Germans : you will see that when we wish to break off relations with you we shall lack no pretext for a quarrel. I warn you to be on your guard ! Let happen what may in Germany ; whether it be the Royal Prince of Prussia or Doctor Wirth who is in power, always be alert at your post with your weapons in your hands . . ."

The reader may well ask why Heine, who could foresee with such clarity the brutal unleashing of a German revolution, did not desert the camp of those who claimed sovereignty for the German people and unity for the German State. The answer is simple. Despite all his forebodings, inspired by an instinctive knowledge of the German soul, he believed in Reason. He thought it possible to prepare the German people to carry out their revolution in accordance with the humanitarian principles that had emerged after the great convulsion that shook France in 1789. He believed in the possibility of a " good German." He dreamed of a great " banquet of reconciliation " ; or, as he wrote in his Italian notes : " The representatives of the German people should take their places at the side of those of other free peoples, and drink a toast to the honour of the French, who had worked for the highest needs of human society—good living and civil equality . . ."

He had set out for Paris therefore in search of a sanctuary and a little fresh air, and not in quest of a new country. Prompted by the same need in 1828 after the publication of *Das Buch Le Grand*, he had wavered between Paris and London. On that occasion he had chosen London, with the intention of going to Paris the following year, where—as he wrote to Varnhagen on October 2 —he would work in the Bibliothèque Royale, observe his fellow men and the world, and gather material for a book that would be " European " . . . Three years had passed since he had conceived this project. Now, in May 1831, circumstances had forced him to put it into effect, for Varnhagen had discreetly given him to understand that he would be well advised to leave Germany.

Cotta was happy to entrust him with the Paris representation of the *Augsburger Allgemeine Zeitung*. Campe was moderately generous in the matter of advances on the fourth book of the *Reisebilder*, the first volume of which included those burning pages that he had written in Heligoland, entitled *Briefe aus Helgoland*.

On the first day of May 1831 Heinrich Heine crossed the Rhine.

CHAPTER TWENTY-TWO

PARIS IN 1831

HEINE arrived in Paris like a man in love. From the moment his diligence neared the Porte Saint Denis he was in a transport of joy. He just could not rid himself of the idea, as he wrote later with charming irony, that the triumphal arch had been erected in honour of his glorious entry.

A pleasant town and a smiling people. What a relief after the morose and frowning North! Ever since his youth he had dreamed of Paris : he had always heard that the Parisians were charming, and now he was actually experiencing that charm in its infinite variety. There was a certain complacency in the air—or perhaps in the Parisian blood. He found himself in a town where coarseness did not exist, or in any case was not apparent. What appeared to him quite marvellous was the fact that the paper-sellers, barrow vendors, waiters and even the children spoke the language of Voltaire and Rousseau. He had brought with him letters of introduction to two well-known bill-changers, Valentine and Véry : those eminent bankers did not fail to mention that they would have been delighted to deal with him without recommendation, as he appeared to be a respectable and very distinguished gentleman. This typically Parisian compliment, however superficial it may have been, filled him with confidence.

Heine now discovered for the first time French cooking, the beauty of the French buildings . . . and French girls. These last he encountered more often behind the shop windows of the Passage des Panoramas and at the *Bals de la Grande Chaumière* than in the Parisian drawing-rooms. Blue-stockings and over-sensitive souls had never appealed to him much—even in Germany, once he had recovered from his romantic passions, he had preferred passing adventures with the fisher-girls of Heligoland, *Gretchens* with fair plaited tresses from Hamburg and the *Kätchens* of Berlin to the friendship of actresses and women of letters. He loved primitive and uncomplicated women, little brainless creatures like kittens, who could lie most innocently.

Amelie and Therese were vanished illusions. Heine sought more and more after facile pleasures. " Give me the flesh," said another great Nordic, Kierkegaard ; and Heine, too, extolled the physical delights, for in the sentimental he had experienced nothing but sorrow and deception.

During his stay in Heligoland he had reflected at length upon the relationship between the body and the mind, upon their ceaseless conflict, upon sexual desire and spiritual love, but without finding any solution. When would the world cure itself of this impetuous tendency to spiritualise and annihilate the material, this foolish error that makes the body and soul suffer at the same time ? . . . He dreamed of a new Hellenism that would re-establish the unity of body and spirit—disturbed by Christian asceticism. Choderlos de Laclos remained his ideal : he combined the frivolous with a passionate revolutionary spirit.

But at heart Heine was not frivolous. On the contrary he was inclined to take his love and passions too seriously. He loved banter and salacious jests ; he would have liked to play the Don Juan among the *grisettes* . . . He conceived the rehabilitation of the body in the manner of the eighteenth-century materialists rather than in the solemn attitude of Enfantin.

His friends, and later his biographers reproached him for having debased himself by his love affairs, these amorous relations with flower-girls and lace-makers, and later by his marriage to Crescence Mirat, herself no more than a lovely working girl. Had he but loved George Sand or the Princess Belgiojoso ! But would he have been happier ? The fact remains that Heine loved Mademoiselle Josephine, called " Fifine," whom he met at the Grande Chaumière and whom he recalls with tenderness in his memoirs as his first French *petite amie* . . . " She was adorable," he wrote, " with her cupid's bow mouth and large dark eyes, and there was something roguish in the tilt of her small *retroussé* nose . . . She was so irresponsible, her smile so caressing, her chatter so sweet that it echoed deliciously in my heart . . ." And after Josephine there were Hortense, Diana, the woman from Biscaya with the heavy eyebrows, and Clarissa whom he had met in the Jardin des Plantes . . . One day he and Clarissa had gone to Montmorency where he had made her ride upon a donkey ; she lost her balance and tumbled into the long grass. He would never forget her fine strong laugh . . . Then there were Yolande and Marie, mother and daughter ; only a few graceful verses give us their names. They taught him *argot* and the little mysteries of the life of the poor folk of Paris . . . Finally he tired of these easy loves, and became more eclectic. He did not visit the writers to whom Varnhagen and Gans had given him letters of introduction until the end of August, when returning from Boulogne, where he had passed the summer. He met Enfantin, the *père suprême*, and Michel Chevalier, the new editor of the *Globe*. They both found a great bond of sympathy with Heine, and their friendship lasted until the poet's death.

The Saint-Simonist movement was at its height. The workers flocked in ever greater numbers to hear the anathemas the Poly-technician prophets hurled against egoism ; Saint-Simonist clubs were also being founded in the provinces. Heine attended several meetings in the great hall in the Rue Taitbout. He acclaimed the orators who protested against the cold selfishness with which the French Government tolerated oppression and the extermination of those generous people who had obeyed their noble impulse and rallied to the appeal of France. The audience understood the allusion, and there were cries of *Vive la Pologne ! Vive l'Italie ! Vive la Belgique !* This was a new experience for Heine, who had never in Germany seen crowds enthusing for the liberty of other nations.

* * * *

He also visited the exhibition of painting at the Salon, and forwarded important criticisms to the *Augsburger Allgemeine Zeitung. The Salon of 1831* is one of his most exhaustive essays, and opens up new avenues in European aesthetics . . . Ten years later the young Baudelaire, to whom Théophile Gautier had recommended this essay, strengthened and elaborated Heine's theories in his own art criticisms and in his fine study of Delacroix . . . Aspersions have been cast on the originality of Heine's concepts in the field of art philosophy : according to his detractors he had merely summed up and wittily presented the ideas expressed by the anonymous critic of the *Globe* in the May 11th and June 11th numbers of that journal, and those of Barrault uttered at a conference on May 2. If, however, one takes the trouble to compare these texts with Heine's *Salon of 1831*, both concordances and divergences will be discovered.

In Heine's opinion—and most of the Saint-Simonists were in agreement—art was not divorced from the spiritual tendencies of the age nor independent of contemporary political and economic events. The artist delved into them for raw material from which to create. If, however, in the " organic " epochs like the Middle Ages the artist remained faithful to his spiritual community— even to the point of anonymity—in " critical " epochs, the individual detached himself from his surroundings and tried to singularise himself ; " romantic " art would appear then to be characterised by the anarchy of its tendencies. " . . . each painter pursues his own particular goal, or works for his own gratification ; each forces himself to work differently from the rest, or to use the ' language of fashion ' only the better to allow his own individuality to emerge . . . " But Heine demonstrates that new artists, if they do not form a school in the old sense of the word, present nevertheless certain common characteristics, in particular a penchant for reflecting great contemporary struggles, and a striving to conquer new domains and new subjects.

He stood for a long time in admiration before Delacroix's magnificent allegorical painting of the July Revolution, and noted with equal interest the canvases of Delaroche, which had been inspired by English History. " . . . the artists of the Middle Ages took their subjects from the Bible and the Golden Legend ; the artists of the Renaissance rediscovered Greek Mythology. The Romantic artist is haunted by world history and the millennial struggle which becomes ever more vast as it leads man on to his emancipation. Like Phidias, Michelangelo and Dante in their time, he, too, wishes to be a participant . . . " Heine therefore repudiated the conception of the independence of the artist. He had a duty to perform : that of reinforcing the hope and belief that animate mankind. In the September number of the *Globe*,

1831, he wrote : " . . . the artists should draw their inspiration from the masses themselves, from their needs and sufferings . . ."

At the same time he stipulated that art should in certain respects be religious. He recognised the first manifestation of a new religious spirit in art in *The Gleaners*, of Louis Robert. " . . . Heaven is on earth and men are the Gods : this is the great revelation that bursts forth in the ravishing colours of this picture." And he added : " Robert is a Frenchman, and like most of his compatriots obeys a doctrine that brooks no conflict between spirit and matter. Robert's gleaners are not only innocent of sin, but are ignorant of its very existence. Their work is their prayer . . ."

He then declared that the artist should portray the drama of his epoch. But—and in this lies his originality—he did not expect him to submit rigorously to moral limitations or to bow before doctrinaire criticisms.

He defended Descamps against the *Figaro*, which had condemned one of his paintings as artificial. " Every original artist, every modern genius," he wrote, " must be judged according to his own aesthetic. Art is not simply a matter of imitation. I myself am a super-naturalist in art. I believe that the artist cannot expect to find all his types in nature, but that the most remarkable of them are revealed to him by his soul as innate symbols of innate ideas." He named architecture as an example, whose elements did not derive from nature but from art itself. " Descamps can answer his critics, who deplore the absence of nature in his canvases, with his trotting horse and the galloping servants of Hadji Bey, because in painting them he has remained true to the fantastic intuition of his dreams . . ."

In defending Descamp's art Heine was defending his own. Like the painter he, too, was seeking a caricatural expression of reality and mixing his styles. Most of his works are, in fact, difficult to define : his poems are not pure *Lieder*, his travel journals are not descriptions of landscapes and his philosophical meditations lack system. He created entirely new styles that must be judged after their own laws. This essay of Heine's furnished aesthetic arguments to the literary anti-naturalistic schools which followed on from Baudelaire to the Surrealists.

CHAPTER TWENTY-THREE

THE BONAPARTISM OF HEINE

Towards the end of September 1831 Heine paid a visit to Börne at the Hôtel de Castille. The German Republican remained in the French capital for more than a year, where he was in communication with Raspail and David d'Angers, the leaders of the *Société des Amis du Peuple*, and took part in the political organisation of the German workers in Paris. They had both changed considerably since their first meeting in Frankfurt. Börne, thin as a skeleton, had nothing alive about him except a pair of burning eyes in a long waxen face ; while Heine, plump and rejuvenated by the Paris atmosphere, felt before his compatriot like a Hellene before a Prophet. Börne was anxious for Heine to associate himself with the political activities of the *émigrés*. Heine did attend one or two meetings held in cafés, but felt ill at ease among his fellow countrymen. On the other hand, his sarcastic remarks with their apparent flippancy irritated Börne. " . . . nothing is sacred to him," wrote the latter to his confidante Madame Wohl after one of the meetings, " the truth is, he loves only beauty, and has no faith at all . . . "

It was in the winter of 1831 that Heine began to send his French articles, which caused such a sensation in Germany, to the *Augsburger Allgemeine Zeitung*. Even Börne was satisfied with the tone and content of the first of these, which violently attacked the regime of Louis Philippe and accused the " citizen King " of having forgotten the revolutionary origin of his Government. " . . . he is trying to maintain himself by means of a quasi-legitimacy, by alliances with the absolute princes, and to follow in the steps of the Restoration." He drew his arguments from the arsenal of Republican propaganda, and Börne hastened to congratulate him. How great was his indignation when he discovered in a later article the phrase : " . . . a monarchist by inclination, I have become more so in this country by conviction." Only a man devoid of principles could have written those lines, thought

Börne. Heine could not plead as extenuating circumstances the attack in the *Temps*, where he was accused of having abused French hospitality by criticising the citizen-King in a newspaper whose policy was never to publish anything against absolute sovereigns. Had Heine been alarmed by this attack, Börne said to himself, he could have abandoned politics and confined himself to writing upon literature and the Theatre. By denying the Republic—even if he had done so in a spirit of political opportunism—he could only sow discord and confusion in the ranks of the party which had hitherto accepted him as one of its champions. After the appearance of this article Börne and his friends regarded Heine as a renegade.

Börne's harsh judgment was actually based on a misunderstanding. Heine could not be a renegade to the republican idea in the true sense of the word for he had never been a Republican. We know that at the time when he was editing and reporting for the *Augsburger Allgemeine Zeitung* he was under the influence of the Saint-Simonists who, although preoccupied with social organisation, professed a complete indifference to the political form of government and considered republicanism to be anachronistic. Once, as he was leaving a meeting of *Les Amis du Peuple*, Heine remarked sarcastically that they emitted an odour like some well-thumbed book, some grease-stained *Moniteur* of 1793. He reproached the Republicans for behaving as though nothing had happened since that date. They did not even ask themselves whether it were possible to achieve a Spartiate Republic in Paris —a town where a hundred and fifty thousand modistes, perfumers and barbers plied their trade. Nor did they ask themselves whether the Puritan and frugal idea had any *raison d'être* in a stage of technical and social development that rendered possible the elevation of the great masses to a material and spiritual level hitherto unknown.

Among the Republicans it was Blanqui to whom Heine felt the closest—Blanqui, who in a famous speech had treated Louis Philippe as " the very quintessence of business." Heine anticipated Proudhon by insisting that the Republican leaders should modernise themselves and replace their " guillotinomania " with a practical and positive social reform : in a word, their conversion to Saint-Simonism. While criticising the leading Jacobins, he retained his passionate attachment to the masses who followed them. When the students and the Parisian workers unfurled the Republican flag on June 6, 1832, Heine was among them.

We can now understand why he had not declared himself a Republican. But this does not explain his monarchist leanings. What did he understand by monarchy? Certainly not absolutism. Every line of his writings is impregnated with irony and accusation against the representatives of absolutism and their French counterparts the Legitimists. Had he in mind then the French form or the English Constitutional Monarchy? Both are improbable. We know that not only his convictions but his aesthetic taste were opposed to equivocal situations. He loved clear-cut formulas, and if in practice he often resorted to compromise, he repudiated in theory the just mean " that hovered, 'twixt heaven and hell." He fully realised that the régime of Louis Philippe in its last phase was nothing more than the reign of the bankers and powerful bourgeois against the true interests of the people. " Casimir Perier," he wrote, " lowered France to raise the Stock Exchange quotations."

He reproached Louis Philippe for " governing too much and yet not enough." Heine was no Orléanist, but was attached by solid ties to another important current in French public opinion, Bonapartism. It gave him satisfaction to say : " . . . the French love the dead Napoleon more than the living Lafayette : Napoleon is to the French a magic word that electrifies and dazzles them. A thousand cannons sleep in that name as in the Vendôme Column, and the Tuileries will tremble if one day those thousand cannons awake . . . " Napoleon signified grandeur, glory and revolution against the traditional European order. The new poets had also placed their talents at the disposal of this new Napoleonic cult, which had become almost a national religion. There was not a single working girl in Paris who could not hum the refrains of Béranger . . . Victor Hugo, who a short time previously had glorified Charles X, became the poet of the Emperor. Heine, however, despite his veneration for the person of the Emperor, did not join in the chorus that heralded the possible arrival of l'Aiglon. He declared categorically that

Hamburg in Heine's time

[*To face p.* 160

View of Düsseldorf at the beginning of the Nineteenth Century

[*To face p.* 161

he considered Napoleon as *the son of the Revolution*, whereas the Duke of Reichstadt was only *the son of the Emperor*. To recognise him would be to pay homage to the principle of legitimacy. On the other hand, he criticised Napoleon's having forgotten his mission : that of making the new spirit triumph throughout the whole of Europe. " . . . in his egoistic pride he engraved his own image on the trophies won by the Revolution."

Heine was not a positive Bonapartist. His political concepts could be defined in the phrase coined by George Brandes : " Caesarist." In his article of April 15 in the Augsburg journal Heine gave an exact definition of what he understood to be the fundamental idea behind the Revolution. " When the intellectual culture of a country and its attendant customs and needs are no longer in harmony with the outmoded political institutions, a conflict is born from this contradiction which brings about the change that is called Revolution. To the extent that this revolution remains incomplete, and in so far as the institutions transformed do not entirely accord with the intellectual culture of the people, their customs and needs, the disease of the social body is not wholly cured . . ."

As we have seen, he did not include the material interests of the people among the causes of revolution. His definition bears the stamp of the period and the surroundings in which he lived.

The opposition to Louis Philippe recruited its adherents less from among the working classes than from the intellectual strata. It had not escaped Heine's notice that the majority of the heroes of the June days were students, lawyers and journalists. Among them relatively few workers were to be seen, and this is understandable because French industry was only in its infancy. It was not only stomachs that were hungry but the spirits that demanded something new and great : the young intellectual defenders of the revolutionary idea were those whose ambitions were unsatisfied by the limited possibilities of the bourgeois régime, and were indignant over the bankrupt sterility of the government. One of Balzac's characters, " Marcus," in the *Scènes de la vie politique*, declares : " August 1830 has forgotten the part played by youth and intelligence. Youth will burst like a boiler . . ."

The " Capacities " was the idea that the Saint-Simonists opposed to the principles of heredity and wealth. They dreamed of a society that would succeed in canalising the spiritual energy of man in the interests of all. That is why Heine thought with nostalgia of the Napoleonic era " where every soldier carried a field marshal's baton in his knapsack." He wrote : " . . . in certain respects Napoleon was a Saint-Simonist Emperor, who succeeded in attaining supreme power by virtue of his intellectual superiority. He fully favoured the idea of ' Capacities,' and his goal was nothing less than the physical and moral well-being of the poorest and most numerous class. He governed less for the profit of the Third Estate, the middle class and the just mean, than in the interests of men whose total wealth lay in their hearts and limbs . . ." Heine found the idea of the Republic too impersonal and anonymous to arouse his enthusiasm. On the other hand—and events proved him to be right—he did not participate in that confidence which the adherents to the Republican idea placed in universal suffrage. Although he was a democrat he did not believe that the majority of the French people supported those who were fighting for its deepest and most far-reaching interests. To bring about the social revolution men of talent and courage were needed, who were capable of dragging the passive majority along the path of progress. A personality with the energy of Napoleon was needed to organise the élite of the nation into a disciplined party. He compared France with the persevering Penelope who wove and unpicked her embroidery every day with the sole object of gaining time until her true husband should arrive. " . . . and who will this husband be? All I know is that he will be able to stretch the long bowstring and that he will nauseate the rash pretenders at the banquet of power . . ."

Heine was in Normandy when the news of the death of the Duke of Reichstadt arrived. He witnessed the mourning and desolation with which the news was received in that Bonapartist province. The old soldiers put on black arm-bands and an *Invalide* shook his head sadly : " Now all is finished ! " He was moved by the sincere grief of these simple folk. " Oh, without a doubt . . . for these Bonapartists who believe in the carnal resurrection of warlike nationalism everything *is* finished. But those who believe in a resurrection through the transmission of the Napoleonic spirit now have a brilliant future before them, for their Bonapartism has no vestige of material elements : it is the idea of monarchy in the highest degree used for the profit of the people . . . Just as Caesar gave his name to authority itself the name of Napoleon will henceforth denote the new power of a Caesar to which only he has sole right who possesses the greatest *capacity* and the strongest will."

Heine was a monarchist or Caesarist in this revolutionary sense of the term, both democrat and socialist, but a partisan of the rule of a conscious élite. His political attitude consisted in the cult of the dead Napoleon, in the hope of a future Napoleon, in a profound contempt for the bourgeoisie and in the recognition of the basic theses of socialism.

Börne saw in this attitude nothing more than the manifestations of a bewildered and Utopian poet. He was under the impression that Heine only conjured up a picture of the far distant future the better to avoid the responsibilities of immediate revolutionary action. Heine on his side could not tolerate suspicion and Börne's characteristic terror of the intellectual. It was not surprising that a rupture occurred between this pair. The German Radicals had to choose between two spiritual leaders whose paths were henceforth separated. The more energetic and active of them joined Börne, but when the armies passed without springing the German revolution, upon which Börne had counted, more and more of his disciples discovered that Heine's apparently flippant remarks concealed deeper truths than Börne's harsh phrases. Heine emerged victorious from the duel.

CHAPTER TWENTY-FOUR

THE TRUE GERMANY

I T was in Saint-Simonist circles that Heine first made the acquaintance of Victor Bohain, with his wooden leg, one of the outstanding Parisian intellectuals who had just founded *l'Europe Littéraire*. Bohain's ambition was to make this review the tribune of all the important French and European writers, irrespective of their political beliefs. He believed that the time had come to put into concrete form the world literature that Goethe had predicted. Obsessed by this idea, and with the enthusiasm of a true inventor, he sought serious financial backing for his proposed periodical and offered shares to the great Parisian bankers of the salons on the Boulevard Saint Germain. He succeeded in attracting three hundred applicants. " . . . our *revue* will be holy ground, a temple raised to universalism, a faithful echo of the literature and arts of all nations, an altar of spiritual solidarity," he declared. " . . . do not laugh, my friends—is it too presumptuous to hope sincerely for this great association of European thought, whose elements already attract each other by their natural affinities ? "

Bohain wished to give his review a presentation worthy of it : it was produced on vellum as a large folio. The first numbers contained a choice of French works : Hugo, de Vigny, Balzac and Sue, Michelet and Dumas, Scribe and Nodier—in a word, the entire Romantic Parnassus figures in the table of contents. He approached Heine for a series of articles on the new German literature, and the poet conceived the idea of revealing to the French not only the literature but the entire spiritual life of Germany in its true significance.

The only source from which the French could draw their notions of the German people and their literature at the beginning of the nineteenth century was the work of Madame de Staël. It was tendencious writing : like Tacitus who, in his *Germania*, contrasted the healthy barbarian customs with the decadence of the

Roman Empire, Necker's daughter held up as an example to revolutionary Napoleonic France an honest, industrious and progressive Germany rich in poets and thinkers. The young French writers who read the German authors enthusiastically analysed by Madame de Staël, gave their literary sympathy to the spiritual and political system of Germany in its entirety: in Saint-Simonist circles Prussia was spoken of as the natural ally of revolutionary France. Heine considered that it was his duty to clear up this misunderstanding. His articles, which appeared in the *Revue des Deux Mondes* after the bankruptcy of *l'Europe Littéraire*, revealed, through the words of the writers and philosophers, the true Germany, the political oppression, the pathetic servility of the people, the isolation and suffering of the thinkers and the hypocrisy of the Prussian Government.

These articles caused a furore in France. " I recall," he wrote later, " that certain eminent thinkers in this country have ingenuously admitted to me that they had always looked upon German philosophy as a strange mystic fog in which the divinity was hidden as though in a sanctuary of clouds." Heine sold them the secret of German philosophy: he proved how that philosophy, beginning with Protestantism and passing through Kant and Hegel, had successively alienated German thought from the idea of a personified deity. " The final conclusion of German philosophy purports to prove that man must make history without a code and without the protection of God, and that it was not God who had created the world, but man who had imagined God. Should this revolutionary lesson once take root in German brains the era of stertorous calm would soon be at an end, as too the veneration of authority and the ingenuousness which has hitherto characterised life in Germany. German philosophy constitutes a declaration of war upon the true Germany and holds out the promise of a revolution. But there is nothing to prove that this revolution will be as generous, liberating and universal in its example as was the French Revolution . . ."

The success of these studies encouraged Heine to give the French public a general outline of German literature. The new series was divided into two parts: in the first he dealt with the great periods of German writing, the second contained a criticism of their Romantic literature. He tried in particular to illustrate the differences between the French and German Romantic schools.

In both countries it was the discovery of the Middle Ages that had given birth to Romanticism. Heine demonstrated that while the French Romantics only rehabilitated the Middle Ages from the aesthetic point of view the Romantic writers in Germany, where Gothic art was not yet dead, wittingly or unwittingly championed the cause of the living mediaeval spirit. He brought to the notice of the French public who had innocently enjoyed the light poesy of *Undine* by de la Motte-Fouqué, the newest German literature, in which the fairies had been banished and which no longer made an apologia for the good old days, but dealt with reality and with modern ideas.

Sainte-Beuve had also rung the death-knell of Romanticism. Writers discovered that modern man was quite as interesting a subject as mediaeval knights and other imaginary heroes. Balzac, whom Heine had met at one of the meetings of *l'Europe Littéraire*, had just embarked upon a series of novels set in the Restoration and in the society of Louis Philippe ; Heine's brother in arms, Immermann, had just written the first realist German novel.

When in the spring of 1833 his collected articles appeared in one volume under the title of *De l'Allemagne*, he dedicated them to his friend Enfantin. He remained faithful to the Saint-Simonists and to his friends even when their attempt on the Church had foundered in disaster and ridicule. We know that the *Globe* ceased to appear, that the community at Menilmontant was dissolved, and that the angelic Enfantin on his release from prison went to Egypt to study the possibilities of sabotaging the Suez Canal. Heine proclaimed the arrival of an heroic and socialist realism, based on a philosophic or rather religious pantheism, which according to him amounted to the divine conversion of the world to a belief in human dignity.

In *De l'Allemagne* he confessed his pantheistic faith ; nothing that he wrote before or later expresses his principles with so much precision and poetry. ". . . God is identical with the world : He manifests Himself in the plants which, conscious of themselves, live a cosmo-magnetic life. He manifests Himself in the beasts who, in the dream-world of their sensual life, lead a more or less unconscious existence. But it is in man that he manifests Himself in the most admirable manner—in man who feels and thinks, and at the same time knows how to distinguish his own individuality from ambient nature. In man the Divinity has achieved self-consciousness : this consciousness is revealed in individual man and in humanity as a whole. God is as a result the true hero of universal history, which is only His eternal thought, His eternal action, words, deeds and gestures. So that one can with reason say that humanity in its entirety is an incarnation of God . . ."

But if humanity is divine in essence whence comes evil ? If humanity is divine is not everything perfect as it is ? Heine tried to give an answer to this question : " . . . evil comes from the imperfection and stupidity of man, from the errors of those who worship the spirit and who consider matter, flesh, the body and its instincts as their enemies. Matter is not evil, it only becomes so when obliged to conspire against the usurpation of the spirit ; or again, when with the hatred born of despair it sullenly takes revenge upon the spirit . . ." Heine, like Freud, came to the conclusion that evil arose from the suppression of the instincts. " . . . pantheism, by reconciling the body with the spirit, tends to re-establish the primitive unity of man . . ."

He refuted the accusation levelled against pantheism : namely, that it would lead to indifference. " . . . pantheism is, on the contrary, a virile doctrine, a new morality that offers perfection to man as his goal . . . The political revolution which takes for its axioms the principles of French materialism will find no adversaries among the pantheists, but only a number of allies who have arrived at their convictions from a deeper source—from a religious synthesis. We pursue the physical well-being and material happiness of races not because we despise the spirit but because we know that the divinity of man reveals itself equally in its bodily form ; that poverty destroys or vilifies the body—the image of God—and the spirit is dragged down in its fall. The great aphorism of the Revolution announced by Saint-Just, " Bread is the right of the People," is translated by us to read : " Bread is the divine right of man." We are not fighting for the

human rights of peoples but for the divine rights of humanity
. . ."

On this issue Heine clearly differed from the Republicans.
He had no appeal for either the *sans-culotte* or the moderate
petit bourgeois. "You demand simple clothes, austerity of
morals and cheap sensations," he snarled at Börne: "we, on
the contrary, are founding a democracy of terrestrial gods, equals
in beautitude and sanctity ; we want nectar and ambrosia, purple
cloaks, the delight of perfumes, the dancing of nymphs, music
and comedy . . ."

Heine, intoxicated with life and imbued with the divine
consciousness of man, demanded a gay and provocative art. He
tried to achieve in his poetic and rather simple fashion a synthesis
between humanist German philosophy and certain French Revolutionary ideas such as Saint-Simonist Socialism. Several
passages in *De l'Allemagne* contain the germ of the grandiose ideas
of Feuerbach, Strauss, Engels and Marx. His work deserved the
popularity it received in France, and several generations—almost
down to our time—have drawn from it their knowledge of the
German spirit and character. The Germans, of course, treated
this work as purely caricatural, for naturally his image of their
spiritual structure did not in the least coincide with their own
conception of themselves.

As for the English, their reaction was at first favourable. The
first of his essays on Germany in *l'Europe Littéraire* had caught the
eye of several Englishmen of letters who, far from being biased
by the aggressive tone of his *Englische Fragmente*, had followed his
activities sympathetically from the start. An *Athenaeum* critic,
reviewing the *Reisebilder*, compared Heine's satirical vein with that
of Swift and awarded him the same place in German poetry that
Kant held in philosophy. The English writers were ready to
excuse him the scant sympathy he had shown for their country,
because of the unfavourable impression the German Junkers had
made upon him in his youth—those Junkers who were allied to
the British aristocracy. In 1833 the editor of the *Athenaeum* pressed
him for a series of articles on German literature, and at the same
time asked Sainte-Beuve to write a study of contemporary French
literature and Quinet for an essay upon Heine himself. Heine's

articles, which were announced in the *Athenaeum*, never appeared. In the February number of 1834 the editor gave the reasons for the abandonment of this project :

" . . . Mr. Heine wished to write a study in four parts : religion, philosophy, history and literature. Despite the great respect we feel for Mr. Heine's genius, we are obliged to admit that he is the very last person whom we should have considered to write a study either of history or of the significance of Christianity . . ."

Thus the English public had to be content with the essay on Heine by Quinet, in which the French critic mentioned the " diabolism " of the German poet, thus illustrating his kinship with Byron.

After the publication of the collected essays on Germany a lively exchange of polemic arose around his works in Great Britain. The *Westminster Review* took up the cudgel in his defence (in October 1836) and suggested that, far from being a renegade to Germany, Heine wished only to point out the unfavourable development of Germany as compared with the Liberal West. But most of the British newspapers—as Sol Liptzin remarks in his scholarly study—were more disposed to attack his perverse poetry, venomous humour and philosophy, which they considered to be impregnated with bad faith. The *Quarterly Review* went so far as to attribute his destructive zeal to the fact that, although born of honest Jewish parents, he had abandoned the religion of his ancestors, without becoming attached to a new faith or throwing in his lot with the national German community. " . . . it therefore only remains for him to espouse the cause of revolution, which alone offers him some scope for bettering his position . . ."

Carlyle himself, that great admirer of German traditionalism, at a later date reproached Matthew Arnold vehemently for having placed " . . . the ignoble Jewish blasphemer in the same rank as Goethe . . ." The Victorian era rehabilitated Heine. It understood perfectly that he had only chastised Germany to arouse her from inertia, and to awaken the conscience of that people to whom he belonged. He had wished to plant in German hearts " a spirit of Spring and gaiety" and to provoke the idea of exuberance and revolt.

No sooner had he voiced his appeal than echoes of friendship came to him from beyond the Rhine : the young intellectuals, Laube, Gutzkow and Lewald asked for his advice and encouragement. Was something brewing in Germany ?

The partisans of the German Republic and of German unity had organised a demonstration at Hambach to which they had invited Börne. More than thirty thousand delegates attended this feast, and noble and hopeful speeches were the order of the day. When someone rose to propose the proclamation of the united German Republic the delegates protested with comic gravity. "We have not the necessary competence." Heine, in Paris, did not take the affair seriously, for he too thought that Doctor Wirth and his friends were far from being " competents." But this harmless event had disastrous consequences. The Diet of Frankfurt, on the initiative of the Prussian and Austrian Governments, introduced a series of repressive measures against those responsible for the demonstration, and profited by the occasion to muzzle the Rhenish Press which had hitherto been comparatively free. Metternich, through the medium of his agent Gentz, ordered Baron Cotta—the director of the *Augsburger Allgemeine Zeitung*—to discontinue the publication of Heine's Parisian articles. Cotta sent a copy of Gentz's letter to the poet :

" For a long time the clergy and the nobility have been unwanted," the confidant of Metternich wrote : " *Requiescat in pace*. But if men like Perier and his colleagues, functionaries, bankers, capitalists and shopkeepers are even more callously unwanted than the princes, counts and barons of bygone days, who then do they finally propose should govern the State ? "

The Metternich clique, supporters of absolutism, were prepared to side with the citizen-King against socialist propaganda.

Less than two years after the July Revolution Germany had taken a new step—but in a backward direction. How did the Germans react to the new measures taken by their rulers ? They calmly and respectfully bowed before them ! Heine recalled the German emigrants journeying towards Le Havre with all their baggage, to embark for Algiers. " Why did you leave Germany ?" he asked them. " Oh, the country is fine, and we should have liked to remain, but we could not live there any longer." They could not live there any longer ! Devil take it ! The tenth part of what these people have tolerated would in France have provoked thirty-six revolutions and cost thirty-six kings their crowns, with their heads into the bargain . . . and these wretched people emigrate to Algiers !

Bitterness, anger and shame stifled him when he compared the German people with the French. In July 1830 provocative French writers and journalists appealed to the public to rise against the Polignac Government and its régime of censorship— and a few hours later they were in the streets in arms. But who had defended Heine, Börne, the Rhenish journalists and Cotta against the Frankfurt Diet ? Was it not insane to demand liberty and bread for a people, who as soon as they received an order obeyed meekly ? Yes, we are mad, and the princes are right. Their defence against the maniacs of liberty, the ridiculous cowardice of the German people, is better than bayonets.

" Oh, the great fool is the German people ! " cried Heine in desperation. " His motley jacket is made in thirty-six different pieces, and on his cap instead of bells hang veritable hundred-weight church-bells, and he carries in his hand an enormous club. His heart is overflowing with grief, but he refuses to think about it . . . If he meets a good friend who wishes to take an interest in his sufferings, who is willing to discuss them and give him some well-meant advice, he bursts out into a rage and strikes him with his club. He sets about all those who wish him well, he is a most implacable foe to his friends and the tenderest friend to his foes . . . "

An immense deception can be felt in Heine's words, but his disillusion did not deflect him from the path he had chosen. The man whom Börne's dogmatic satellites had accused of con-spiring with Metternich, and of soliciting a post from the Prussian Government, declared in the preface to his book *De la France* (a collection of articles from the *Augsburger Allgemeine Zeitung*) that, if he had been moderate and had not violently attacked the Prussian Government in his articles it was in the hope that the Government would keep its promises of liberal reform. He perceived that he had been tricked, but he profited by the occasion when the Republicans were being tracked down all over Germany to contract a solemn alliance with them, " . . . without doubt they will misinterpret me less today than formerly, at this moment when they thought to see their wishes realised, and when victory seemed within their grasp. I have had no share in their foolish illusions—but I demand my share of their misfortunes. I will not return to my country so long as a single one of these brave fugitives languishes on foreign soil. I would rather beg a crust of bread from the poorest Frenchman than serve in Germany under those proud protectors, those men who take moderation for cowardice . . ."

Thus Heine, who for years had observed a self-imposed moderation, finally unmasked Prussia. "The most dangerous enemy of the German people is the Prussian Eagle with its greedy beak and hooked claws. The corrupter of the German people is the hypocrite Prussia, that State Tartuffe who, with diabolical skill and Jesuit cunning, knows how to exploit the aspirations to liberty of the best Germans, such as Hegel, Arndt, Schleiermacher and hundreds of thousands of others . . ."

CHAPTER TWENTY-FIVE

CARNIVAL AND CHOLERA

THE July Revolution had awakened immense hopes among the French. " The future is magnificent," cried Victor Hugo in a poem of great exaltation. The French Democrats Carrel, Lammenais and the young Quinet heralded the advent of the Holy Alliance of the people. Italian, Belgian and Polish patriots rose and the Spanish Liberals rallied to the flag of the Cortes of 1820. Ten years later Louis Blanc affirmed that if the French Government had dared it would have been able at that moment to tear up the Dictate of 1815. Heine nursed the same hopes as the Polish, Italian, Belgian and Spanish revolutionaries. " . . . let the French people loose the cry of liberation : To arms ! To arms ! as it was written in the Constitutional of March 1, 1831 . . . " These enthusiasts did not take into account the empty coffers of the State and the army, reduced to two hundred and fifty thousand men, barely sufficient to guard the national frontiers and certainly not enough to wage a European offensive. But the Democrats counted less on the army than on a simultaneous uprising of the peoples.

The awaited summons never came. Only " the barking of the police dogs " that the aristocracy let loose on the representatives of Liberal ideas was heard. The risings were suppressed everywhere. Despair succeeded exaltation.

The power in France passed into the hands of the cautious bourgeois who did everything within their means to steer the people well clear of social and political adventures. The Saint-Simonists were prosecuted ; the sources of republican revolution were nipped in the bud. The prices on the Stock Exchange became stabilised and revolutionary hopes vanished ; nevertheless, incorrigible and rowdy Paris continued its glowing life in unrest and trepidation.

Neither his revolutionary and patriotic preoccupations nor his literary activities hindered Heine from throwing himself body and soul into this teeming life. " In Paris one can dispense with happiness," he said, quoting Madame de Staël and promptly distorting her, " Paris *is* happiness, Paris is the whole of France—which is but a huge suburb of Paris. Paris is the whole world ! " He sang veritable panegyrics to the glory of Paris.

" . . . here is gathered together all that is great in love, hatred and sentiment, as well as in thought, knowledge and power, of the future and of the past. Here is created a new art, a new religion, a new life : it is here that the creators of the new world busy themselves . . . "

Heine was presented to the Princess Belgiojoso at a fête given in honour of Lafayette ; she invited him to her salon, which was frequented by de Musset, Lammenais, Mignet, Thiers, Bellini, Ballanche, Victor Cousin and many others. At the Royal Academy of Music, Meyerbeer's *Robert le diable* was being performed, and Geoffroy St.-Hilaire was demonstrating his discoveries at the Academy of Science . . . In the cafés every new number of the *Revue des Deux Mondes* aroused passionate discussion . . . There was the Carnival, too, with its thousand quips, balls and public rejoicings ; masked and painted figures, singing and jesting, drove through the illuminated streets in flower-decked carriages. The Republicans spread the report that these masked revelries were sponsored by the police in order to give the impression that the people were gay and happy, but Heine discounted these slanders : the people were making merry because there was always Paris, forgetting their cares and sorrows because it was carnival time, and because it was good to be young and to laugh and dance even with an empty purse and a hollow stomach. On Shrove Tuesday madness reigned supreme. " . . . the Fat Bull is king, and the music is the only means of expression . . ."

With Lent the town regained its calm. Heine edited his articles with chilblained fingers in his badly heated hotel room. At the end of March a brief insertion in the newspapers announced that a few cases of cholera had broken out . . . But since the sun was shining and a gentle breeze blowing the Parisians paid scant attention to this news. The streets and boulevards were always thronged. At night in the dance halls thousands of couples waltzed or sipped their iced drinks.

Heine went to one of these dances with his cousin Carl, the son of Salomon, who had arrived in Paris that day. They were both dancing with two charming grisettes whom they had just met when suddenly their attention was caught by one of the attendants, who collapsed, tore off his mask and, to the consternation of the onlookers, displayed a mottled purplish face. The laughter faded, couples began to separate and the crowd melted away. A few carriages bore away to the Hôtel Dieu several young revellers, whose faces were hideously convulsed with fever.

The fête was over. Heine accompanied his young cousin home ; Carl was trembling with fright and his anxiety had brought on a high fever.

Heinrich nursed him devotedly, and on his account remained in Paris while the epidemic claimed its thousands of victims. He took part in the tragi-comic riot of the rag and bone men : as a protest against the decree issued by the Commissioner of Health, ordering the transportation of excrement and rubbish beyond the city walls immediately after collection, these men had come to an understanding with their friends the second-hand dealers and thrown several new rubbish carts into the Seine, having first demolished them.

Hardly had the echoes of this revolt died away than rumours spread through the town that the thousands of dead were not really victims of the cholera but of mass poisoning : according to some it was the legitimists and to others the priests who had poisoned the food stocks. The frenzied crowd lynched two men in the Rue de Vaugirard whom they suspected, and upon whom they found a white powder, which when subjected to analysis proved to be chloride . . . A deathly calm succeeded the cries of rage, and the boulevards, usually teeming with people, became deserted, with scarcely a passer-by to be seen. In the salons discussions took place in lowered tones, the theatres closed their doors. On April 10 in one single day over two thousand persons perished of cholera morbus. From behind their padded windows the Parisians watched the hearses filing past, followed neither by friends nor relatives. There were not sufficient funeral carriages and all manner of vehicles were used, which looked very strange with their crêpe coverings. Finally there were not enough of these, and Heine saw coffins being transported in cabs; they were placed transversely so that the ends extended through the doors. A morbid curiosity drove him to visit Père Lachaise.

" . . . as I arrived in the neighbourhood of the cemetery my coachman suddenly stopped. I looked around. I could see nothing but the sky and coffins. We had become entangled among several hundred funeral carriages. At this moment one of the coachmen tried to pass another at the entrance to the cemetery and the file became disorderly; the gendarmes on their prancing horses swung their drawn sabres, cries and oaths arose on all sides and several carriages were overturned. The coffins broke open and the corpses fell out of them . . . I think that this was the most terrifying riot I had ever seen . . . a riot of dead men."

Heine took refuge from this spectral scene on the high ground above the cemetery. It was from this same spot that the youthful Balzac often used to observe with fascination and nostalgia the alluring town below. But Balzac saw in Paris the town of secret crime, of temptation and fatal rivalry, a town that he would have liked to seduce like some beautiful mature and experienced woman; whereas Heine leaned at this moment over an ailing Paris wrapped in her twilight fog as though in a shroud, and he wept bitterly " . . . for this unhappy town, town of equality, enthusiasm and martyrdom; the redeemer who has already suffered so much for the temporal deliverance of humanity . . ."

Salomon Heine, the Hamburg Banker, Heine's Uncle

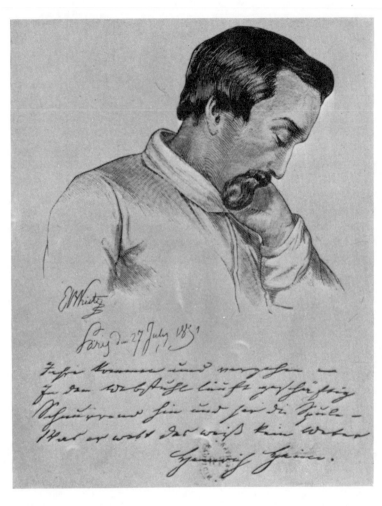

Heine in the year 1851.   A portrait by Kietz

[*To face p.* 177

CHAPTER TWENTY-SIX

PARISIAN FRIENDS

1832, 1833, 1834. . . . The years flew rapidly by in work, discussion and amusement. Heine, since publishing two volumes in quick succession—one with Renduel and the other with Heideloff—had become a personality in the Parisian literary and artistic world. Michel Chevalier and his young friends read with pleasure his paradoxes on the conflict between the spiritual and the sensual : they hardly raised a murmur when he tore to pieces the latest work of Père Enfantin who while in Egypt had addressed an open letter to Heine in reply to his dedication of *De l'Allemagne*. In this letter, which was very pointed, *le père suprême* invited Heine to portray to the French public, subsequent to German philosophy and literature, German politics. He then proceeded to assist him by sketching certain major outlines for this great new work. According to Enfantin the guarantee of the greatness and future of the German people lay in Austria, the only German country that had resisted the temptations of the " imperfect " ideal of liberty and equality, and which represented the principle of order in a chaotic world. It can be well imagined what effect these words had upon Heine, who, like his democratic contemporaries, saw in Austria the arch enemy of progress.

Chevalier, who no longer followed his master, gave Heine the probable reasons for Enfantin's burning friendship for Austria : that man who was as honest as he was ingenuous had met Marmont, who was travelling with an Austrian passport, in Egypt, and who told him that Metternich was keeping a close watch upon his activities. " If the Saint-Simonists knew how much I studied them they would take me for a proselyte," the leader of Austrian Foreign Affairs was supposed to have said to Marmont. This information must have aroused high hopes in Enfantin. Gustave Eichtal, another Saint-Simonist, shared in these hopes, in the belief that Metternich would help in the emancipation of the

Jews, who were destined to fulfil a new religious mission . . .
Eichtal actually went to Vienna at this time and requested an
audience with the Archduke Karl, but was refused admission.
Heine enjoyed the snub to this Jewish "Tyrtaeus" as much as
his friend Michel Chevalier : he expected neither a new revelation
from the Jews nor social justice from Austria, and to avoid
compromising himself with democratic public opinion he had the
dedication to Enfantin suppressed in the second edition. He
remarked ironically in his new preface : " . . . martyrs
no longer carry crosses—unless they be those of the Legion of
Honour— ; they no longer trudge the desert barefooted, but get
married like good bourgeois and build railways . . ."

Théophile Gautier, who for more than twenty years remained
a faithful friend, first became attached to Heine during these years
when he represented the apostle of *joie de vivre*. One would have
said that Heinrich's pagan beliefs had transformed his outward
appearance : most of the bitter traits had disappeared from his
face, his complexion was clear and his eyes sparkled ; it was no
longer the harassed, nervous Heine, but a new man at peace with
life and devoid of acerbity. If he still wished to change the
world it was not through discontent with his own lot, but
through force of creative will and solidarity with the
disinherited.

He continued to frequent the salon of the Princess Belgiojoso,
that exquisite aristocrat who was interested in all new ideas.
The walls were covered with black velvet and the room was dimly
lit by little silver lustres, which formed a piquant contrast to the
vivacity of the hostess and the light and easy chatter of her guests.
The Princess was not exactly pretty, but her large gentle eyes,
graceful figure, velvety voice and, above all, her passionate temperament, seduced all the men in her circle. Heine became one
of her admirers, not because he was in love with her, but for the
triumph he might derive from abducting her from a de Musset or
a Mignet who disputed for her favours. The Princess stimulated
him and calmed his spirit. As regards his heart, incomprehen-
sible though it seemed to him, only the midinettes, figurantes
and dancers from the Opera could move it. His love for the
Princess—which was actually non-existent—did not survive the

first friendly and tactful refusal. Their relationship, once freed from desire, became more cordial, intimate and sincere.

It will be remembered that Heine had first met the philosopher Victor Cousin, with whom he had had such violent discussions on the subject of German philosophy, at the Princess Belgiojoso's. Heine made no secret of the fact that he found the " eclectic synthesis of Cousin, that gave philosophic argument to the doctrinaires of the just mean" too timorous. He tried to convert Thiers to Saint-Simonism. He admired Michelet and Edgar Quinet enormously for their idealism, and he was on excellent terms with Mignet, the Secretary of the Academie, who had become the *cavalier servant* of the Princess.

Sometimes he visited the Princess at her *Château de Marly* in company with Bellini, who was then at the height of his fame. The young maestro with the charm of a Donatello angel had a superstitious fear of sickness and death . . . One day in the billiard room Heine went up to him looking very serious and said in a solemn voice : " Hurry up and live, my dear Bellini."

" Why ? " asked the musician, scowling.

" Your colossal talent condemns you to die young."

The billiard cue clattered to the floor, Bellini went pale and beads of sweat broke out on his forehead. But Heine, with sibylline unction, continued with his joke.

" You will die young, very young, my friend—like Raphael, Mozart, Jesus . . ."

" But it's horrible ! " wailed Bellini, covering his face with his hands. " Princess, forbid him to speak of death ! "

The Princess came up. Bellini, trembling and nonplussed, his eyes moist, continued to complain. She found the scene puerile but charming, and reprimanded Heine with mock severity.

" It's only a joke," she consoled Bellini.

But Heine was adamant. " I only said what I think, Princess : all geniuses die young—it is a law. And I only warned our friend in a kindly manner—unless, of course . . ."

" Unless ? "

" There is just one hope : let us hope, my dear friend, that the world has exaggerated the renown which it has awarded you . . . "

It is hardly surprising that after this scene Bellini studiously avoided Heine—the *Jettatore* as he called him in his terror—and that he took even more precautions to protect his body against the wind and rain and his soul against violent emotions.

One day they waited for Bellini in vain ; he neither arrived nor sent excuses.

" Well, Heinrich, what have you done with him ? " asked the Princess. " You are most surely the cause of his absence, for he is afraid that you will cast a spell on him with those eyes of yours."

" No," replied Heine, " he must have some appointment."

Shortly afterwards they learned of his death. After that the " evil eye " of Heine gained a redoubtable reputation.

*   *   *   *

There were others who feared Heine's banter. De Musset, for example, never forgave him for having one day referred to him as " a young man with a fine past." His ironical and cutting reflections aroused many dislikes. Victor Hugo, after a few meetings, refused to see him again ; he found Heine too frivolous and lacking in respect, while Heine in return could not endure Hugo's rhetorical emphasis, his stilted attitude and lack of humour.

Heine loved carefree comrades—like Gautier, Alphonse Noyer, Béranger and Dumas. He criticised the new French literature as being too solemn, heavy and severe. It is strange that as a poet he showed so little appreciation for French poetry. " The French," he said, " are born materialists ; thus the charm of naïveté, the secret language of the soul, creative impulse and the possibility of identifying themselves with nature, are all forbidden to their poets. With them everything confines itself to reflection, passion and sentimentality."

He only recognised one poet as authentic, and that was Gérard de Nerval. It is possible that jealousy was at the root of this attitude. In the course of the last few years he had hardly written any poetry ; it was as though the source of poetry in him had run dry. He may have tried to convince himself and others that the poem in verse no longer corresponded with the feelings of modern man . . .

A sincere friendship developed between himself and George Sand and Balzac. He had met both of them in the offices of the *Revue des Deux Mondes*. Curiously enough, Heine shared Sainte-Beuve's opinion that, although he admired the fertility and creative force of Balzac, George Sand was the more balanced artist of the two. Her *Lélia* was one of Heine's favourite stories. He prided himself on being attracted solely by the talent of this great woman novelist rather than by her physical attraction. When, after the famous break in Venice, the friends of George Sand and de Musset split up into two camps, Heine placed himself without hesitation and not without a certain satisfaction on the side of George Sand.

From this moment on he was one of the elect for whom the house on the Quai Malaquais was always open. One day he took Laube along with him, one of the champions of " Young Germany." Witnesses and documents of the period enable us to reconstruct this visit.

The two friends mount the staircase, which has a thick red carpet, preceded by a liveried valet who introduces them into George Sand's boudoir. In a dimly lit alcove with blue and white furnishings an elegant little woman is seated among a heap of downy cushions upon a divan . . . Heine kisses the hand of his hostess with gallantry. She smiles and shows her fine white teeth. Heine presents Laube, who bows to her and then sits down awkwardly on the edge of a chair upholstered in rich Lyons silk . . . Heine installs himself familiarly on the divan and begins to chatter. The young German studies George Sand with interest : her eyes are large and really magnificent but perhaps a little too close-set, her look has something in it rather strange, lack-lustre—cold almost. Her dark hair parted above her high forehead is tied with two simple ribbons. Is she beautiful ? Laube asks himself. By no means . . . but she is bursting with youth and full of energy. George Sand opens a Venetian leather box that is standing on a near-by stool, takes out a cheroot, places it in the corner of her mouth with a somewhat masculine gesture, and lights it.

The valet enters and whispers something in his mistress' ear ; she nods her head and winks maliciously at Heine. Some minutes later a little, poorly dressed man enters. Wrapped up in a dark green, very out-moded overcoat, and wearing coarse leather slippers over his grey stockings, he advances with all the clumsiness of a provincial and bows to Laube. The newcomer, who is obviously myopic, casts a hesitating look around him and then places a large pair of thick-rimmed spectacles on his nose.

Laube leaned over to Heine. " Who is he ? " he asked in a low voice.

" Don't you know ? It's Lammenais, the Breton priest."

" As you suffer from persecution, Monsieur Lammenais, I can only offer you my esteem," said Heine, smiling. Then turning towards George Sand : " Don't you think that it is only when religions are more persecuted than persecuting that they become great and worthy of veneration ? "

" Silence, demon ! " she cried, spreading out her arms, throwing back her head and roaring with laughter.

Lammenais remained silent and confused. The Breton priest did not like banter. He leaned his narrow head forward, a forced smile played about his large, thin-lipped mouth, and he passed his hands nervously through his hair which was combed forward.

" But admit that your politics are appalling," cried Heine. " Christianity is a religion for the oppressed, a religion of sorrow : its emblem is the crucified Christ . . . The principal virtues of the Christians are patience, humility and calm suffering, whose recompense is pleasure beyond the grave. It is another philosophy which claims them now, a philosophy which does not recognise the existence of an after life, and in which sorrow is not considered a merit but an accident and a fatality."

" Christ, crucified by us, promised to deliver us," retorted the Republican priest passionately.

They continued to argue, Heine with his habitual irony and Lammenais with the gravity of an apostle ; Sand intervened only on rare occasions. Heine explained later to Laube, who had been surprised by her silence, that he had never heard her make a witty remark. " She never invents anything, but only collects and develops the ideas of other people. She hardly speaks, and perhaps she doesn't even think; only dreams. That is the reason why her silences are so eloquent."

In the meantime the hostess had prepared coffee, which was served in minute Sèvres cups. Heine went on to complain of the German censorship; by their deletions the censors completely deformed articles submitted for publication. "Can you imagine—" he commented with a laugh, "the other day I wrote, 'Professor Raumer is the best of the bad Prussian authors.' After it had passed the censor the phrase read as follows, 'Professor Raumer is the best of the Prussian authors.' They had cut out the word bad!"

It was Shrove Tuesday. As the two Germans, after taking leave of George Sand, were strolling along the quay they fell in with a strange carnival procession, which seemed like a page from *La Caricature*. On the back of a giant monster, a Pegasus with bat's wings and serpent's tail, sat Victor Hugo with his brown beard and wide forehead. Dressed in his velvet jacket, he was waving a large striped flag which bore the coarsely traced inscription: "The Ugly is the Beautiful." Heine raised his hat and waved to Hugo, who turned his head away—for he did not like this foreigner with the viper's tongue, who had once had the temerity to call him "cold".

The monster advanced slowly, and behind it, serious and full of unction, filed the French Romantics: solemn Lamartine, charming Gautier, amiable Alexandre Dumas, and a little behind them, staggering somewhat, Gérard de Nerval. As soon as he saw Heine, de Nerval stepped out of the ranks.

"Come, come, my dear Heine, your place is certainly here."

"But I am not a Romantic."

"You are a defrocked Romantic," cried de Nerval, teasing him.

Gautier came to the rescue and took Heine by the arm. "I quite agree with him," he said.

"Not a Romantic?" insisted de Nerval, and started to declaim: "*The beautiful Loreley whose long fair hair cascades over her adorable white shoulders like a stream of gold overflowing into the green waters of the river . . .*"

"The Beautiful is the Ugly," chanted the crowd, who formed a single line and applauded.

" The Beautiful is the absence of the commonplace," corrected Gautier gently. "I dream of an elegant, aristocratic and scintillating literature . . ."

Heine walked among them, a little moved and rather shame-faced. Behind them came de Musset and Jules Janin arm-in-arm. "I don't like atheists," said de Musset, as he caught sight of Heine.

" What ? " asked Janin, " are you a believer then ? "

" No, I doubt—" he answered, " but with a great gnashing of teeth. Heine is an artificial person."

It began to drizzle.

" Don't you think," said de Musset to his friends, pointing to the crowd of onlookers, " that the black costume which the men of our age affect is a terrible symbol ? " And he murmured, with a sob in his voice : " We all suffer."

" You know how to suffer," agreed Janin.

" Since he has returned from Italy," Gautier remarked to Heine, " he is unrecognisable. I think he is finished."

It was raining softly. The strange procession was swallowed up in the fog as night fell.

CHAPTER TWENTY-SEVEN

CRESCENCE MIRAT

Don't you want me to introduce you?" whispered the Princess in Heine's ear.

"Good Heavens, no—I should have to be a hero. A single look from her disturbs my spirit."

The Princess burst out laughing. "To please you I will once more play the *Proxénète*, my dear friend."

He kissed her hand gratefully.

A moment later he was in front of Kitty. The Princess revelled in his amorous agitation : despite his thirty-five years, Heine blushed and stammered like an adolescent, while he devoured the English girl with his eyes. She was a dashing creature with jet black hair. At first she was embarrassed by his insistent looks, but from then on they never left each other during her short stay in Paris. They were beautiful days, which even the prospect of a dull marriage that awaited her on her return home could not cloud.

Was this happiness ? Rather, a gentle intoxication. There was something unreal and bewildering in this love, approved by the Princess Belgiojoso, which blossomed so swiftly and was condemned to die at its birth.

After Kitty's departure Heine felt quite desolate. Could this have been the woman of his destiny ? Perhaps he should have followed her, or refused to let her go . . . He gave himself over to his grief and entered upon a period of unrest, haunted by the desire for death just as in the time of Amélie. *Nimmer vergeht die Liebe !* he had avowed to an incredulous and smiling Kitty.

And now already he, too, was smiling. In the street he would turn round and look at new faces. He resigned himself to having lost the capacity for love. Perhaps it is nothing but a green sickness, a trouble which accompanies the awakening of the senses. . . . A man does not love one woman among all others—he abandons the ridiculous pursuit of the ideal and loves all the women who cross his path, as they are all only different aspects of the " unique ", of her whom Balzac called " the dangerous being ".

One afternoon in the autumn of 1834 during a stroll, Heine entered a glove shop in the Passage Choiseul, and saw a pretty girl behind the counter. She was a ripe, fresh country wench, full of Parisian grace. Her name was Crescence Eugenie Mirat, whose large dark eyes would in future accompany Heine to the end of his days.

He was no longer to be seen in society, and spent every moment of his time trailing after the young girl who worked in her aunt's shop.

Crescence, whom Heine called Mathilde, found the stranger to her taste, as he styled himself poet, dressed impeccably and showered presents upon her. A simple girl—the curate of her village had barely taught her to read and write—foolish, proud of her beauty and youth, she did not wish to yield except of her own accord and to a man who would pay the price. Heine's passion did not surprise her. Ever since her arrival in Paris she had been awaiting precisely that : a successful man, bourgeois or officer, who would fall in love with her. Then she would know how to arrange matters. She was not afflicted with the least sentimentality but was more than eager to escape from her modest circumstances and become a lady, to wear fine clothes, to ride in a carriage and change over to the sunny side of life. She had refused all the well-to-do farmers who had asked for her hand. With her good commonsense she had known how to wait. " Mathilde has not a German soul : she is a Frenchwoman," Heine said later. But during the autumn of 1834 he noticed only her bright eyes, attractive figure, provoking carriage and slender ankles. To reason was useless : he was obsessed with the desire to possess this woman whose healthy laugh made the walls of the little shop ring.

For weeks and months he continued the siege. On Sundays he would escort the young girl and her aunt to Montmorency, never obtaining a caress, a kiss—or even a five-minute tête-à-tête. Finally his patience was exhausted, and approaching her aunt he asked her permission to install Mathilde in his house as his accredited mistress. The aunt considered the offer from the practical aspect : Crescence was to her, she explained, an indispensable help. Heine offered to recompense her materially for this loss. The aunt finished by giving her consent. All these negotiations took place in the absence of the girl . . .

Heine asked his French publishers for an advance on work in preparation and, in addition, for substantial aid from his Uncle Salomon. One summer day he rushed triumphantly into the shop and paid the ransom. In the literal sense of the word he bought Mathilde, to whom her aunt intimated in front of Heine that she could go and live with him.

Mathilde protested and threatened to return to her village, but Heine succeeded in calming her with illusory promises. The girl packed her bags, took leave of her aunt, and the same evening they celebrated their new life with a dinner *à deux*. Mathilde, having consented, was in high spirits. Heine could hardly control himself. " She is a French girl—but her kiss is magical, intoxicating . . ." The philosopher of the rehabilitation of matter, the prophet of the exaltation of sensuality, the poet of tender love, discovered woman in her raw animality and insatiable natural greed. He hoped for miracles from their " wedding night ". The miracle was accomplished, but in a different sense to which he had expected. Mathilde, whose lovely Greek body he held in his arms, remained reserved even in her abandon. He had wished to possess her, and she was there, delivered to him, bought like a slave, and still she remained the stronger. Taciturn, with her solid peasant temperament, Mathilde humiliated Heine.

He later related the details of his wedding night to an intimate friend. Mathilde had sat down on the bed and calmly, in a cutting, almost hostile voice had said : " Don't imagine that I don't know you bought me from my aunt : I am not such a fool as you think." Heine, with the egoism of the male, would have liked to forget the hardly elegant way he had acted—he liked his illusions, and wished to know nothing of the past nor to think of the future. " Don't speak of that now, Mathilde, I implore you. Is it not enough to know that I love you ? " But Mathilde was insistent ; she wanted to clarify the position there and then and not later.

" Whether you bought me or not," she continued, " I did not sell myself. I would have you know that of all the men who have courted me you are the only one who has pleased me."

There was nothing in this declaration of love of the playful, easy tenderness of the German girl. She uttered it in a voice which might have said : " I have never hated anyone but you."

" Be quiet," Heine implored her again.

" No, I will not be quiet. I have given you everything that an honest girl can give a man. I did it because I wished to . . . because you pleased me. But from now on I will never leave you again—whether you love me or not."

" But I do love you," protested Heine pitifully.

" Whether you love me or not, whether you are good or evil, whether you marry me or not, I will never leave you again— never ! Do you understand ? Never, never, never again ! "

It was like a vow or a curse, like a solemn promise or a deadly threat. Heine shivered with agony, joy and remorse. Until then he had not thought that his adventure with Mathilde could have any deeper or more lasting consequences than the others. He had desired her savagely, madly, but only considered her as a magnificent and lovely object, incapable of having plans or making decisions contrary to his own.

" Do you understand ? " asked the girl obstinately.

" Don't be a child," Heine admonished her, at the same time trying to calm her.

Mathilde shook her head with its loosened tresses. " I love you too—otherwise I should not have done what I have. But do understand me, it *is* for ever, even if you cease to love me. For ever ! " And as though the words had disturbed her, she burst out sobbing in the darkened room.

Thus began Heine's affair with Mathilde, which his contemporaries—and the majority of his biographers—considered to be a harmful if not fatal influence upon the development of the poet. Mathilde was, they maintained, stupid, uncultured, obstinate, extravagant and vulgar. She was anything but the understanding mistress who might have offset Heine's Bohemian leanings, assisted him in the difficult passages of his life and stimulated his spirit.

It is even more difficult to refute Heine's own judgment of her, for he often complained quite openly to his friends and family that she was unworthy of him. He related laughingly that Mathilde had only begun to take an interest in his works after they had lived together for four years—and then only because she had heard someone speak of them. On that occasion she gave Heine no peace until he had brought her a copy of the *Reisebilder* from one of his publishers. No sooner had she read one page than she grew pale, began to tremble and closed the book. She had stumbled upon a love passage.

In her eyes Heine was neither a poet nor a great writer, but a man whom she loved and who kept her, and to whom she was attached by a jealous and ferocious passion, like a peasant to his land, his house and his beasts. But Heine was, in fact, bewitched by this elemental love which was devoid of all semblance of civilisation. As we have already observed, he did not care for refined and intelligent women and his senses were fired by vigorous and sensual creatures. He did not seek intellectual stimulus from a woman, but tension, danger, suffering and carnal delights. Mathilde was his criterion. This untamable wench filled his life to overflowing. Before she had become his mistress she had remained chaste on account of her poverty, but now she gave free reign to her caprices. She was tyrannical, fickle and insatiable as any child. Greedy, vain and pleasure-loving, everything bright and luxurious that she saw attracted her, and she would not rest until *mein Mann* had procured it for her. She showed herself as grateful for the smallest present as a starving man into whose hand someone had placed a thousand-franc note ; at other times she rebuffed the sweetest tendernesses with the coarseness of a market slut. She had the fiery and unstable character of a world whose laws Heine had never really fathomed. Her unexpected replies often amazed him : cooings, rustic songs, wild embraces, mad rages, during which she would break anything that came to hand, followed one another in quick succession.

Life with such a woman implied ebullient joy, tortured nerves, pride and hatred. Mathilde cared little whether they were at home, in the street or in a restaurant ; whenever something irritated her she would raise her voice and the storm would break.

The neighbours and sometimes hundreds of strangers would learn that Heine was a vile seducer who had taken her virginity and broken his promises, who let her go about in rags, ran after girls and deserved to be hanged.

One day, after a particularly violent scene, Heine decided to put an end to their relationship, however painful the consequences. Like a white man who has fallen among natives in the jungle, he sighed for a more gentle climate and civilised customs.

" I hate you . . . I shall leave you . . . I shall forget that I ever knew you ! " threatened the woman.

" Go to Hell then ! " Heine raged in return, taking her at her word.

" Ah, so it's like that ! " Mathilde grew pale ; but too proud to go back on her words—or feeling too sure of her hold over him —she went off and packed her trunks.

Heine shrugged his shoulders, laid his remaining money on the table and left the house. So it was no more difficult than that ! He sighed with relief : he had extricated himself more easily than he had imagined. It could not have continued, he thought. For six months he had not had a free moment ; he had been a complete slave to the glover's assistant. He looked at himself in a shop window : his face was drawn and his features haggard, as though he were recovering from a long illness. It was high time to stop his downhill career . . .

He went straight to the Princess Belgiojoso and confessed his adventure. Christine shook her head and listened compassionately to his pitiful tale.

" How can it be," cried Heine, " what is this curse that makes me love the maddest and most evil creatures ? Take care of me, Princess, be my guardian angel . . . help me to surmount this crisis, for I am desperate. If I really thought that Mathilde would give herself to the first comer—she threatened this and is quite capable of it—I am sure that I should rush like a madman to the Passage Choiseul, and if I found a man with her I should knife him like a dog. I am like those refined Greeks whom Circe changed into swine : it is useless offering me nectar—pig-swill is my true beverage . . ."

The Princess invited him to stay at the Château de Jonchères, for a merry company awaited him there : there were Mignet, Gautier, Alphonse Royer . . .

Heine accepted. He stayed for the whole of July, resting and wandering through the woods and playing billiards. His nerves grew calmer and his face filled out. The Princess had restored him to life. Sometimes he caught himself waiting for a sign from Mathilde. He had a vague presentiment that at the first gesture from her this beneficent charm would be broken ; his organism was already used to the poison and his passion only slept a while. He was, in fact, an exile in the rarified air of these heights, among this witty company : his place was elsewhere—at Mathilde's side. Could she have realised her power ?

The Princess, half seriously and half in jest, forbade him to leave the Château grounds. He had already imposed this ban upon himself, but was always considering the possibility of breaking bounds. Jonchères was not far enough from Paris.

He left for Boulogne and the seaside that he adored. He stayed there for several months—until December—renewing old acquaintances, and making love to several attractive women. He tried to work—to put his shame and the stigma of remorse into verse. But his grief was still too acute, the experience too recent to produce harmonious songs . . .

One dark wintry day he received a letter from Paris in an unknown woman's handwriting. It was from one of Mathilde's friends, writing from the Passage Choiseul and purporting to be unbeknown to Mademoiselle Mirat. She wrote that if Heine had a vestige of pity left he would not let his fiancée suffer any longer, as she had not smiled since the day of their separation : she neither laughed, sang nor danced, and thought continually of him who had treated her so badly, and whom she never expected to return . . .

This letter, with its childish handwriting full of spelling mistakes, reopened Heine's wound. Despite his good resolutions and all his plans, life without Mathilde was but the life of a ghost. Reason and advice were useless : he would have sold his soul for one of Mathilde's kisses. He bade farewell to Boulogne, the sea and solitude. He was under no illusions : he knew that he was choosing, not happiness, but heaven and hell combined. He knew that he would suffer a thousand shames and tortures from the vulgarity and caprice of his mistress, that he was deliberately selling himself into bondage, but could not do otherwise. It was impossible to live without her. And, after all, she might have changed; perhaps this separation of more than six months had made her think, perhaps in the interests of their mutual life she would make some sacrifices. He reproached himself for not having tried to influence the young woman, to fill the gap in her education and raise her to his standard.

On his arrival in Paris he did not go directly to see Mathilde, but first set about finding a little furnished apartment such as she had always wished for, where she could busy herself with the household. After a few days of search he hired a " warmly and voluptuously appointed apartment." He ransacked the florist's shop to fill the three rooms with roses, chrysanthemums and carnations ; then he sent a carriage to the Passage Choiseul to inform Mathilde that a friend of Monsieur Heine's had just arrived from Boulogne and wished to see her. An hour later Mathilde knocked at the door.

Heine's first words were : " You've made yourself look very beautiful—did you want to seduce my friend ? But, you know, your hat doesn't please me at all . . ."

Thus ended the first and last attempt at escape by Heine.

CHAPTER TWENTY-EIGHT

THE TRUE STORY OF A SUBSIDY

WHILE he was still at Boulogne, Heine had received disturbing news from Germany. His friends informed him that the Prussian Government were preparing a new prosecution against the Liberal writers of " Young Germany." Their name was taken from a young author, Ludolf Wienbarg, who had dedicated his *Aesthetische Feldzüge* to " Younger Germany." In this book Wienbarg had tried to define the political and aesthetic position of the new generation. He designated Heine as the magister of the new German literature, and drew attention to the disciples of Heine and Börne—Laube, Gutzkow and Mundt.

Of these three Gutzkow was certainly the most important. Of bourgeois descent, he was still an enthusiastic member of a *Burschenschaft* (a student society imbued with feudal principles) at the time of the July Revolution. He despised the French, and had very confused ideas of history and politics ; he dreamed of a new peasant revolt. Girardin Saint-Marc, the Berlin correspondent of the *Journal des Débats* to whom Gutzkow had given German lessons, was amazed at the naïveté and ignorance of this young intellectual. But the French newspapers, Börne's Parisian letters, Heine's writings and the information that he obtained from Saint-Marc led the young man to modify his ideas. An old friend of Heine's, Professor Menzel, director of the Stuttgart *Litteraturblatt*, then engaged him as chief collaborator. But their agreement soon became impossible, for Menzel became opposed to Liberalism in French politics, whereas Gutzkow fell more and more under the influence of the French Republicans. He therefore left his employer and went to Frankfurt where, doubtless on Börne's recommendation, he was given the editorship of the literary supplement of *Der Phönix*.

Menzel, who would have liked to insure a kind of monopoly for his *Literaturblatt*, looked unfavourably upon the foundation and progress of a rival paper. His disfavour changed to rage when he learned that Wienbarg and Gutzkow wished to found yet another periodical, under the title of *Deutsche Revue*, to group together all the important personalities of Left Wing literature. They appealed above all to Laube, who had just put a year of prison behind him—he had been denounced by the parents of one of his pupils who had accused him of inculcating revolutionary and immoral ideas in their offspring—and begged him to obtain his friend Heine's support for their enterprise. Heine advised prudence to his friend from Silesia, while at the same time declaring that " . . . these young people, with whom I am not in agreement on all questions, will always find a support in me." Börne, although seriously ill, Eduard Gans, the Hegelian, and Theodore Mundt, the champion of women's emancipation, promised their co-operation. The success of the *Deutsche Revue* seemed assured. It was then that Menzel—on the intervention of a Prussian police agent, Rochow—undertook a campaign which earned for him the epithet of " informer " in the history of German literature. In the December 11 number of the *Literaturblatt* he wrote a venomous article attacking the " conspirators " who, renouncing all national and moral German traditions, would be prepared to disseminate their destructive ideas under a literary guise.

The German Diet, which was then sitting at Frankfurt, reviewed the accusations formulated against the young writers, and on November 30 Gutzkow was arrested at Mannheim ; ten days later the Diet passed a resolution forbidding the printing and sale of the works of the writers of " Young Germany "—Heine, Börne, Gutzkow, Laube, Wienbarg and Mundt.

Heine was all the more outraged by this brutal measure, which deprived him of his principal financial resources, because he had played no active part in the direction of " Young Germany." Apart from Börne and Laube he did not know any of the writers who figured on the list. Furthermore, he had broken with Börne some years before, and had never ceased to recommend prudence and moderation to Laube. On the other hand, at the moment Gutzkow found himself in the hands of the Prussian *sbires*, and the Radicals were being hunted all over Germany, it would have been cowardice on his part to disassociate himself from those youngsters. They were possibly clumsy, but animated by excellent intentions, and having been influenced by his own writings, found themselves in a more serious position than he himself, whose personal liberty was not in danger. Some days after the publication of this interdict Heine sent a declaration to the *Augsburger Allgemeine Zeitung*, in which he declared that he would not have hesitated for an instant to have participated in the editing of the new *Deutsche Revue*. On January 30, 1836, he published the following letter in the *Journal des Débats* :

" To the High Diet of the German Confederation :

" My Lords,

" The decree which you have issued at your thirty-first session in the year 1835 fills me with the deepest affliction.

" I must admit that this affliction is mixed with a sentiment of extreme amazement. You have accused, judged and condemned me without a hearing, with no one charged to appear in my defence, and without the customary *subpoena*. It was not thus that in a similar case the Holy Empire, whose place the Germanic Confederation has taken, was wont to proceed. Dr. Luther, of glorious memory, was able, under a safe-conduct, to present himself before the Diet of the Empire, and there to defend himself publicly and in all liberty. Far be it from me to have the presumption to compare myself with the man who has given us freedom of discussion in religious matters ; but it is natural for the disciple to avail himself of the master's example. If you do not deign to grant me a safe-conduct to come and plead my cause in person before Your Lordships, render me at least the facility to defend myself in the German Press by temporarily lifting the ban with which you have struck at my writings both present and future.

" The step that I am taking is not a protest, it is simply a plea. It is impossible for me to remain silent, for public opinion would interpret my silence adversely. It would see in it an avowal of the culpable tendencies imputed to me, and a disavowal of my writings. I flatter myself on the contrary that no sooner have you allowed me to defend myself than it will be easy for me categorically to prove that my pen has been guided by no immoral or irreligious impulse, but by a highly moral and religious synthesis, to which for a long time not only a few writers of this or that literary school designated by the name " Young Germany," but the greater part of our illustrious authors, both poets and philosophers, have paid homage. Whatever may be your decision on the subject of my present request, My Lords, you may be confident that I shall always obey the laws of my country.

" Do not think, Your Lordships, that I should dream of taking advantage, in order to flout you, of the fact that I am out of your reach ; in your persons I respect and shall always respect the supreme authority of our beloved Germany. The personal security which my stay abroad guarantees me is precious to me only insomuch as it should represent a pledge of the sincerity of the sentiments of perfect consideration and profound respect that I profess for you . . ."

This open letter, which evidently remained unanswered, drew down attacks upon Heine's head from Left Wing circles, and he himself was displeased with the tone of his acquittal. There had been in effect no question of trickery with an adversary who was perfectly cognisant of the quality of the " highly moral and religious synthesis " that Heine represented. The Saint-Simonist Luther' had received a safe-conduct neither from the Emperor of Austria nor from the King of Prussia . . . The only result of the open letter was a polite communication from the Prussian Legation in Paris to the editors of the *Revue des Deux Mondes* informing them that if articles by Heine continued to appear, the import rights into Germany for the periodical would be withdrawn. Campe also informed Heine that for the moment he was unable to publish his works without the permission of the censor.

His financial resources dried up just at the time when he was abandoning his bachelor existence. In addition to the money which his French publications brought in, his only income was the allowance of four thousand francs from his uncle Salomon. Under these circumstances, Princess Belgiojoso, to whom Heine confided all his worries, interceded through Mignet with Thiers, who appreciated Heine's works, to subsidise him out of the secret funds for Foreign Affairs. Twelve years later, in 1848, following the February Revolution, the *Revue Retrospective* published a list of secret subsidies paid by the former Government, in which Heine's name appeared. The Parisian correspondent of the *Augsburger Allgemeine Zeitung* immediately reported the scandalous revelation to his newspaper. In this way a new accusation against the much maligned poet was born—that of having sold himself to a foreign power. Heine, who was seriously ill at the time, protested vigorously against this calumny. We can believe him, for if Thiers or his successor Guizot had demanded political services in exchange for the subsidy he would have refused them without hesitation. Although officially the minister for Foreign Affairs granted the pension, it was in reality a friendly aid from Thiers to a man whom he esteemed personally, and held as a proven friend of France. During the years that followed the granting of this subsidy Heine did not write a single line which could have been considered in the light of a service rendered in exchange for financial aid. When he renewed his collaboration with the *Augsburger Allgemeine Zeitung* he criticised the French political situation more harshly even than in 1832, as though he wished to prove to himself that gratitude in no way influenced his political opinions. At the beginning of the 1840's we shall see Heine, under the influence of his young German friend Marx and his comrades, drift still more towards the Left, thus risking expulsion from France.

When Guizot succeeded Thiers at the head of foreign affairs he informed Heine, who had attacked him more than once for his reactionary opinions, that he would continue to pay him the subsidy. Heine craved an audience to thank this generous statesman for his impartiality. Guizot brushed aside his thanks with genial dignity. "I am not the man to refuse a crust of bread to an exiled German poet."

After this interview Heine continued to attack Guizot's home and foreign policy just as violently. The majority of Heine's German biographers—even the most indulgent—could never bring themselves to understand how French statesmen, capable of distributing a considerable pension to a foreign writer without a *quid pro quo*, could possibly exist. In Germany it would not have been possible, but in France, where reaction was represented by a Guizot—whom Ortega y Gasset rightly called one of the most distinguished spirits of the nineteenth century—it could appear quite natural. Let us add that the Princess Belgiojoso, whose political idealism and moral integrity were above suspicion, would never have consented to serve as intermediary in a dubious transaction. The Princess did not see in Heine a venal agent, but the champion of the Spring of German thought.

CHAPTER TWENTY-NINE

COMPLICATIONS

THEY were installed in a little apartment at the foot of Montmartre in the heart of the country. The sun, the twitter of the birds, the beasts that grazed in the field and the *va-et-vient* of the harvesters created an atmosphere of harmony for Heine. And there was Mathilde, a child of nature, voluptuous and dangerous, whom he forced himself to tame. At the beginning of their reconciliation she had seemed more tractable, as though she had learned from her hard lesson, but she found a means of avenging her recent humiliation : she made her lover jealous.

In Paris and, above all, in Germany, various reports circulated around Mathilde : people pitied Heine, who was living with a *grisette* who cuckolded him. He got wind of these rumours and protested violently. " These calumnies do honour to the German people," he wrote to Lewald, his friend in Stuttgart, who had passed many pleasant evenings with the Heines. But if he suffered from these slanders he was tortured all the more by jealousy, for Mathilde was very coquettish ; she loved to please, to dress well and to attract attention, but most of all to prove conclusively to *mein Mann* that other men also found her seductive.

However, his most intimate friends did not believe that she had ever been unfaithful to him. Although she was sensual and a flirt, her dominating passion was Heine and all that he represented to her : material security and an assured bourgeois position. Even when she was most carried away and in her most capricious moods, she never allowed herself to be led into an action which might have compromised her plans—the chief of which was to make the poet marry her. Her coquetry, which irritated Heine more and more, was all aimed towards this goal. Once his amorous rage nearly had serious consequences : they were dining at a well-known restaurant, the Boeuf à la Mode in the Rue des Bons Enfants, when Heine suddenly noticed that some young dandies at the neighbouring table were insolently quizzing

Mathilde. He rose from his seat and slapped the face of one of them. They met three days later in the Bois de Boulogne to fight a duel, but the witnesses succeeded at the last moment in bringing about a reconciliation.

"We are very happy—that is to say, I never have an instant's peace night or day," Heine lamented with a touch of pride to his friend Lewald.

Mathilde, like a spoiled and tyrannical child, demanded constant attention. Sometimes his patience was sorely tried ; he would have liked a little solitude to concentrate upon his writing. He started a tale for the *Revue des Deux Mondes*, "*Florentinische Nächte*," in which in the bantering style of *Das Buch Le Grand* he aimed to portray Paganini, Bellini and Italian moonlight. But he did not succeed in staying away long enough from Mathilde. He needed her presence ; no sooner had she been absent for a few hours than he became a prey to ridiculous suspicions. In the month of May he hired a villa at Coudry, near Plessis. They walked in the Forest of Fontainebleau where Mathilde, true to her peasant nature, joyfully returned to the birds and flowers of her youth. Heine was tired of Meyerbeer, Duprez and the theatre. The glorious spring of the Ile de France brought him rest. The village children took their coats off and frolicked in their shirtsleeves near a giant tree that stood by the little country church, and which served as a belfry. "The tree, all covered with blossoms, looked like an old powdered grandfather, smiling calmly at his fair-haired children leaping round him." But suddenly the weather changed, a northerly wind sprang up that made the doors and the ill-fitting windows rattle. The following day when he opened the shutters the countryside was white with snow. Mathilde put on a shawl and went to the cellar to fetch logs. They sat around the crackling fire and Mathilde, in a sudden fit of economy, started to make a shift with her nimble fingers, humming as she worked. Her lover pretended to read, and blowing on his fingers from time to time watched her surreptitiously. He felt an infinite tenderness for the young woman.

But these idyllic moments were rare. The neuralgic pains which had spared him for some years returned in 1835 with redoubled violence. Towards the end of the summer he had contracted jaundice, with terrible cramps and bilious vomiting, and at the same time his eyes started to trouble him. His doctor, Sichel, ordered a change of air, and Heine thought of making his way slowly across Provence to Marseilles—which he had not yet seen. During his absence Mathilde was to visit her mother in her native village, Vinot, where Heine would fetch her on his return journey.

The change of air did not produce the expected results. Marseilles—the French Hamburg—with its insidious mistral, irritated his nerves even more. He arrived in Mathilde's village thin and depressed, and looking older than his forty years. The family received him with great respect, and both the mayor and the priest appeared at a lunch given in his honour. Mathilde concealed from her family that she was not married to Heine. Her mother took her infant clothes and little shifts from the chest, and Mathilde showed him the school, the stream in which she had bathed in her youth, the field she had hoed and the meadow where she had tended the cows. In her village she behaved very sedately ; on Sundays she walked proudly down the main street, on the arm of *mein Mann*, wearing a fur and a plumed hat.

This visit brought them closer together. Mathilde was grateful to him for having played the role of distinguished husband so impeccably : polite and tender towards herself, simple and friendly with the peasants, who, from Mathilde's descriptions, took him for a minister or a bishop. Heine was moved by his own generosity. But at the same time he reproached himself, and wondered why he did not marry her, as this would have made her so happy.

He surprised himself by these thoughts. He could not help smiling ; the idea of marriage appeared to him so unpractical, for he set great store by his independence. But was he still free, and could he leave Mathilde ? What would happen to her without him ? Her aunt was no longer in Paris to take her back, as she had sold the shop and returned to her village. Admittedly, Mathilde was still young, but she was no longer a girl . . . Ridiculous, why should they separate—and why should they

marry? Her threatening voice still echoed in his ears: "for
ever, do you understand, for ever!" Now, he thought, she
had more need of him than he of her. But Mathilde had no
need to fear a possible separation any longer; nothing need now
put a brake on her caprices and extravagance. All the authority
and influence that he retained over her was due to this threat.
Had not Balzac recently said to him as they were walking in the
gardens of the Palais Royal: "He who in love forgets for one
minute that he is in the face of an enemy is irretrievably lost"?

Heine wrote in his note-book, in which he entered ideas for
future works: "Married people in every country, as is the case
in general between a man and a woman, are at war with each
other; but everywhere except in France the fair sex is deprived
of liberty of movement. Elsewhere the woman may rebel or at
most create some small insurrection, but here the two adversaries
are armed with equal force . . . At home in Germany, as in
England and the other Germanic countries, every possible
liberty is granted to young girls, whereas the married women
live in absolute dependence on, and under the strictest sur-
veillance of, their husbands. In France it is quite the contrary:
young girls live in claustral seclusion until their marriage, but the
doors of the salons are flung wide open to even the most shameless
Messalina so long as her conjugal ram walks patiently by her
side. But the young girl who gives way to a burst of generosity,
or takes a lover, is ostracised by Society. It is true that this
happens very rarely," added Heine with bitter irony, "chiefly
because the young girls of this country never love, or if they do
love they try to get married as soon as possible so as to enjoy
the liberty that custom grants only to married women . . ."

Heine had no desire to play the role of "conjugal ram."

He had once seen a performance of *Mariez-vous* at the New
Theatre near the Porte St. Antoine. It was a comedy by an author
whose name he had forgotten, which treated of the conjugal
misfortunes of a man who, instead of marrying respectably had
wedded a girl of the people. The wife took her cousin for a
lover, and the stepmother, wife and lover formed a clan against
the husband, who was plunged into misery by all this disorder.
Finally, in order to provide for the needs of this family, the poor

devil was forced to open a sordid tea-garden at the gates of Paris. It was in this state that a friend found him, and the unfortunate man related snatches of his married troubles as he fiddled on his violin. Heine thought with a shudder that his might be the same fate once he bound himself irrevocably to Mathilde . . . He must not yield then to her tenderness, to her sallies, nor forget that however much he loved her he was always faced with danger. She would not fail to take his kindness for weakness, and she would abuse it as she had hitherto always abused his indulgence.

On the other hand, Heine felt with regret that Mathilde definitely had the advantage of youth and robust health, whereas his strength was on the decline. He often appeared much older than he really was, and on certain days an intolerable lassitude overwhelmed him. His doctor did not attach much importance to his eye trouble, in spite of the fact that neither the drops, the compresses nor the change of air had brought him any relief : actually, he could hardly see out of his right eye. His capacity for work had diminished, too, in recent years. The French edition of the *Reisebilder* was a great success, but in Germany ill-disposed critics already spoke of him as a worn-out author. For a year Lewald had urged him to fulfil his promise and write a study of the French Theatre, and thence continue with French customs. He had, furthermore, spent the advance that he had been paid for this work.

When brought to bay by his extravagant life, his illness and his debts, he asked for additional help from Uncle Salomon, who refused him boorishly. How could he explain to Mathilde that they would have to live more modestly ? Where could he find the money to pay his debts, which were at least fifteen thousand francs ? Should he propose the publication of his collected works to Campe ? Most of his editions were now out of print : perhaps the Prussian censorship would now be more indulgent . . .

Mathilde entered the room where Heine, seated in an old arm-chair, was brooding over his worries.

" What are you doing, *mein Mann* ? " she asked with the coy laugh of a spoilt child, ruffling his hair and placing her cool lips on his sick eye. " What are you thinking about ? Who ? "

" About someone I don't want to love, whom I ought not to love, and whom I cannot help loving."

And it was true : he could not prevent himself from loving her. Each day and each year spent together, each quarrel and reconciliation, their cares, joys and jealousy, had drawn them closer together.

As winter came Heine began his study on the French Theatre, and reached an agreement with Campé for the publication of his collected works. The twenty thousand francs thus obtained enabled him to pay his debts and to renew Mathilde's wardrobe. The following year they spent two happy and carefree months at Granville. The state of his eyes improved and a taste for work returned. He dreamed of a book on the July Revolution . . .

CHAPTER THIRTY

"MEIN MANN" MARRIES "MEINE FRAU"

HEINE learned of Börne's death while he was at Le Havre. It is a strange thing, but the death of his rival increased his animosity rather than appeasing it. Börne and his disciples had calumniated him for years and proclaimed him a renegade before the youth of Germany. Heine had not been unduly disturbed, but when Gutzkow and other Radical writers, in paying tribute to the dead Republican, called him " the only representative of consequence " and " faithful progressive spirit," he felt it was time to react and to defend himself before his contemporaries and posterity. The pamphlet *Börne* is one of Heine's cruellest pieces of writing. Against a background of emotions, hopes, and the illusions and deceptions of the July Revolution two men, the one a Nazarene and the other a Hellene, confront each other with their opposing ideas. The ancestors of the former are the Iconoclasts, Pharisees, Puritans and Jacobins, while the latter evokes the lovers of life, the outstanding figures of Greece and the Renaissance and the Saint-Simonists. The future did not belong to the Spartiates but to those who proclaimed the possibility of happiness . . .

Börne's faithful followers were highly indignant over the cruel and satirical tone of the pamphlet, and the prominent personalities of the new Left Wing literature, Gutzkow, Rüge, Wihl, Auerbach and Venedy attacked Heine most venomously. Even his friends could not excuse his impertinent allusions to Madame Wohl-Strauss, who had for ten years cared for the ailing Börne with admirable devotion. Heine was even more blameworthy for having spitefully rehashed the Platen affair.

It was as a result of a far from savoury incident that after years of vacillation he decided to marry Mathilde. Strauss, the second husband of Börne's *amie*, demanded reparation for the insult to his wife. In June 1841 he accosted the poet in the Rue Richelieu near the Bibliothèque Nationale and—according to Heine—stammering and gesticulating furiously, insulted him. Heine was disturbed, but retaining his sang-froid handed the grey-haired Chevalier his card. Heine declared that he was leaving the next day for the Pyrenees and could not postpone his holidays for such trifles, but that on his return he held himself at Strauss's disposal. Whether in his excitement he had misinterpreted the poet's impassivity, or because he could not resist the temptation of playing the hero, Strauss gave his friends quite another version: he asserted that he had slapped the poet's face, who had thereupon taken to his heels, crying "We shall meet again!" and that on the following day he had taken the train for Cauterets . . . A few German papers, who never lost an opportunity of blackguarding Heine, published the second version.

On his return at the end of August, Heine learnt of this campaign, and immediately prevailed upon two of his friends, Gautier and Royer, to call on Strauss, who in turn called as his witnesses Raspail and a Republican named Kolloff. According to the *Breslauer Zeitung* there was apparently some discussion as to who was the offended party, and who in consequence had the choice of weapons. Strauss wanted to fight with swords, but Heine insisted that as it was a case of a public insult, that is, a slander and a serious offence, according to the French custom pistols were the only correct weapons; and further, that although he had the right to fire first, he renounced this prerogative and left the decision to a throw of the dice. As they could not come to an agreement the respective witnesses withdrew. In reply to a strong letter from Heine, Strauss proposed a compromise—swords and pistols alternately.

The date of the duel was fixed for September 7. Heine, who was a prey to evil presentiments, felt the need of settling affairs with Mathilde. On August 31, escorted by his friends Gautier and Royer, he conducted his mistress to the town hall. It was raining in torrents, and the mud squelched under the carriage wheels. "The road to marriage is very miry," remarked Heine. Mathilde, who was extremely moved, snubbed him. From the town hall they went to Saint-Sulpice. His Radical friends described his marriage as a secession to obscurantism. To this accusation he replied : " I did in fact visit the church in question, which was previously a church of the Jesuits and which is called Saint-Sulpice ; there I submitted to a religious ceremony, which was by no means a hateful abjuration, but a vow of conjugal fidelity, extremely edifying and bourgeois. After the civil marriage I obtained the church's blessing on my union with my beloved wife because she, who comes of a strict Catholic family, would not have considered herself married without this ceremony. Had I refused this, I should have troubled a pious soul who for her own happiness should remain faithful to the religious traditions of her ancestors, and," he added ironically, " it is in any case a good thing for a great number of reasons that a woman should be attached to a positive religion . . ."

Heine, in order to contract a mixed marriage, had to obtain a dispensation from the archbishop and undertake to bring up his children in his wife's religion. He signed the undertaking with a wry smile, for he knew that he would never be able to have children.

After the marriage he made his will, naming his wife as sole legatee, and wrote a letter to Salomon asking him to continue paying his allowance after his death to Mathilde.

Some days later, on September 7, at seven o'clock in the morning, the duel took place in the valley of Saint Germain. Strauss displayed more courage than his adversary had expected. His bullet grazed Heine's thigh. Heine shot into the air.

He had to remain in bed for a few days, and Mathilde nursed him devotedly. Never had the eyes of *Meine Frau* shone with such tenderness, never had her caresses been so gentle. She was the real victor of the duel and Heine grudgingly admitted that he was happy in his defeat. He was delighted with the idea that Mathilde had made her peace with the Church, and that she once more went regularly to Mass, Confession and Communion. Like the bourgeois who, fresh from their experiences of the Revolution, had abandoned Voltaire and returned to the Church, believing that the only antidote to radical and materialist propaganda rested in religious education, Heine hoped that Mathilde, through fear of punishment in the after life, would remain more or less faithful to him. It was all very well reprimanding himself for "his grocer's outlook"; the Hellenic morality which he had preached a few years previously had satisfied him as little as the religion of reason proclaimed by the Republicans. Marriage, like all social institutions, ought to rest on firmer bases.

In the month following his marriage Heine made friends with a delightful German writer from Bohemia, Alfred Meissner, to whom he freely confided his struggles of conscience, jealousy and doubt. One day while waiting with growing impatience for Mathilde, who had gone out with Pauline, her best friend, he began to discuss his wife's coquetry.

"Mathilde loves to attract men, but that is all. I am convinced that she would never deceive me."

"I am quite sure of it," stammered the young man, with great embarrassment.

Heine seized hold of Meissner's hand, and his fingers were trembling. "Swear that you believe that."

"I swear it," he replied without hesitation.

"I am grateful to you," said Heine, much relieved, as he flung himself down in his chair. "I know that my friends relate all sorts of nonsense on this subject, but it's just pure slander. Do not laugh, my friend, when I tell you that it is not an easy thing to be the husband of a beautiful woman in this Babylon. Some years ago I laughed like everyone else when I went to the theatre and saw Arnal play the part of the cuckold husband with his inimitable comedy. As long as one belongs to those who trust, all goes well, but afterwards . . . the great and truly deadly passion is jealousy. Love is only the prelude to the real drama, which begins with marriage. It is easy to conquer the body of a woman, but her soul, her desires, her hopes, her dreams . . . It is a terrible disease, my friend, an incurable disease. And do you know that sometimes in the night, when I wake up and light a candle, I study her face for hours trying to divine her dreams? Sometimes in the morning I question her, and when she says that she has dreamed of nothing I do not believe her. I know that it's altogether mad, for Mathilde, awake or asleep, is a child who dreams of nothing but ball dresses and parakeets, sweets and silk skirts . . . She is happy and grateful that I have married her, but all the same, all the same . . . But do not believe for a minute that I am unhappy. I am beginning to realise that the jealous man is not unhappy, but on the contrary is more deeply and more genuinely happy than one who does not know its pangs, admitting of course that his jealousy is groundless—like mine."

There was a sound of rapid footsteps in the corridor, and the hall door opened.

"There they are," he cried with relief, as though he had feared that Mathilde would not return.

The two women rushed into the room with their arms full of packages.

Mathilde kissed her husband on both cheeks. The rustle of her skirts brought a sense of well-being into the room.

CHAPTER THIRTY-ONE

THE BEAR HUNT

Surrounded by dark mountains which seem to scale the heavens, and lulled as in a dream by the noise of hidden waterfalls, Cauterets, the fashionable hamlet, lies in the hollow of the valley. Its white houses are ornamented with balconies ; beautiful women lean upon them . . .

HEINE spent the summer of 1841 at Cauterets with his wife. One day, in the main square of the little mountain town, he witnessed a strange scene. A showman was making his bear dance and do its tricks before the assembled crowd, when all of a sudden the bear, which his master called " Atta Troll," broke his chain and ambled off down the narrow street leading to the church. Women and children ran off with cries of terror. The showman kept his presence of mind, and quickly recaptured the fugitive. Holding him by his chain he began to thrash him with a stick, and " Atta Troll " lowered his head in pained remorse.

The flight of " Atta Troll " gave Heine the idea for a poem. He had cogitated for a long time on a satire of the German patriots who had dragged his name in the mud. At last he had found the symbol that would enable him to hold up his adversaries to ridicule.

For years now he had suffered from the belief that the sources of his poetry had dried up. The author of *Das Buch der Lieder* had not written a single poem that satisfied him. We have seen him propound his new doctrines, in which he invited the young German writers to abandon pure poetry and descend into the political arena, and his appeal had been better answered than he could have hoped. The young German poets, Georg Herwegh, Ludwig Freiligrath and Hoffmann von Fallersleben, saturated with this ideology, proudly declared themselves poets " of the thesis." But the rising generation began to see in Heine the representative of a past era, who had stopped half way between romantic and modern poetry.

Heine was jealous of these young poets ; he did not like their verses, and considered them dull and dry. He felt attacked by an ever-increasing nostalgia for the poetic impulse of his youth, for the azure flower of romanticism, which he had pursued in company with Chamisso, Brentano and La Motte-Fouqué. He regretted having abandoned his old brothers in arms.

Had he not judged the romantic poets with the same severity as he himself was judged today ? Had he not deprecated Goethe for remaining detached from the great problems that assailed mankind ? Did not his own theoretical writings contain a veritable arsenal of new tendencies inimical to poetry ?

Atta Troll, however, was conceived in Heine's mind as a diatribe against those who stifle poetry in a prosaic atmosphere of utilitarian consideration. For is it not the poet, above all, who should reflect the hopes and sorrows of the world without a vestige of restraint ? Heine felt that he had committed a sin against poetry and himself by renouncing the free inspiration of his first poems. He thought of Balzac, whom he had recently defended against Pierre Leroux and George Sand, who were indignant at seeing the Parisian underworld portrayed without sympathy or repulsion and with the precision of a zoologist. George Sand, of course, embellished or deformed her characters at will according to her own standards and moral conceptions. Poetry ultimately has a purifying effect upon man ; it arouses his solidarity with his neighbours and his feeling for nature, but only masterpieces touch the ethical. Heine had discovered the idea that Gide expressed a century later : " It is with good sentiments that one makes bad literature . . ."

In the Pyrenees, amidst pungent smelling pine forests, and walking by crystal-clear streams, Heine rediscovered the young man who had wandered through the Harz mountains. *Atta Troll* breathes refound youth, the joy of liberty regained. The bear's showman brandishes the whip of his irony over the clumsy beast's head.

" . . . Atta Troll, sans-culotte bear, equalitarian and wild ; worthy husband and serious spirit, religious soul and enemy of frivolity—dancing badly though, and bearing his virtue in his shaggy breast ; often stinking, devoid of talent, but a powerful character . . ."

The path of literary mediocrity, like the path of Hell, is paved with good resolutions. As Jesus once chased the money-changers out of the Temple, so Heine wished to cleanse the sanctuary of poetry of the Philistines who encumbered it. His anger was directed against those who, without understanding the pliancy of ideas, schematised them to the point of making them tyrannical rules.

This poem, *Atta Troll*, published several years later, was a breath of liberty to spirits benumbed by the desiccating atmosphere of growing capitalism. " We need a new Voltaire," said Proudhon himself. Stendhal, too, declared that the French bourgeoisie had deserted Voltaire, and to escape from the exigencies of the masses had taken refuge more and more in the citadel of religiosity. But republican bourgeoisie could not escape from puritan hypocrisy, which muffled it in a doctrinaire shroud.

Heine and his friends, with Théophile Gautier at their head, replied to the suffocating constraint of bourgeois pragmatism with the war-cry of " Art for art's sake." Heine was proud to have been one of the first to proclaim the autonomy of art. ". . . the defence of the sovereign independence of poetry," he wrote in the preface to *Atta Troll*, " has been the chief preoccupation of my life . . ."

But had he not said elsewhere that the struggle for liberty and justice for the people was the vocation and glory of his existence ? True, he did wish to lead this struggle—but without abdicating his independence as poet and artist. Once it was a question of art, Heine was no longer a democrat : he observed only the discipline of the Beautiful. He often quoted the words of a Hungarian he had met at a watering-place, who had said to him as he stroked his moustache : " It never worries me if a man be Christian or Jew, Republican or Monarchist, Prussian or Turk, provided he is in good health." All Heine demanded from the artist was that he be gifted. Did not Balzac's works, despite the vague monarchist principles that the writer professed, serve the cause of democracy better than the republican orthodoxy of hundreds of militant mediocrities ?

CHAPTER THIRTY-TWO

THE AFFAIR OF THE DAMASCUS JEWS

FROM February 1840, Heine resumed his regular contributions to the *Augsburger Allgemeine Zeitung*. His articles, which appeared unsigned and were published several years later in a volume under the title *Lutetia*, constitute one of the most important documentations of the reign of Louis Philippe. In truth, French society and artistic life of the 1840's had no clearer observer than Heine. The author of *Atta Troll*, the defender of the sovereign rights of art, was also one of the most brilliant publicists of the nineteenth century. The secret of his success lay in the fact that he devoted the same care to the writing of a newspaper article that he did to the composition of a poem. The journalist Heine reacted in the poet, and he commented upon events with his customary vivacity and irony. He did not limit himself to commentary but criticised and judged his contemporaries, taking up his stand with boldness and courage. Péguy's phrase could be aptly applied to him, " . . . the revolutionary is he who courageously meddles in affairs which do not concern him . . ."

Heine interfered in French life, despite the subsidy the French Minister for Foreign Affairs continued to pay to him, and always said unequivocally what he thought and felt. Let us recall, for example, his relations with Thiers : in spite of their close friendship he never failed to oppose the President of the Council with violence on every occasion his conscience demanded. He once opposed the entire French Press when he considered—as in the affair of the Damascus Jews—that they had adopted an ambiguous attitude.

The persecution of the Damascus Jews was one of the episodes in the Near Eastern conflicts which had become acute in 1840. French external politics devolved on the Syrian Catholics, who stirred up an intensive anti-Jewish propaganda among the Arabs, in order to deflect from themselves the hatred felt by the Mussulman for the Infidel. The French Consul in Damascus, Count Ratti-Menton, circulated pamphlets of the type of " The Wise Men of Zion" throughout the country, accusing the Jews, among other atrocities, of using unleavened bread at their Passover prepared with the blood of Christians. This propaganda, both written and oral, inflamed the people's minds, and when at the beginning of 1840 the missionary Thomas was killed in mysterious circumstances, the authorities of Damascus accused the Rabbi of the town of having committed, or at least ordered, a ritual murder. They subjected the accused to " questioning," using mediaeval methods, which were still recognised in that country. Under torture the Rabbi admitted to having killed Father Thomas. The crowd invaded the Jewish houses, pillaging and massacring several hundred of their inmates. These acts of violence were only put a stop to by the intervention of the Austrian and English Consulates. The English, who had watched French expansion in Syria and Egypt with growing jealousy, seized upon the occasion to point out the responsibility of the French Consul in these inhuman machinations to world opinion.

Heine thought that Thiers would at least reprimand Ratti-Menton, but the President, espousing in his Near Eastern policy the interests of the clergy, contented himself with an inquest conducted by the Vice-Consul. Furthermore, he published an ambiguous declaration in which—according to Heine—he condemned the massacres with nauseating weakness, while affirming that he did not hold it entirely beyond the realms of possibility that the Rabbi of Damascus, " . . . with the best intentions, and faithful to the archaic prescriptions of his religion, could have committed the crime . . ."

Heine denounced this accusation with the same pamphleteering passion as Voltaire in the Calas affair, or later, Zola, in the Dreyfus case. He protested, in the name of humanity and progress, against the indifference of his contemporaries. " Wherever there is murder, baiting and torture, there must be a protest, intervention and the exaction of reparations. Today they are killing Jews : tomorrow the mob, drunk with blood, will attack the Christians. If we wish to deserve the name of man we should show ourselves in sympathy with all oppressed peoples . . ." His prophecy was realised ; twenty years later, in 1860, hundreds of Christians perished at the hands of an infuriated mob in Damascus.

Heine was not content with castigating Thiers for having sacrificed the broad interests of humanity to the immediate interests of French policy and national prestige : he directed his caustic wit also against the Parisian Jews ". . . whose God is gold and whose religion is industry . . ." who had avoided taking part, either by word or deed, in favour of their co-religionists in Damascus. Although he by no means advertised his own Jewish origin, he hated more than anything else in the world the Jew who denied his race. Heine, the convert, who placed himself always and without hesitation on the side of the persecuted Jews, considered that he had the right to indict the Worms de Romilly who ". . . hesitated to give a hundred francs, even to save the entire race of Israel . . ." the Foulds who discussed the budget in Parliament while their fellow Jews perished in pogroms, and the Baron Delmars who founded institutions for the daughters of the impoverished nobility but never dreamed of helping destitute Jews. He despised and ridiculed them on every possible occasion. His brotherly sympathy went out to the tortured Rabbi of Damascus and to the Jews who had— as Christ had done on earth—suffered for centuries under the cruelty of the Pharisees, while the crowds roared for their deaths and the Pontius Pilates washed their hands.

CHAPTER THIRTY-THREE

THE RETURN OF THE ASHES

ONE of the first acts of the new President of the Council was to submit to Parliament his long-nursed project for the return of Napoleon's ashes. This was a personal matter for Thiers : he had devoted many years of his youth to elaborating a work on the great Corsican, and took no pains to hide from his friends that his major ambition was to continue with his Napoleonic studies. Thiers was no more Bonapartist than Heine : the failure of Louis Napoleon's *coup d'état* had merely amused him, and Heine had not even deigned to mention it. Their cult was for the person of Napoleon, his glory and the idea of French hegemony that the " Son of the Revolution " personified, and not for the Bonaparte family. Thiers' aim was to revitalise French foreign policy, and the bold patriotic tone he adopted provoked violent reactions in Germany. He decided to break with the cautious policies of the former Ministers for Foreign Affairs under Louis Philippe. In bringing back the ashes of Napoleon and in organising his solemn obsequies, he was not only seeking to fulfil the last wishes of the Emperor, but trying to rally all the fanatics of the eagle, to mobilise those Frenchmen who were Bonapartists by nature, and—as Heine said—to stimulate their patriotism.

In the Chamber of Deputies Lamartine thundered against this plan for making a national idol of a man who was the enemy of liberty, egoism crowned, and the incarnation of tyranny. Heine immediately took sides against Lamartine—for he liked neither his poetry nor his character. " It is true," he exclaimed, " that Napoleon was an egoist and a despot, an enemy of liberty and a traitor to the Revolution ; but the homage that the French people and the whole world will pay him in placing wreaths on his tomb will not be addressed ·to the historic Napoleon, but to the man who, opposed to the old Europe, represented Young France."

The poet, who in his childhood had seen Napoleon riding through Düsseldorf on his white horse, rendered during the hard winter of 1840 a deep homage to the dead Emperor :

" . . . I saw his funeral with my own eyes ; I saw the golden chariot and the golden Victories which bore the coffin. The convoy passed slowly down the entire length of the Champs Elysées, and beneath the Arc de Triomphe, in foggy weather and on a carpet of snow. The musicians played funeral marches ; their noses were blue and their fingers stiff with cold. The eagles on the standards seemed to salute me with a piteous air. Men stared with haggard eyes at once happy and afraid, as though they had seen the apparition of a beloved phantom. In their hearts old memories of the Imperial dream were rekindled ; the fairy tale of the Empire with its heroic splendours lived again before them.

" I wept that day ; the tears came to my eyes when I heard the long-forgotten cry of love resound again : ' Long live the Emperor ! ' "

It had not escaped Heine's notice that the enthusiasm of the crowd had not been as fiery and as spontaneous as when they had celebrated the return of their Emperor in the July sun ten years earlier. The German writer was one of the first to perceive that in the course of the last decade the French people had undergone a profound change ; words of glory and victory no longer had their old effect. There was no joy of future revenge for Waterloo ; the people of Paris received the body of Napoleon with a sorrowful emotion . . . a filial piety.

He realised with a shudder that not only had he withered since the time he had admired the Emperor on his white horse, but that the French people too had aged, and that Thiers, the *enfant terrible* of French politics had been superseded by Guizot, the representative of immobility. " The era of viceroys and marshals must give way to the industrial middle classes who worship other heroes, like the virtuous Lafayette, or James Watt, the cotton-spinner." The great events of the day were no longer battles, the overthrowing of thrones and the curbing of usurpers, but the laying down of railway lines between Paris and Rouen or Paris and Orléans. Encyclopedias gave way to account books ; the importance of the Court was eclipsed by the Stock Exchange—of which Parliament was only the effluvium. The French bourgeoisie were willing to renounce Syria, the left bank of the Rhine and the prestige of France, on condition that their political representatives protected them from the anger of the workers and intellectual fanatics.

The prediction of the Saint-Simonists had come true. The heroic and military age was followed by an industrial age whose chosen people were the English, whose uncrowned emperor was Rothschild, and whose missionaries were the bankers.

Heine saw in the fortifications of Paris, carried out by Guizot, the symbol of the change that had come to pass in the French mentality. A Danton or a Napoleon would never have dreamed of constructing lines of defence around the French capital. The towns of the Roman Empire were never encompassed by protecting walls until confidence had been lost in the power of the Empire. A live race defends itself against danger by attack or by being ready to attack.

The obsequies are over . . . Here and there a few stragglers are to be seen making their way home . . . The valets begin to snuff the candles round the bier . . .

But was he not premature in mourning the French and their evanescent grandeur ? Heine dreamed of the Republicans, the Communists and the young students who still believed in France and in her mission and future. Powerful forces remained latent in the soul of the French people, and their volcanic explosion could again astonish the world. But in order that the spirit of Napoleon should rise again from his ashes it would be necessary to roll away the heavy tombstone under which the bourgeoisie had buried him. The bourgeois were afraid of the people, and Guizot, the representative of bourgeois virtues, feared to undertake a forceful foreign policy which might force him to arm the people.

Like most of the members of the opposition, such as Lammenais, Lamartine and Louis Blanc, Heine actually wanted a war, hoping it would lead to a revolution and the rejuvenation of France and Europe. He believed that the masses, well organised and conscious of their goal, were ripe to wield political power. Proudhon was perhaps the only Left Wing representative who did not have confidence in his comrades ; he considered the French working class too immature, and their social doctrines too primitive to replace the bourgeoisie and capitalist organisations.

Heine rallied to the French patriots, condoning even their excesses, for like other German Radicals he believed that only French arms could bring liberty to his country. One day he saw Guizot outside an antique shop on the Boulevard des Italiens examining an Overbeck engraving. He accosted the President of the Council, and they spoke of German and Dutch painting. Guizot made no allusion to Heine's attacks, which had appeared in the *Augsburger Allgemeine Zeitung* ; he may not have seen them, but this is improbable since Eichtal, a collaborator on the same paper, visited him every week in his study to keep him in touch with German affairs. In the Passage des Panoramas, just opposite the confectioner Marquis', they stopped, and as Guizot took leave of him he asked the poet point-blank : " What is the meaning of all this German blustering ? Why do the German patriots resent us, when we feel so benevolently towards them ? " Heine replied that the true patriots thought like himself : they desired a strong France. " As for the others—those who claim Strasbourg and Alsace Lorraine—they are jokers who should be silenced with the whip."

CHAPTER THIRTY-FOUR

HEINE THE CRITIC

AMONG the great contemporaries whom Heine met during the second half of his stay in Paris, and for or against whom he took up his position, the most important of mention was Franz Liszt. He first met the composer and his friend the Countess d'Agoult at George Sand's, and although he was enormously impressed by Liszt's virtuosity he felt absolutely no sympathy for the man. In a criticism published in 1837 he accused him of adapting his music to one philosophy after another ; for enthusing immoderately over the Saint-Simonist teachings and the metaphysical structures of the gentle Ballanche. In a number of the *Musical Gazette* Liszt replied that Heine's criticisms were far more applicable to himself, inasmuch as since his arrival he had openly declared himself a Saint-Simonist, and that later they had both followed and enjoyed the lectures of Ballanche together. In actual fact, Heine was not criticising his Saint-Simonism or his friendship for Ballanche, but the catholic-liberal inspiration of his latest works under the influence of Lammenais. " The Great Pagan " had persecuted the spiritual even in the realms of music, and considered the art of Beethoven to be too ethereal. On the same grounds Heine reproached Liszt for seeking his effects as much in his playing as in his composition, and of organising his publicity in a manner unworthy of a great artist.

Liszt for his part suggested later that Heine had been severely disposed towards him because he had been unwilling to pay Heine for his reviews. It is possible, as Liszt affirms, that he really had approached him in a moment of financial embarrassment, knowing that the musician dispensed money generously among the musical critics. But this suggestion of blackmail was voiced by Liszt in 1844, and several years previously Heine had spoken of him with great reserve. Later, perhaps he thought that by criticising the composer less harshly he might earn as much money as his colleagues, who were paid for showing their sincere enthusiasm. If Heine really tried to obtain money from the musician, only the peculiar customs of the literary world of that period—to which he had not been able to subscribe—were his excuse. However, he extolled the musicians whose personalities intrigued him : he called Chopin " the Raphael of the pianoforte," he described the colossal talent of Berlioz as " antediluvian," and praised the gentle melodies of the magician Rossini. The frail and melancholy Chopin, however, was his favourite. He had often heard him play in George Sand's drawing-room ; he was the complete antithesis of Liszt. Of the German musicians he was most in accord with the young Wagner who, among other themes, had borrowed from him the subject for *The Flying Dutchman* and possibly *Tannhäuser*.

His friendship with Wagner was born of their common aversion for Meyerbeer. In one of his fits of vanity Heine asserted that although he had written a great deal on the subject of music he understood nothing about it ; all the same, he did not allow himself to be dazzled by the spectacular productions of Meyerbeer's grand operas. He was perhaps the first critic to realise and to point out to the public that the extravagant décor and effects, combined with the florid passages of his music, hid a lack of true inspiration and originality.

Heine's aesthetics, however, were far less intransigent than his politics. Already in his youth he had summed this up with delightful sarcasm : " Professor Hugo affirmed that I am a great poet, which proves that Professor Hugo is a great jurist."

Among his contemporaries he only praised those whom he liked personally and who returned his affection, but oddly enough his judgments were usually correct. If he over-estimated George Sand in calling her " the greatest master of French prose," Sainte-Beuve later committed a similar error of judgment, for it was he who dubbed Balzac " Shakespearean."

During 1839 and 1840 Heine saw a great deal of Balzac. The *Prince of Bohemia*, which appeared in the *Revue Parisienne*, bore this charming dedication :

" My dear Heine, this study is for you, who represent the spirit and poetry of Germany in Paris, as in Germany you represent the spiritual life of France ; for you will know better than anyone how to discern in it the criticisms, jests, loves and truths."

In this short love story Balzac cited Heine's aphorism: "Love is perhaps the secret malady of the heart," and called it superb.

At this period Heine became reconciled with de Musset, and acclaimed him as the greatest of all French poets. But Victor Hugo and his poetry still aroused his antagonism: Hugo offended his human and aesthetic ideal and his love of lightness and spontaneity. He preferred the songs of Béranger to the mournful poems of the author who had written *Les Burgraves*. He was no doubt unjust towards Hugo, but we must not forget that even the critics of posterity, while declaring Victor Hugo to be the greatest French poet, have never failed to add: " Alas, the greatest ! "

Among the young men, Heine appreciated Michelet and his inseparable friend Quinet the most. When, at the beginning of the 'forties, the clericals, agitating for liberty of instruction, launched an attack concentrated against the State and University educational system, and Michelet fulminated from his professor's chair in the College of France against the Jesuits, who were leading the offensive, crying: " To expel you we have overthrown a dynasty, and if necessary we will overthrow another six dynasties to banish you," Heine embraced the excitable young professor. He recalled his own early career, when he had entered the arena with the same zeal and indignation to attack the Jesuits and the aristocrats. The friendship between Michelet and Quinet reminded him of that which had bound the Immermann who had written the *Adventures of Baron Münchausen* to the Immermann whose recent death had so profoundly affected him. Pierre Leroux, the almoner to George Sand, gained Heine's respect by his chastity and devotion to the people. In one of his articles the poet called him, with incredible exaggeration, the greatest of French philosophers. " . . . Pierre Leroux is a man whose strength of character is allied—a rare thing indeed—to a spirit which rises to the highest spheres of thought, and a heart which is capable of plumbing the very depths of human suffering . . ." he remarked on the subject of this Utopian philosopher.

Heine naturally continued to follow the activities of the early Saint-Simonists and to read the pamphlets of Louis Blanc, the Fourierists and Proudhon. He esteemed them and campaigned for them, but realised that " . . . they are not compelled by a demonic necessity; they are not the predestined artisans of a Supreme Will, capable of executing its terrible decisions as intermediaries . . ." When Heine wrote these lines he had already read some articles by a young Rhenish Hegelian, in which he sensed the wind of this demonic necessity.

CHAPTER THIRTY-FIVE

RETURN TO GERMANY

HEINE was prostrated by the news of the fire of Hamburg. The flames had destroyed the greater part of the town to which the most moving memories of his youth attached him . . . the town of Amelie and Thérèse. He waited with feverish anxiety for word from his home, and did not rest until he had received a letter from his old mother. It mattered little that his manuscripts and youthful notes which he had left behind were destroyed : his mother was alive. He read the old lady's description with tears flowing freely down his cheeks. She spoke of the heroism of Lotte, who had rushed into the street with a packet of her brother's letters under her arm just as the flames had caught the roof of the house opposite. The young woman, who had fainted, was dragged away with the crowd in its mad flight ; a stranger had rescued her, but when she had regained consciousness the letters had disappeared . . . The tower of Saint Peter and the statues of the Emperors which had decorated the façade of the Rathaus had collapsed, and the Breitengiebel, where Heine used to eat oysters, had been burnt to the ground.

The half-blind Heine wept like a child, and thanked Destiny for saving the two beings who were dearest to him. " . . . my mother is now never out of my mind. It is twelve years since I pressed her to my heart. Germany will live for ever ; it is a country with a healthy and robust body, with its oaks and lime trees. I shall always refind it. I should not burn so much to see it if my mother were not there ; the fatherland will never perish, but my old mother . . ."

The old lady might die any day. It was a miracle that she had come unscathed through the danger. Nostalgia, or rather the desire to see his mother, so long repressed, burst out in Heine with primeval force. In his first excitement he wanted to take the next coach to Germany, but his friends counselled prudence—it would be better to make sure that the Prussian authorities were not still on his trail. Mathilde was also opposed to the journey—perhaps because she feared that the family would not allow *mein Mann* to return. Heine's sight had deteriorated a great deal ; not only the eyes but the facial muscles were attacked by a mysterious disease. The doctors ordered complete rest. Having always told his mother that he was in good health, he did not wish to arrive home broken down and half blind, and even to the Hamburgers he wanted to show himself still a buck. A man of forty-five is not old. He therefore postponed the journey from month to month—autumn to winter, and spring to summer. Finally, having made his peace with the Prussian Legation, and his health having somewhat improved, he took leave of Mathilde one foggy November day :

> *Ada, mein Weib, mein schönes Weib*
> *Du kannst meine Qual nicht fassen,*
> *Ich drücke Dich so fest an mein Herz,*
> *Und muss Dich doch verlassen . . .*

He took the coach for Germany, and at the frontier the Prussian Customs Officers ransacked his baggage in their search for lace, jewellery, and perhaps forbidden books. Heine smiled maliciously. He would have liked to shout at them : " Imbeciles ! You rummage in my trunks, but you are looking in the wrong place : all my contraband is hidden in my head."

He halted for half-an-hour in Aix-la-Chapelle, where he saw the soldiers of the Prussian garrison in their grey capes and high red collars, march past. They had not changed since he had seen them the last time. " . . . it is always the same genus of pedantic puppets ; always the same angular movements, and on their faces always the same icy and stereotyped complacency. They march just as stiffly and unnaturally as before, straight as a die. One would say that they had swallowed the corporal's stick, with which a short time before he had thrashed them . . ."

At Cologne he sat down, with an excellent appetite, to a dinner consisting of scrambled eggs with ham, washed down with mellow Rhenish wine. From Cologne to Hagen he took the covered postal wagon, and passed through Mülheim, the dainty little village which he had last visited in 1831. Then it had been spring, and hope had run high in every heart : the hope of being freed from the Prussians. But alas, the Uhlans still mounted guard on the Rhine.

He lunched at Hagen, and slept at Unna in a downy bed, —" one can always sleep and dream well in Germany." Under a fine rain the coach clattered through the forest of Teutoburg along a muddy road lined with tall stern lime trees. Minden, Bückeburg and Harburg—no more than an hour from Hamburg —passed before his eyes. Night was falling, and a gentle breeze was blowing from the near-by sea which dispersed the clouds and revealed the first few stars.

" . . . and when I arrived at my mother's house, her joy was almost akin to terror : ' My beloved child,' she cried, clapping her hands. 'My dear, dear child, it is thirteen years since I saw you. You must be hungry—tell me, what would you like to eat ? There is fish, goose and oranges from Portugal ? ' ' Well, let it be fish, goose and oranges from Portugal . . .' And while I ate, with a great appetite, my mother, transported with joy, asked me a thousand questions. ' My dear boy, do they look after you there ? Is your wife a good housekeeper, and does she mend your stockings and your shirts ? '

' The fish is excellent, little mother, but it must be eaten in silence. A bone gets stuck so easily in the gullet : don't disturb me for a moment ' . . .''

Old Betty van Geldern moved about painfully on her rheumaticky legs, but age had not quenched her spirit, and she was as witty and malicious as ever. Lotte, whose hair was growing grey, brought her son and her little girl for him to see. Julius Campe, the publisher with whom he had quarrelled and been reconciled a hundred times, arrived to pay him a visit, leaning heavily on his walking-stick. Uncle Salomon came too, and in the joy of reunion promised to increase his allowance ; "—on condition that you don't commit any stupidities," he added immediately with a frown, regretting his hasty generosity. His brother Max arrived from St. Petersburg, and the Doctor told him that his books were already well known and appreciated in Russia.

Old acquaintances and new admirers flocked to visit the poet, to the great pride of his mother. Since the night he had fled from Hamburg the Liberal camp had increased, and they spoke anew of the revolution. In Campe's bookshop Heine met the famous tailor, Weitling, the Communist agitator. He was by no means impressed by the poet, and did not even touch his cap, but remained seated on his stool, and raising his right foot from time to time so that his knee almost touched his chin, rubbed his ankles with his hands. On Heine's asking him if he suffered from gout, Weitling shrugged his shoulders and replied that it was not gout but the trace of the manacles—the natural appanage of revolutionaries—by which he had been attached to the walls of the prison, that irked him.

Weitling was convinced that the day was at hand when the German proletariat would wave the red flag of revolt. There was something insufferably conceited in the manner of this tailor, which disgusted Heine. He remembered that as a young man, on his way through Münster, he had reverently kissed the chains of the heresiarch Jan van Leyden, the assistant tailor and "King of Zion," and also the pincers which the *sbires* of the feudal Germans had used to martyrise him. He now found himself face to face with a living tailor, martyr to the cause for which the "King of Zion" had previously suffered, and which was also his own. How can we account for this antipathy to Weitling from one who sympathised with the proletariat, and why should he turn away from this class-conscious proletarian? Is it possible that despite his faith and convictions he was a bourgeois at heart?

Before his departure Heine entered into a new agreement with Campe, who consented to pay him an annual fee of eighteen hundred marks for the right to publish his future work. According to Heine's contract, Campe would continue to pay the same amount to his widow.

Rejuvenated, enlivened and bristling with projects, he returned to France. He stopped at Cologne, where a banquet was given in his honour by his admirers. The anti-Prussian feeling had greatly increased in the Rhineland; the bourgeoisie was clamouring with increasing energy for the right to vote, and the number of separatists was growing. Heine was delighted with the progress of the ideas that had been dear to him since his youth : he believed that a free Rhenish Republic would at once establish a bridge between France and Germany and curb Prussian ambition—which was already brooding over schemes for reconquering Alsace and Lorraine. He rejected the idea of German unity, for it entailed the sanctioning of Prussian power. " German unity and grandeur," he said, " should be based on liberty and democracy. I will honour your flag," he told the Pan-German patriots, " when it is deserving of honour and is no longer the plaything of extremists and knaves. Hoist your colours on the peak of German thought, make them the standard of free humanity, and I will shed for them the last drop of my blood. The Lorrainers and the Alsatians will voluntarily rejoin Germany when we have accomplished what the French began— universal democracy, the great work of the revolution. When we shall have pushed the thought of the revolution to its ultimate consequences, and have destroyed servility in its last refuge, Heaven ; when we shall have chased poverty from off the face of the earth, and have returned to the disinherited peoples their dignity, their baffled genius and their profaned beauty—as our great masters the thinkers and poets have said and sung and willed that we their disciples should do—then, not only Alsace and Lorraine, but the whole of France, Europe and the world, which will have been saved, will belong to us. Yes, the whole world will be German ! I have often thought of this mission, of this German hegemony, as I walked among the eternally green pine trees of my country. That is my patriotism ! "

This was the patriotism of Heine, which distinguished him as much from the ancients, Socrates, Plato, Seneca and Diogenes— who proudly extolled *Apolis* (without country), and went so far as to consider the apatrid state as a divine gift—as from the humanists like Dante, Ghiberti and that strange Petrus Alcinius who, in his work *De Exilio Libri duo*, asserted that the truly wise man is he who considers the whole earth as a single town, and finds his country where virtue, honesty and decency reign, and where science and free art flourish best.

This cosmopolitanism of the most distinguished minds lasted until the Revolution. Did not Montaigne, who was essentially a Frenchman, say that he embraced the universe, and note in his diaries: "I am first a man, and then a Frenchman"? But this quality, to which Herder, Schiller, Goethe and Jean-Paul also subscribed, had more of a Utopian and spiritual character than the constitution of a political standpoint.

Heine was also a universalist and cosmopolitan—but after the fashion of the French Revolution patriots, who wished to make their own country the chosen people of ideals and humanity. ". . . French patriotism," he had written ten years earlier in a preface to the *Salon*, "comprises love of country, which should be at once a country of civilisation and human progress . . ."

All the outstanding Frenchmen of the nineteenth century were at one in declaring that the interests of humanity were superior to those of country. But at the same time they considered France to be the leading representative of these universal interests. Auguste Comte, in his *Système de la Politique Positive* said: ". . . for the positive spirit the individual does not exist; nothing exists outside humanity . . ." But he hastened to add that Paris meant France, the West, and the whole of the earth. Joseph de Maistre himself, who was little disposed to new ideas, affirmed that ". . . truth has need of France . . ." The anarchist Proudhon—at least before 1848—professed equally his faith in the universal mission of France, as did the Creole, Flora Tristan—the "woman of light and shade," as Jules Janin christened her.

Heine could easily have broken with his country, following the ancient humanist adage *Ubi bene, ibi patria*. He could have broken the ties that bound him to Germany by becoming naturalised French. But when he was asked why he had abandoned his plan for naturalisation he replied jestingly: "For fear of loving France the less—as one cares less for a mistress once one has led her before the Registrar." He wished to live in wedlock with France, but had the deepest reasons for not wishing to divorce his unhappy love, Germany. The chaste ironist had never made this admission publicly, but all his writings testify to it. The German chauvinist Nationalists understood Heine's mentality; they condemned him less for his cosmopolitan apatrid Jewish attitude than for his aggressive and active patriotism. He had said to them : " You always play upon what is bad in the German people, upon national hatred, religious and political superstition—in a word, upon their stupidity."

Heine taught a French type of patriotism, designed to harmonise with universal interests, and based on national virtues.

In his pamphlet against the informer Menzel he compiled an inventory of the German virtues. Fidelity, chastity, honesty and courage figured in his list. " The German is the most courageous of all men," he wrote, but added that his tragedy lay precisely in the fact that his government always abused his national virtues, which were not accompanied by farsightedness and an instinct for liberty. And without these two factors no people can give anything great to the world. To turn to account the German virtues and create new ones, and to transmute German philosophy—that is, the moral and social ideas of the greatest Germans—into a popular force : this was Heine's patriotic programme, which became also that of the Liberal and Democratic German Youth of the 1840's.

While the French professed the theory of a " chosen people," Heine and his followers worked to elevate the Germans to the French standard, and to make of them a second chosen people with the ideas of liberty and justice. The check to the French Revolution was—he thought, resuming his Saint-Simonist theories—due to the lack of economic knowledge on the one hand, and to the antagonism of Germany, the second greatest power in Europe, on the other. A Germany dominated by a modern social and political doctrine formulated by the Hegelian school, a Germany with a foreign policy based on her friendship with France, could achieve the height of moral and economic reforms, and save humanity.

But how would it be possible to eradicate from the German soul that Francophobia which their educators instilled in it from earliest infancy ? Heine asserted bitterly that the German chauvinists Becker, Schneckenburger and Scharnhorst were trying to revive the 1813 mentality in Germany, and denounced French immorality just at the time when in France men like Victor Cousin, the friend of Hegel, and Charles de Remusat " . . . who knew all the heights and depths to which the German spirit could rise or fall . . ." were struggling with obvious goodwill to create an atmosphere of mutual understanding between the two countries separated by the Rhine.

Heine also gave his French friends to understand that he required from them more than a knowledge of the great German minds ; he demanded of them a more positive policy, by assuring them that a Germany whom they helped to become democratic would be the surest ally in their attempt to found " . . . a liberal society of the European nations."

"God desires a Great France and a Great Germany," sang Victor Hugo. Today the magnificent dreams of these poets awaken in us nothing more than a sad smile.

CHAPTER THIRTY-SIX

HEINE AND MARX

" Had I been correspondent to the newspapers in Ancient Rome," wrote Heine on his return to Paris in the Augsburger Allgemeine Zeitung, " I should not have taken into account the banquet given by Agrippa to the Diplomatic Corps of Rome, but the Galileans whom they flung on the bonfires . . ."

HEINE was convinced that posterity would be grateful to him for not having spoken of the sumptuous receptions given to the ambassadors accredited to Paris, but for having drawn attention to the working-class world and the beginnings of Communism.

Heine often visited the Saint Marceau quarter and the workshops, and argued with the workers. He examined the books and pamphlets that they read—Robespierre's works, Marat's broadsheets, Cabet's history of the Revolution, Buonarotti's book on ideas and the Babeuf conspiracy. The workers received him with confidence, and often invited him to take a glass of wine with them in their cafés, and some of them even invited him to their homes.

He was touched by the simple familiarity of the French workman, by his gaiety and commonsense. He contrasted them favourably with the bourgeoisie debased by their thirst for gain and fear of the proletariat. If the French bourgeoisie was rotten to the core he recognised among the workers generosity, enthusiasm and hope. Liberty was for them more than a formula, it was a question of justice and the right to bread and work. Perhaps the day is not far off, he thought, when the bourgeois comedy will come to a close.

"How many of you are there?" Heine asked a young revolutionary worker.

"Many, many," he replied. "Perhaps four hundred thousand in Paris alone."

He also followed with great interest the development of the English working-class movement, and considered the alliance between the Chartists, who were clamouring for the right to vote, and the proletarians, who were struggling for higher wages, as one of the most important events of the epoch. Everything was coming to pass as he had foreseen ten years earlier at the time when the Saint-Simonists were disbanded :

" The failure of the Utopians does not signify the defeat of Socialism ; on the contrary, it makes possible a deeper teaching by the best-informed minds . . ."

" The economic side of the theory concerning the right of ownership must be carefully elaborated," he wrote to Varnhagen.

The English Chartists and the French Blanquists—Louis Blanc and his friends—who amalgamated the idea of social revolution with the requirements of political Democracy, in other words, the claims of the working classes, brought a considerable advance into the practical and theoretical domain of Socialism. A thinker should arise who would evolve a philosophical and historical philosophy to unite the fragmentary theories of these fore-runners. Heine did not think that the master capable of making the synthesis of Communism would come from England. " The English," he said, " proceed too much by inference ; they concentrate on immediate facts, which oblige them to remedy the most striking legal injustices. They have not enough imagination to embrace an action in its totality or in its most far-reaching aspects. The English working-class movement dis-tinguishes itself from the French movement precisely by the fact that while the latter is animated by ideas, the former is stimu-lated solely by famine and poverty . . ." On the other hand, the French mentality appeared to him too sceptical to create a lasting system that would prescribe the laws of social organisation and mobilise the will and belief of the human élite."

*   *   *   *

Along with Heine, certain young German writers and philoso-phers—Moses Hess, Karl Marx and Friedrich Engels, who had been working since the beginning of 1842 on the *Rheinische*

Zeitung—were following with sympathy and interest the Socialist and Communist literature in France and England. It was a curious coincidence that the same *Augsburger Allgemeine Zeitung* in which Heine's articles on the working-class movement appeared, accused the intellectuals of the *Rheinische Zeitung* in one of its October numbers of wishing to establish a Communist organisation in Germany. Karl Marx replied to this article.

" . . . we are firmly convinced," wrote the young Hegelian, "that the true danger is not to put Communist ideas into practice, but rests rather in their theoretical elaboration. An actual revolt—even if it is based on a mass movement—can always be answered with cannon. The ideas which convince our intelligence and conquer our sentiments, on the contrary, constitute chains that cannot be seized from us without tearing out our hearts at the same time . . ."

The Prussian Government very soon realised the danger of "the theoretical elaboration" of Communist ideas, and banned the *Rheinische Zeitung*. This interdict only confirmed Marx's decision to devote himself entirely to social problems. " Communism and the suppression of private ownership are not the same thing," he wrote to his friend Rüge, the director of the *Hallisches Jahrbüch* in September 1843.

Communism, as it had been presented in the *Icarie* of Cabet, and in the rather primitive writings of Pecqueur, Dezamy and Weitling, did not satisfy this young philosopher brought up in the Hegelian school. " It is not by chance only that Communism has provoked a reaction," he wrote, "which has manifested itself in various socialist theories, like those of Fourier, Proudhon and others, for Communism only represents one of the aspects of the Socialist principle, which in turn is only one aspect of human reality. We must take into account also the *theoretical* existence of man, religion, science, etc. . . ."

Moses Hess, one of his friends on the Rhenish paper described Marx in the following terms to the writer Auerbach: "Imagine Rousseau, Holbach, Lessing, Heine and Hegel all rolled into one, and there you have Doctor Marx." Marx envisaged a synthesis that would embrace man in his entirety, in all his aspects, that would explain his past, determine his future and reveal the meaning of all his tendencies and hopes. He thought of a synthesis in which the German criticism of religion would unite with the teachings of the French social and political revolution.

This theoretical idea of fusion was in the air. Another Left Wing Hegelian, Feuerbach, published his famous theses in the same year, which his partisans compared somewhat exaggeratedly with those that Luther had nailed to the door of Wittenberg University. Feuerbach demanded the combination of French materialism and German spiritualism. " The true philosopher, who identifies himself with man and with life, should be of Gallo-Germanic ascendancy . . ." Moses Hess was of the same opinion. In an essay published in Switzerland in 1843 he wrote : " Without absolute equality and French communism on the one side, and German atheism on the other, it would be impossible to achieve either individual liberty or true social equality." After the Prussian Government had banned the *Rheinische Zeitung* and the *Hallisches Jahrbüch*—the scientific review of the young Leftist Hegelians—the director of that publication, Arnold Rüge, decided to launch a revue in France that would preach " . . . the combination of German philosophic radicalism and French democracy." He proposed to Marx that he should collaborate with him in the editorship of this organ. They thought first of installing it in Strasburg, that Franco-German town where Calvin had found refuge and where Herder had initiated Goethe into the cult of cathedrals, popular poetry and universalism. But owing to technical difficulties they renounced this plan and decided upon Paris, hoping that the eighty thousand German workers who lived there would support them.

Marx arrived in Paris on November 11, 1843, and took up his lodgings at 38 Rue Vanneau. Some days later he paid a visit to Heine, who received " . . . this young Titan with his tousled hair and glittering eyes . . ." like an old friend. He had read his articles in the *Rheinische Gazette*, and knew that he had defended him in the struggle with Börne. Marx was a Rhinelander like himself ; they had both studied at Bonn University, both loathed the Prussian spirit and they had a common admiration for Hegel.

Marx seduced Heine with his pitiless and incorruptible logic. What he as a poet had only sensed—the revolutionary character of the dialectic theory taught by Hegel—Marx the philosopher explained with method. The idea to him was not a pre-existent entity in the Platonic sense, but the expression of the intelligent will of social man. Marx loved the truth, not tenderly and timidly, but with violence and obsession. While recognising Heine's contradictions, he loved the forerunner in him who, like some John the Baptist, had announced the new Saviour—the Proletariat. He valued the inimitable mastery of German prose of this caustic polemist, who had tried to awaken the German people from their stertorous sleep. He achieved a reconciliation between Heine and Rüge, who had previously sided with Börne against him, and also gained his collaboration for the revue which they proposed to found in Paris. Heine presented him with three satirical poems, in which he made fun of Ludwig II of Bavaria. Marx himself published two important studies in the first issue of the *Franco-German Annals*, one on the Jewish question and the other on the Hegelian theory of Law.

The German philosophers were mistaken in thinking they would win the support of the French Socialist writers for their publication. Louis Blanc, Considerant and others refused their collaboration more or less politely, or made promises which they never kept. Proudhon was the only one who, without going so far as to write an article for the *Revue*, at least evinced a desire to acquaint himself with the trends and ideas of the German revolutionaries. The others only listened with sceptical smiles to the explanations of Hess, Rüge and Marx, who claimed that French politics could also find inspiration in Hegelian philosophy. They regarded them as bone-setters who wished to apply a panacea of which they themselves did not make use.

The *Franco-German Annals* was short-lived. The Prussian ambassador in Paris, von Arnim, warned his Government in advance of the appearance of a subversive publication. The first number was confiscated at the Prussian frontier, and in April 1844, the Prussian Minister for the Interior issued a warrant for the arrest of the principal collaborators of the review : Marx, Heine, Rüge, Herwegh and Bernays. Heine, to keep the promise he had made to his mother to pay a visit to Hamburg with Mathilde, was obliged to use the sea route to avoid crossing Prussian territory. After the disappearance of the Annals, Marx and his friends grouped themselves round the *Vorwärts*, which had been launched at the beginning of January by a certain Börnstein, an able though suspect publicist, with material support from Meyerbeer. The Marxist group succeeded in eliminating Börnstein, and the direction of the paper from the first of July fell into the hands of Bernays.

At this period Marx and Heine saw each other nearly every day. Mathilde did not care very much for the philosopher, and left the house every time he began his interminable discussions. Heine also frequently went to visit him in the little apartment where he lived with his wife and small daughter. He played with the child and regained his youthful outlook among these enthusiastic young people. His scepticism softened, and he was completely carried away by the faith of Marx and his companions.

> *Ein neues Lied, ein besseres Lied*
> *O Freunde, will ich euch dichten ;*
> " *Wir wollen hier auf Erden schon*
> " *Das Himmelreich errichten.*
>
> " *Wir wollen auf Erden glücklich sein*
> " *Und wollen nicht mehr darben,*
> " *Verschlemmen soll nicht der faule Bauch,*
> " *Was fleissige Hände erwarben.*"

> A new song and a better song,
> Oh friends, for you I'll sing :
> " Now here on earth the Heavenly land
> " Let us swiftly bring.
>
> " Here on earth we'll happy be,
> " And we shall want no more ;
> " The lazy belly shall not squander
> " The fruits that strong hands bore."

Contact with Marx stimulated him. He, who a short while previously, at the period of *Atta Troll*, had pleaded for free poetry and art for art's sake, now began to write numerous *Zeitgedichte*, —pamphlets in verse—which eventually appeared in a volume entitled, *Neue Gedichte*. Friedrich Engels proudly announced in the English radical paper, *The New Moral World* :

" Henry Heine, the most eminent of all living German poets, has joined our ranks, and published a volume of political poetry which contains also some pieces preaching socialism."

Heine's *Die Weber*, which appeared in *Vorwärts* on July 10, 1844, was written at the instigation of Marx on the occasion of the revolt of the Silesian weavers. The insurrection marked the beginning of the German working-class movement. Even today, thanks to this poem which has become a revolutionary song, Heine still lives in the hearts of the German workers.

The collaborators of *Vorwärts*, who met every day in the smoky editorial offices at the corner of the Rue des Moulins and the Rue Neuve des Petits Champs, violently attacked the Prussian régime, and made intensive propaganda for Communist ideas.

In the spring of the following year, the Burgomaster, Tschech, attempted to assassinate William IV of Prussia. *Vorwärts* congratulated him in an audacious editorial. " Socialism cannot be realised without revolution," wrote Marx on May 10, 1844.

The Prussian Government approached Guizot to ban the paper. The French authorities showed themselves indulgent at the beginning, however, only bringing an action against Bernays, the editor, under the pretext that he had omitted to deposit the surety required by law at the registry of the Tribunal ; whereupon Bernays declared that the paper would appear in future as a periodical. Upon new steps being taken by the Prussian Ambassador, the French Minister of the Interior issued a decree of expulsion against the principal collaborators on January 11, 1845. The name of Heine figured on the list.

Heine warned his friends among the French journalists, and the Liberal and Radical Presses violently attacked the Government for its servile obedience to the Prussian demands. As a result, the Minister of the Interior modified his decision : exceptions were made in the cases of Heine, on account of his fourteen years' residence in France, George Herwegh who was Swiss, and Rüge who was a Saxon citizen. Marx and Bakunin, however (in 1844 the Russian revolutionary was connected with the group of German Communists, and worked on their paper), were obliged to leave the country.

Marx's departure for Brussels did not put an end to the friendship between the poet and the revolutionary philosopher. A year after his expulsion his best friend Engels arrived in Paris. He went often to see " Papa Heine," kept him in touch with the development of the Communist movement, the activities of Marx and also frequently transmitted to his friend news of and commissions for Heine. When Marx returned to Paris, attracted by the February revolutions, Heine was seriously ill in a clinic in Auteuil, unable to receive anybody. From this period onwards Heine had no more direct relations with the German Communists, but he never ceased to think of his friends, and some years later, although he had abandoned his atheistic convictions, he wrote in his *Confessions* :

" The more or less recondite leaders of the German Communists are great logicians, the strongest of whom have issued from the school of Hegel ; and they are without doubt the most capable heads and the most energetic characters of Germany. These Doctors of Revolution and their ruthlessly determined disciples are the only men in Germany who are truly alive, and to them belongs the future . . ."

And although he added, " . . . I do not express here my wishes and regrets : I am relating facts and speaking the truth," it is quite obvious that this spirit, struggling against God and Death, defying the decrepitude of his body, desired nothing more deeply than the triumph of a single idea, " . . . that would destroy the old world where man exploited man . . .", the idea that was imbedded with ruthless logic and savage passion in the man whom Heine, in his *Political Testament* referred to as " my friend Marx ".

CHAPTER THIRTY-SEVEN

UNCLE SALOMON'S LAST TRICK

IN the summer of 1844, Heine set out for Hamburg in company with his wife. Mathilde insisted at all costs in taking her favourite parrot Cocotte with them, as she did not dare to leave her in the hands of strangers. At the port of Hamburg Charlotte's husband, Moritz Embden, met the couple. Anxious to be of service, he carried the bird-cage into the carriage, but as they arrived the infuriated bird nipped his fingers through the bars of the cage. Heine's brother-in-law let out a yell of pain and dropped the cage, and Mathilde, forgetting her husband's admonitions, began to scold him. " My God, how anyone can be so clumsy ! My poor little Cocotte, who has already suffered so much from seasickness . . . and now in addition you must go and frighten her . . . " Mathilde began to cry, the parrot squawked, and Moritz Embden apologised profusely ; Heine laughed till the tears rolled down his cheeks.

The visit passed off without further incident. Mathilde forced herself to behave correctly and to be pleasant to Uncle Salomon, who was racked with gout and nearing his end. Heine visited his uncle on his own and, although it was extremely painful to him, begged his uncle not to forget Mathilde and himself. Salomon asked his nephew to express himself more clearly. He had granted him an annual pension of four thousand eight hundred francs since his marriage, but Heine would have liked to extract a promise whereby Salomon's heirs would continue with the payment until Mathilde's death. Furthermore, he would have liked assured annuities from Campe made in his wife's favour. " Why don't you live more economically ? " growled the old miser, not forgetting to reproach Heine for his relations with the Communists. But he finished by agreeing, and reassured him with the words : " I will think of you."

A few weeks after his nephew's departure for Paris the banker died of an embolism. In January 1845, his son Carl, the principal heir, communicated the contents of the will to his cousin.

Heine opened the letter with trembling fingers. Mathilde and his secretary " little Weil," a small man with glasses and tousled hair, waited impatiently to hear the contents.

Salomon, who had left several hundreds of thousands of marks to various charitable organisations, had allotted to Heinrich only eight thousand marks—without any allusion to the allowance.

Heine rose incredulously from his chair, his face ghostly pale, gave a groan and fell senseless to the floor. Mathilde and Weil lifted him up and carried him to his bed. Half an hour later he came to his senses, and immediately noticed that he could no longer open his left eye. He burst into a fit of violent sobbing. Doctor Sichel, who had arrived by this time, diagnosed that he had *icterus*. Mathilde leant stiffly against the chimney-piece and listened while the Doctor gave instructions for complete darkness.

During the critical weeks that followed, Heine only held on to life by his rage and a desire for vengeance. The image of old Salomon appeared constantly before him : a leering, tyrannical old Shylock, dictating his will. He must have derived a vicious pleasure from playing this last shabby trick on his nephew, even from beyond the grave ; and his son Carl, who was as miserly— if not more so—as his father, but lacked the Balzacian carriage of the old man, had always borne him a grudge. He had never forgiven him for having thrown Clara Fould into his arms : she had always preferred Heinrich to himself. But Heine could not bear the thought of having been outwitted by Uncle Salomon. The " assassination", as he called it, had only been half success-ful : his left side was paralysed, but he could still raise his right hand to show his rage and threats. If Carl thought that he was only a phantom and an impotent invalid (his spies had certainly in-formed him of his cousin's condition), he would show him that his triumph was premature !

As we have already mentioned, Heine had always felt that the rich members of his family owed him support, and that, whether the will provided for his pension or not, it was due to him. To whom could a poet apply, who had renounced a lucrative career and devoted his life to the search for truth and the cult of beauty, if it were not to the wealthy members of his family ? Had they not been blinded by jealousy, fear and hatred, they would have been proud of him for having made the family name famous to posterity. Heine had no love for these business *condottieri* who did not participate in his passions and opinions ; he saw their faults clearly, but he was none the less a member of their family. If he had often threatened to voice his judgments upon them in public, up to the present he had spared them. But the moment that Salomon and Carl proved to him that they were indifferent as to whether he had enough to eat in his old age, or whether after his death his widow would have a roof over her head and firing to warm her, the anger which had lain dormant all his life and the memory of all the humiliations he had endured from Salomon exploded.

This burning rage put new life into his paralysed body, and even if it did not cure him, helped far more than the medicines of Doctors Gruby and Sichel. Some weeks later Heine was able to leave his bed. Wearing a goatskin cape and black glasses, and leaning on a stick, he visited two of his lawyer friends, Emmanuel Aragot and Crémieux. On their advice he sent a letter to Carl requesting that he recognise the allowance promised by his uncle. He informed him in passing that he proposed to write his memoirs, in which his dear family would figure prominently.

This veiled ultimatum started the conflict which reached its culminating point eighteen months later, when Carl Heine spread the report in the German Press that his cousin had gone mad and had been shut up in a sanatorium. By way of reply, Heine wrote in the *Augsburger Allgemeine Zeitung*, on the election of Carl's uncle, Achilles Fould, as deputy of Tarbes, that " . . . the last traces of mediaeval intolerance have disappeared at a moment when even the Jew, with no other quality than that of being rich, can, like his Christian brother, reach the *Chambre de Députés*—the highest dignity in France." He announced in his article that he was preparing a great historical work on the national wealth of the Jews, from Abraham to modern times, and in the course of his work he would have the opportunity of speaking of Benoît Fould, the father-in-law of Carl. His cousin must have realised that the book, if ever it saw the light of day, might contain certain very disagreeable revelations as to the inside workings of the Frankfurt bank. However, he did not yield, perhaps because he thought that in view of Heine's failing health his threats could not be carried out. The poet himself shivered at the idea that he might die before he could force Carl to give way. He approached his friends Prince Pückler-Muskau, the witty globe-trotter, Humboldt and Varnhagen, who never lost their interest in him, Mendelssohn-Bartholdy the musician, and the young Lassalle, begging them to write to Carl and to intercede for him.

The banker showed himself disposed to negotiate, provided that Heine apologised for his insults. Finally, in the month of September 1847, mutual friends prevailed upon Carl, who was passing through Paris, to go and see his cousin whom they gave but a few days to live. A scene worthy of Balzac's pen was enacted in the sick man's darkened room. Carl, with his hand on his heart, reproached Heinrich in breaking tones for having doubted for one instant the friendly sentiment that he and his wife felt for him. Moved by his own generosity he promised to pay, in the event of Heine's death, *half* of the pension to his wife. At this solemn moment the poet seized his cousin's outstretched hand with a sudden frenzied movement and, in order to drink the cup of humiliation and hypocrisy to its very dregs, raised it to his lips. Disturbed by this sudden outburst, Carl recoiled, muttering words of excuse. Heinrich winked maliciously and told him that at that moment he was indistinguishable from his Uncle Salomon, whom he had always loved like a father, and whose hand he had always kissed when he wished to express his affection. Carl then grasped that the hand-kiss was by no means a capitulation but a highly equivocal gesture, and that so long as his cousin lived he would have to be on his guard.

CHAPTER THIRTY-EIGHT

THE FEBRUARY REVOLUTION

Once Heine had recovered from his jaundice he immediately forgot his suffering and refused to take the malady seriously. From early youth he had been a prey to more or less violent neuralgic pains, and had become accustomed to looking upon himself as in perfect health between attacks. On this occasion he simply considered it a more severe attack than usual; he had an unshakable confidence in his organism, as though it were a friend whom he did not possibly imagine could betray him. Mathilde supported him in this conviction. In the course of the last few years she had become a little plumper and more untidy—but she had retained her irresponsibility and gaiety. She shrugged her shoulders when she heard the doctors anxiously discussing the gravity of her husband's illness. She continued to treat him like a healthy man who merely thinks he is ill.

They spent several months at Montmorency, where Gautier and Royer, accompanied by their mistresses, often visited them. One day, as he watched the three women chattering and laughing, he could not refrain from crying: "I have never seen three more beautiful creatures than our mistresses." Mathilde prepared a magnificent dinner in her guests' honour: as *hors-d'œuvre* there were oysters in Sauterne, followed by cutlets *à la Provençale*, a fine Brie and iced meringues. After lunch they sat in the orchard, and Mathilde regaled them with cool drinks concocted from beer, lemons, oranges and sugar. At a later date Gautier evoked with nostalgia these Sunday afternoons when Heine's spirits sparkled and they talked pell-mell of Communism, Descamp's pictures—Gautier considered him too trivial and Heine defended him—of Chopin, George Sand, rich Jews and Prussian pedantry, little actresses and grisettes. The more Heine's youth and health deteriorated the more he became obsessed by women. After Marx's departure, too preoccupied with his cares, pains and recovery, he had retired completely from politics. He had never been quite as frivolous, lacking in respect, and pagan as during this period at Montmorency.

On his return to Paris at the beginning of autumn, this half-blind man with his tired limbs, who stumbled along with a bizarre smile on his lips, began to pursue the girls of the Palais Royal. During his walks he often met Lassalle, who was then only twenty and who was working at the Bibliothèque Royale collecting material for his book on Heraclitus. Thin, elegant and amazingly handsome, he easily won the ladies of easy virtue so desired by Heine. However, instead of resenting him, the poet cultivated and encouraged the young man, whose ardour and temperament filled him with boundless admiration. In his own mind he placed Lassalle almost above Marx, for Marx was a man of single passion whose ideas and energies all centred on the revolution, whereas Lassalle with true dillettantism sought to taste everything and conquer everything : power and truth, women and luxury ; he dreamed with romantic devilry of becoming at once philosopher, politician, military leader, poet, millionaire and great lover. Heine looked upon him as his disciple, and both loved and envied him for his strength, his pride—and his resolution, which was like that of a new Siegfried in search of the Absolute. Nothing is superior to life, and the whole meaning of life is joy. From the moment that there is joy and happiness life becomes worth living. Asceticism, resignation, abstinence and the thousand modes of torturing oneself are only victories of death over life. The man who believes in himself, in happiness, in the sun, bread, wine, women and poetry, in the truth of appearances and in dancing and youth, is of the company of the gods.

Heine had never proclaimed the glories of life and youth with so much vigour and solemnity as now—since he had been touched by death. He refused to recognise the power of his affliction, he behaved like a banker who on the verge of bankruptcy continues to dissipate his assets.

One afternoon as he was leaving the Montpensier Gallery reading-room, he ran across an old friend, Madame Jaubert. She experienced some difficulty in hiding her surprise, for she hardly recognised him : " . . . his eyelid hung down over his left eye, and the whole of that side of his face had become immovable, presenting a singular contrast with the lively movements of the other . . ." Heine took the arm of this young woman whom he had courted a long time before in the Princess Belgiojoso's drawing-room. " Stroll with me, my dear. At least you will be able to boast that you have walked along the boulevards with a living corpse."

During the winter his condition grew worse, the disease spread to the lower part of his face and the muscles around his mouth became affected. " I kiss, but I cannot feel anything, for my lips are so paralysed . . ." He found difficulty in masticating and swallowing, suffered from loss of appetite, and for weeks on end lived on infusions alone.

With the first sunny days his doctor, Wertheimer, sent him to Barrèges, hoping that the tonic waters of the Pyrenees would bring him relief. The long journey exhausted him to such a degree that near Bagnères-de-Bigorre he could no longer stand the jolting of the carriage, and had to descend and be transported over the mountains in a sedan-chair. But even then, half-blind and paralysed, he enjoyed the forest landscape they were crossing with intensity. To live was the thing : to live in spite of everything, to conquer the most agonising pains and still enjoy this luxuriant country . . . where from time to time he could see the light colours of a herd and the graceful gestures of a young shepherd waving his hat.

He submitted grudgingly to the necessities of the cure. He entered the black cage that so resembled a crypt almost morosely, and slid resignedly into the bathing-pool where he had to remain for an hour with outstretched legs and crossed arms, as though preparing for the quiet of the grave. He hated the ominous calm, and missed the noise of Paris ; he missed Mathilde, who had returned to her village for a few months, and grew increasingly ill at ease among these invalids who reminded him constantly of his own condition. And what was more, his health was declining instead of improving. The least noise exasperated him, and he had no appetite whatsoever.

Towards the end of the summer, thin as a skeleton and terribly depressed, he returned to Paris and to Mathilde, who received him amidst a flood of tears. During his stay at Barrèges his beard had grown white and his whole left side had become completely paralysed. Engels, who came to pay him a visit some days after his return, was shocked at his appearance and told Marx : " It is appalling to see such a man disintegrating piece by piece."

Heine's spirit, however, remained intact, and though he was isolated and chained to his bed, he still took part in the life of Paris. He was *au courant* with all the events, interested in everything, and surprised his visitors by the vivacity of his conversation, his good humour, and the malicious tone he adopted when speaking of his approaching death. He looked upon every day he lived as a gift. He wrote often to his mother—who had one day read the news of his death in the German papers with dismay—and tried to persuade her that he was in excellent health. ". . . the gods do not abandon those who have sung their glories." With the aid of his secretary he carefully prepared an edition of his complete works ; he collated his studies and corrected each of his articles, revising each line, adding and deleting, disputing every hour with his malady, to leave a completed work to posterity.

After a terrible and depressing night he drafted his will, appointing as sole legatee his wife who, " . . . by her goodness and fidelity, has embellished my life." He wished to be buried as simply as the most humble man of the people. In the event of his dying in Paris he chose to be buried in the cemetery of Montmartre and nowhere else, " . . . for I have lived my best days among the people of the Faubourg Montmartre." He specified that he was to be interred in that part of the cemetery reserved for Catholics, where later Mathilde would join him. At the end of his will he wrote :

" My great and noble mother, thou who hast done so much for me, I bid thee farewell !

" To you, my dear brothers and sisters, with whom I have lived in peace, to you an eternal farewell.

" Farewell to thee too, my German fatherland, land of mysteries and sorrows ; may you be resplendent and happy.

"Adieu, witty and good Frenchmen, whom I have
loved so much ; thank you for your cordial hospitality."

He took leave of life and of all those whom he had loved, but
the hope that he would survive did not leave him even in the
midst of his adieus ; and in fact, after the crisis he recovered,
and by the spring he was able to leave his room once more.

One morning he paid a visit to Gautier, whom he had not
seen for a long time. His friend looked at him with wide open
eyes as though he had seen a ghost.

"Is it the devil or is it Heine ? "

"It is Heine . . . God become man," the ghost replied.

In the streets he would cast lecherous glances at the courtesans,
and blow them kisses. He rebelled more and more against his
infirmity. Charming grisettes, *figurantes* of the opera with their
puffed skirts, overcoming their disgust in their pity for him like
good Samaritans, caressed and spoiled him. One afternoon he
visited the Louvre Museum. An ailing Hellene, he sat in front
of the Venus de Milo. Had he been alone he would have knelt
before the admirable goddess and confessed his sorrows to her.

No, he would not give in to death : lucerous or leprous, he
adored youth and beauty. Oh, that he might fall dead there and
then ! That would be a poetic, pagan and superb death—a
death worthy of him.

He rose with an effort and, hesitating and stumbling, made
his way to the reading-room to peruse the French and German
papers.

In the garden of the Palais Royal he found a huge crowd
assembled. There were cries of "Long live the Reform ! "
"Long live the Republic ! " and "Down with the corrupt ! "
For some weeks the atmosphere of Paris had been more tense
and restless than usual. The Orleanist opposition with Thiers
at its head had launched an attack against the Guizot Government,
who had refused to consider any new reforms. The Republican
Party also mobilised its militants. Revolutionary agitation
found a fertile soil in the working-class districts, which were
experiencing the first great economic crisis. The industrialists,
incapable of selling their products, were dismissing their workmen by the thousand. The Guizot Government could find no

other answer to the demonstrations of the hungry unemployed than to oppose them with the sabres of the National Guard. The revolution that Heine had predicted and wished for, the revolution that was hatched in the suburbs, now emerged into full daylight. It was the dwellers of the Faubourg Saint Antoine and Saint Marceau, men with burning eyes and clothed in workmen's blue blouses, who ventured now as far as the gardens of the Palais Royal: these were the soldiers of the revolution !

For the moment they were content to demonstrate peaceably. At an order from the National Guards they dispersed good-naturedly ; but tomorrow, perhaps even in a few hours, they would have weapons in their hands and would be shooting at the representatives of authority from behind hastily constructed barricades.

Heine smiled maliciously when he thought of Thiers, gullible enough to imagine that he could hold in check the storm that he had unleashed. These men in their blue blouses and their comrades, the artisans and students, would no longer be content with electoral reform ; they desired nothing short of a complete reformation of society, a Socialist Republic ; they wanted to continue from where Robespierre and his friends of the Convention had left off, to repair their mistakes, avenge Thermidor and revive the experience of the great unappreciated Babeuf.

These dwellers of the suburbs and garrets would hoist the red flag of insurrection on the *Hôtel de ville*, proclaim the *Lex Agraria* in the villages, and declare war on all privileges and privileged in France and throughout the world—from the English Lords to the Prussian Junkers, Metternich, the Czar and all tyrants of all countries.

He thought with beating heart that the Universal Republic, his aspiration and hope for years, was now about to materialise, thanks to the will and struggle of the French people. Engels brought him the *Manifesto* he and Marx had compiled, and which had already been circulated throughout the whole of Germany by the members of the Party. In this slender booklet the two Hegelians recorded with irrefutable logic the aims and methods of the class struggle. He made his way to the smoky and crowded reading-room, sat down at the table and began to glance through the *National*, the *Reform*, and the *Débats*. And all of a sudden, for no apparent reason, the idea crossed his mind that *this was not yet the moment*. To bring the revolution to fruition it would be necessary for the leaders to be in agreement, and to know exactly what they wanted. He thought of the chiefs of the French Left—Lamartine, Odilon Barrot, Ledru Rodillon, Leblanc and others. He saw in none of them the energetic qualities that the control and leadership of a vast revolutionary movement demanded. They would recoil before difficulties, betray the confidence of the people and be deceived themselves. Would it not have been better to soothe the masses instead of exciting them? The men in blouses and the students would spill their blood on the barricades in vain, and it would be the best, the most generous and the purest among them who would fall.

He would have preferred to warn the opposition leaders and draw their attention to their terrible responsibilities, beg them to reflect before taking action, not to undertake lightly an historical task whose accomplishment required long and careful preparation. He would have liked to beg them to wait a little longer . . . But could it be that he desired the postponement of the revolution because, like the bourgeois who cast anxious glances about them, *he feared it*? Did he fear the noise, the volleys, barricades, disorder and change? Did he fear the loss of his pension and the interruption of his relations with Germany, or no longer having enough money to pay his rent or buy Mathilde new dresses? He began to feel ashamed for thinking of *himself* when the fate of the world was at stake, when others younger than himself, who had neither lived nor loved, were ready to sacrifice everything for their ideal.

Suffocating in the stuffy air and oppressed by his thoughts, he rose from the table and tottered into the street where he could breathe more freely. Should he return home? Mathilde had gone to visit a friend with Pauline, and would not return before nightfall. If at other times he had liked to enjoy the solitude, interrupted only by the screeches of the parrot, the idea of being alone at that moment appeared to him extremely distasteful.

Suddenly he thought of Madame Jaubert, whom he had not seen for some time. That charming woman was just the person he needed; he could open his heart to her, confess his contradictory sentiments and muddled ideas. Hailing a cab, he gave the address of Madame Jaubert; he took care to warn the driver in advance that she lived on the second floor, and that he would be obliged to carry him upstairs because he was too tired to climb them alone. After much haggling they agreed upon a fare, and on their arrival at the entrance to the house the cabman carried the poet on his shoulders and set him down before the door of the lady's apartment.

Madame Jaubert clapped her hands with joy, installed her visitor on a couch among innumerable cushions, wrapped a shawl round his legs and hastened to prepare the tea. Heine, joking away quite merrily, suddenly gave a groan: he told her how he had recently gambled on the Stock Exchange—on the advice of Friedländer, Lassalle's brother-in-law—and had lost nearly all his savings in the shares of the Belgian gas company.

"But it served me right," he added; "the Rabbi Ben Chloime of Prague was right—do you know that story? An old Jewess rushed up to the Rabbi one day as he was crossing the bridge over the Moldau . . .

'Rabbi, Rabbi,' she lamented, 'oh, what a misfortune!'

'What is the matter, my dear Rebecca?'

'My son Itzig—he has broken his leg.'

'How did he do that?'

'He was climbing a ladder . . .'

'Climbing a ladder? Well, he got his deserts—what on earth was a Jew doing climbing a ladder?'

. . . or a poet on the Stock Exchange?" he concluded with a sarcastic laugh.

Madame Jaubert laughed with him, but suddenly she stopped, her face went pale, and with a cry of alarm she hurried over to Heine.

The poet had been seized with a terrible attack. Cramps shot through his body from head to foot. It was a terrible sight: he gasped, his weakly frame was torn with convulsions, his face contorted terribly and took on hideous animal expressions.

Madame Jaubert sent for a doctor and gave the poet morphia. His sufferings were somewhat eased, and they were able to transport him to his house. On the following day he summoned Doctor Gruby.

When the doctor entered the little room in the Rue de Berlin he found Heine utterly immobile in his bed, a complete human wreck. He was suffering from a salivary flux and was incapable of taking the least nourishment. In this impotent body, which exhaled a pestilential odour, only the weak smile on his deathly pale face and a sorrowfully ironic look from his half-open left eye betrayed that he was alive. He tried to move his lips, but found it impossible to articulate.

" All is not lost," said the doctor, smiling wanly.

He arranged for the poet to be taken to a private clinic in the Rue de Lourcine. Heine had need above all of " rest and professional care." Mathilde understood the hint that lay in the doctor's words ; her eyes moist with tears, she acquiesced with a nod of her head. As soon as Doctor Gruby had shut the door she flung herself on her husband's bed and sobbed.

" Don't leave me, Henri, don't leave me. Tell me you won't leave me," she whimpered, and lovingly stroked his hand.

In the clinic they soothed him with morphia pads, placed along his spine. After several weeks he recovered : his vitality was fantastic. Mathilde came to visit him for a few hours every day, and read the papers to him. " . . . the revolution has broken out ; the Government is resisting, but the victory of the rebels is not in doubt . . ."

" Everyone is in favour of the Republic," said Mathilde who, following the fashion, had pinned a tricolour cockade on her breast. Although her husband had forbidden her to go out during this dangerous period, she and Pauline wandered about the city the entire day, playing at revolution with its crowds and brawls, as though it were carnival time or a more than usually exciting fourteenth of July.

The church bells were ringing. On the boulevards the crowd had torn down trees, lamp-posts and window gratings. No one paid the slightest attention to the volley of shots. The cafés remained open during the street fighting ; in the middle of a battle, when the insurgents were thirsty, they would leave the barricades, go and have a drink, or smoke a pipe—and then return to their " work."

A rumour spread—Mathilde told him—that the King had fled. In the street cries were to be heard : " There is no longer a King ! " " The whole world is free ! "

A wicked smile played about his lips. He was delighted to have lived long enough to learn of the King's flight, who in his eyes was the very incarnation of the bourgeoisie, and to be present at the downfall of the Louis Philippe who had sabotaged the promises of July. The whole world is free—but what use would it be to him if he could not stand upright ? Perhaps he would never be able to walk again, never be able to wander in the Tuileries Gardens, never return to Germany—which was still not free, but which might become so . . . The King had fled, and the country was free. But he, Heinrich Heine, must submit to the most terrible tyranny of a mortal and humiliating malady. Never more would he be able to climb a mountain, embrace a woman or savour delicate dishes. He thought of Gunther, Burger, the great Kleist and the wretched Lenau who had died a madman. There seemed to be a curse on the German poets, as though life betrayed precisely those who were attached to it with the greatest ardour. Friends were inconstant, too ; his early brothers in arms forgot him as though he were already in the tomb. Only his enemies were unforgetful. When the *Revue Retrospective* published a list of the journalists and writers who had been subsidised by the former Governments, they hastened—by distorting the truth—to pillory his name in the eyes of the German public.

The revolution which he had summoned with all his strength, which he had served and heralded, turned against him now it had arrived. This man, powerless and paralysed, whose body was at regular intervals tortured by cramp and unbearable suffering, turned away offended from his epoch and from the revolution. He perceived with an almost perverted pleasure the difficulties of the young Republic, Lamartine's powerlessness, the reverses of Louis Blanc and the clumsiness of the German Republicans.

Mathilde rented a little pavilion for the summer in the quiet main street of Passy, and Heine could at last leave the clinic. Towards the end of the year they returned to 62 Rue d'Amsterdam. His condition remained unchanged. This human scarecrow whom they transported on a stretcher to the newly decorated apartment, and who for months had awaited death as a deliverance, had finally become inured to his suffering. Experience refuted the rather naïve materialism which had sufficed in his youth. Now, in his purulent paralysed frame, half-blind, his spirit was untouched, his heart sound and his capacity for work unchanged. " I really think there must be something divine in us," he remarked dreamily to Madame Jaubert, who never ceased to admire the serenity of her sick friend.

The doctors, completely baffled by this remarkable phenomenon, gave him permission to work, provided he did not over-tire himself. He continued with the preparation of his collected edition. The gentle and melancholy Gérard de Nerval, whom Gautier had brought to see him, suggested that during the course of the winter he should translate his youthful poems *Lyrisches Intermezzo* and *Nordseereise*. They decided to do the translation together, and while parties and passions clashed viciously in Paris, during the long grey winter days the two poets—the most German of the French and most French of the Germans—applied themselves to the transposing of Heine's texts into prose. They did not stop until they had breathed into the current language the sad charm, subtlety and blithe gaiety of the original verses.

Heine worked on a writing desk which a carpenter had ingeniously constructed over his bed. Nerval sat nearby at a little round table. He would correct a few lines, declaim them, and then push back his chair and sink into a reverie, from which he would be awakened by Mathilde as she brought in the tea tray. " I'll warrant you are still thinking of Adrienne," she would scold kindly. She preferred Nerval to all her husband's other friends. He had once told her the story of his unhappy love for a little dancer, who had made a mockery of him, scorned him and rejected his advances. Heine, as he rewrote these poems, seemed to relive his youthful passion for the fair-haired Molly : he saw again the image of " Loreley " combing her hair with a golden comb. He would be irritated with Mathilde for breaking the spell, and for bringing him back from the enchanted countries of his dreams to his " mattress tomb."

" Let me work," he would growl, " and don't chatter."

Mathilde would hesitate for a moment, not certain as to whether she should throw the tray on the floor or not. But instead she would shrug her shoulders, remove the papers from the table, saying : "You have only to pour out, Gérard," and leave the room.

Nerval would follow her with his eyes and smile. He had obviously not heard a word she had said. Then his gaze would fall on Heine, who would be biting his lips. Evidently they understood each other without speaking :

> *Zuweilen dünkt es mich, als trübe*
> *Geheime Sehnsucht deinen Blick*
> *Ich kenn'es wohl, dein Missgeschick ;*
> *Verfehltes Leben, verfehlte Liebe !*

> *Du nickst so traurig ! Wiedergeben*
> *Kann ich dir nicht die Jugendzeit—*
> *Unheilbar ist dein Herzeleid*
> *Verfehlte Liebe, verfehltes Leben !*

CHAPTER THIRTY-NINE

THE GOD BECOME MAN

IN the sick man's room news of the outside world arrived distorted and only irregularly. The election of Louis Napoleon to the Presidency, the dissolution of the Frankfurt Parliament, the lamentable crumbling of revolutionary hopes, failed to disturb his calm. Only the defeat of the Hungarian Revolt succeeded in moving him :

> *Wenn ich den Namen Ungarn hör,*
> *Wird mir das deutsche Wams zu enge*
> *Es braust darunter wie ein Meer*
> *Mir ist als grüssten mich Trompetenklänge !*

> If I do hear of Hungary's name,
> My German coverings tighter grow,
> And underneath I seethe, the same
> As when I hear brass trumpets blow !

He felt ashamed, both as a German and as a European, that the whole world had abandoned that small country to the mercy of Russian and Austrian reaction—that people who had struggled for a year and a half for their independence. But he had resigned himself to the fact that he would not live long enough to see his political dreams mature. It was up to the healthy men to carry on the struggle. It was up to Marx, Engels and their friends to prepare for a new revolution—new revolutions. He himself had struggled enough. He had now lain down his arms to use the short time that remained to him in putting his house in order. The publisher Lévy offered to print all his poems and prose works in the French language. It was an immense task, and without a thought as to whether he could finish it he was determined to devote all his strength to the task.

One terrible night, haunted by nightmares, the poet experienced a profound shock. As he lay tortured with pain, a sudden fear of death welled up in his soul, and he cried out in his agony : " God ! "

" But He does not exist ! " he scolded himself, as though some stranger had suggested this " vile subterfuge " to him. " But He does not exist," he declared cruelly and obstinately to his wasting body. After living almost half a century in the conviction that only that which is perceptible exists, that man is the creator and master of the world, after having been a good pagan, was he now to call upon the God of the Jews and the Christians to help him in his misfortune ? It appeared to him like cowardly treachery. He had lived as a good pagan and he would like to die as one : he had lived without a God and he would like to die without one. *If God existed*, and if He were more than the despairing cry of a man at bay or his vain hope, he thought, He should have revealed Himself to him when he was still full of strength and able to look Him in the face.

But the sufferer reasoned with himself in vain. " The spirit is strong but the flesh is weak." Mathilde, horrified by his condition when she tended him, sometimes gave vent to the cry : " My God ! " And the poet, clenching his teeth, his forehead pearled with sweat, would echo : " God help me, God have pity on me ! " Was this faith ? Was this insensate and delirious hope God, Whose Spirit had hitherto been unable to disclose Its existence and unlimited power ? Had he to discover Him through his wounds, afflictions, agonies and paralysed limbs ? Was this then God, the simple evocation of Whom solaced him as though He had wiped his forehead to ease his fever ? Heine felt like a soldier who remains at his post for the sake of honour, and will not surrender while he still has ammunition—but after having fired away his last cartridge puts down his weapon with an easy conscience. During his long nights of insomnia he continued his grievous meditations.

Humanity is perhaps great and legitimately proud of its achievements, but a man by himself is very small and helpless. Formerly, Heine had proudly declared that religion was only a means of deluding oneself, only good for children, old people, invalids and the weak-minded. It was a compensation for the multitudes who had failed, but now life was forcing him to place himself, too, in this category. Formerly, he had accused physical impotence of giving birth to supernatural illusions : he began to think now that even his atheistic humanism and his cult of physical beauty were perhaps another form of illusion even more deceptive. Why was pride more human than humility? He discovered that there was also a joy to be gained from resignation, suffering and solitude. The Gods of Greece had abandoned him, they knew no charity; like selfish and carefree holiday-makers they only frequented the sunny landscapes of life; disease, boredom and death are banished from their world. Consolation is not in their province. He needed a God, however, who would be ready to visit him in his distress.

One afternoon Immanuel-Hermann Fichte, the son of the great philosopher, himself a philosopher and professor at the University of Tübingen, came to see him and to thank him for the lines of friendship and enthusiasm he had written about his father. They discussed at length the new philosophical trend, Hegelianism, and Proudhon—who had just been condemned to a prison sentence by the Republican Tribunal. Suddenly Heine, raising himself with the aid of a cord that hung above his bed, and lifting his paralysed eyelid with his right finger, asked Fichte anxiously:

" Tell me frankly, Professor, do you believe in another life? Do you believe that the soul is immortal? "

The young professor, who was wearing a long black overcoat cut like a toga, rose, and caressing his fair beard, solemnly declared as though he were making a profession of faith:

" I believe in the invisible world of ideas."

"But you do not believe in a God—in a living God personified?"

" I do not," the professor replied without hesitation, shaking his head.

Heine let his eyelid fall, and sinking back on to his pillow, remained silent. The young Fichte added, by way of explanation:

" I believe in the Spirit, and I believe that there is something imperishable in us which has existed since eternity, rising, disappearing and returning. I believe in the ideas which are inherent in us, but the conception of a personal God is contrary to my conviction, for personality signifies limitation."

" And I, I cannot imagine that ideas can exist that have not been conceived by someone," growled Heine.

Fichte stared at the sick man with astonishment. "Is it possible that you have been converted to the belief in a personal God?"

"Believe me, Sir," replied Heine, "my conversion was not voluntary—if the word 'conversion' expresses what is happening to me. Agreed, when I was young like you—and even a few years ago, even a few months—I believed that God was myself . . . only . . . only the entertainment expenses of a god who spares neither his purse nor his person are enormous. To maintain this generous role, one must have a great deal of money at one's disposal and a great deal of health. Well, one day I discovered that I had no longer money nor strength . . . What can I do, Sir—what would you do in my place? I have resigned myself, do you understand? I have abdicated my divinity before God, just as the French Republicans have abdicated in favour of Louis-Napoleon."

"You are jesting."

"Obviously I am jesting, but as is always the case when I jest—I speak very seriously. *Andere Zeiten, andere Lieder*. It is said that humanity is sick, and that the world is a great hospital. It would be even more appalling, Sir, if the world hostel were without a Host."

"But can one not endure sickness and suffering without God? Does not the knowledge suffice that the spirit—the spirit of humanity—survives our body? Think of Socrates . . . think of my father . . ."

"I think a great deal of them, and in any case I should be presumptuous to compare myself with them. But what can I do? God—or should I call Him Death—has defeated me. Why deny my defeat? I have spoilt my life: I have lived badly. He looks at me now with irony. 'What have you done for yourself?' He asks. He is right. But now let us see what He can do, He . . . If He wishes to command, let Him command. I have no more ambition, neither in theology nor in politics. It is for you, the young ones, to continue the revolution that I began. I want to die in peace."

Heine raised his voice. "Let us see a little what He can do. It is easier and more pleasant for me to submit to His Will. What do you want me to undertake? With all my will I can do nothing in any case. I am sick, do you understand? For a year and a half I have not been able to stand. Do you want me to walk without crutches? Is that it—that paralysed I can be free?" And he added, lowering his voice: "I have need of God; at night when my wife goes to bed I feel so alone. Sleep will not come; I toss and turn, and the pains shoot through my body from head to foot. Every moment I think that it is the end, and in these moments it is pleasant to think that there is someone in the sky—or no matter where—to whom I can cry in my distress; someone whom I can accuse, whom I can make responsible."

Fichte, his hands clasped and his head bowed, nodded gravely. "I understand. But—"

"Between ourselves, I will confess something to you—that you may understand me the better. The malady has not weakened my brain. I am not abdicating the rights of the spirit— I have not yet come to that!" With his right hand he seized a sheet of paper from his bedside table. "If you will allow me, I will read you the poem that I wrote last night." In low, languid tones he recited:

> *Unser Grab erwärmt der Ruhm.*
> *Thorenworte! Narrenitum!*
> *Eine bessre Wärme giebt*
> *Eine Kuhmagd, die verliebt*
> *Uns mit dicken Lippen küsst*
> *Und beträchtlich riecht nach Mist.*
> *Gleichfalls eine bessre Wärme*
> *Wärmt den Menschen die Gedärme,*
> *Wenn er Glühwein trinkt und Punsch*
> *Oder Grog nach Herzenswunsch*
> *In den niedrigsten Spelunken,*
> *Unter Dieben und Halunken,*
> *Die dem Galgen sind entlaufen,*
> *Aber leben, athmen, schnaufen,*
> *Und beneidenswerter sind,*
> *Als der Thetis grosses Kind.—*
> *Der Pelide sprach mit Recht:*
> *Leben wie der ärmste Knecht*

In der Oberwelt, ist besser,
Als am stygischen Gewässer
Schattenführer sein, ein Heros,
Den besungen selbst Homeros.

Glory does make warm the grave.
A foolish phrase ! Words of a knave !
A better warmth indeed we'll find
From a lovely cow-girl kind,
Who kisses us with full lips sure
Though smelling highly of manure.
A more enduring warmth, likewise,
In your bowels (I surmise)
You feel when drinking punch or wine
Or grog to make your heart feel fine,
Drunk in filthy tavern's mire
Mid thieves and rogues and rascals dire,
Who have slipped the gallows' noose,
Yet eat, live and are on the loose,
And are to be envied in a way
As Thetis' eldest child one day.—
For Peleus' son did speak aright :
To live here as the humblest wight
In the upper world is better I ween,
Than on the Stygian flood to have been
A prince of shades, a hero bold,
Sung by mighty Homer old.

The professor of philosophy, his face buried in his hands, listened to the magnificent and sombre strophes.

" What do you think of it ? " asked Heine, letting the paper fall from his hand.

" It is your most beautiful and most moving poem," replied Fichte. " May I copy it—just for myself ? "

" If you like."

In effect, Heine had not renounced his Faith : he still insisted that his relations with God had no connection with positive religion. He had need of neither Jewish, Catholic nor Protestant doctrines, nor did he need the intercession of a priest, to find the way that led to God. As a young man he had read the Bible passionately, and it had become his bedside book. The God whom he glimpsed in the midst of his agony and despair resembled the irascible and vengeful God of Job and Moses. This God was a father—but not in the Christian and indulgent sense of the word. He was much more like Uncle Salomon who, even dead, still did evil, than his own good father. He was a God, nevertheless, with Whom—despite His proud and tyrannical nature—one could speak, discuss and bargain. He was a God of destiny and history, an absurd God, Whom one could ask why He had instilled in man a desire for justice—which He Himself never applied—and why He had aroused in man the hope of eternity when He Himself caused him to die.

> *Warum schleppt sich blutend, elend*
> *Unter Kreuzlast der Gerechte,*
> *Während glücklich, als ein Sieger*
> *Trabt auf hohem Ross der Schlechte?*
>
> *Woran liegt die Schuld? Ist etwa*
> *Unser Herr nicht ganz allmächtig?*
> *Oder treibt et selbst den Unfug?*
> *Ach, das wäre niederträchtig!*
>
> *Also fragen wir beständig,*
> *Bis man uns mit einer Handvoll*
> *Erde endlich stopft die Mäuler—*
> *Aber ist das eine Antwort?*

> Why does he drag with bleeding steps
> His cross, the Man of Righteousness,
> While the other, like some great conqueror,
> Bestrides his horse in unrighteousness?
>
> Where lies the fault? Our Lord, perchance
> Is He not might omnipotent?
> Or doth He urge the wrong Himself?
> How vile indeed such discontent!
>
> So ask we never ceasingly,
> Until with half a clod of earth
> Eventually they stop our mouths—
> Is *that* an answer of any worth?

Like the prophet Jonah in the belly of the whale, Heine on his bed of suffering reproached God for His inconsistencies, and when he prayed he infused a bitter irony into his chant.

> *O Gott, verkürze meine Qual,*
> *Damit man mich bald begrabe ;*
> *Du weisst ja, dass ich kein Talent*
> *Zum Martyrtume habe.*
>
> *Ob deiner Inkonsequenz, O Herr,*
> *Erlaube, dass ich staune :*
> *Du schufest den fröhlichsten Dichter, und raubst*
> *Ihm jetzt seine gute Laune.*
>
> *Der Schmerz verdumpft den heitern Sinn*
> *Und macht mich melancholisch,*
> *Nimmt nicht der traurige Spass ein End'*
> *So werd' ich am Ende katholisch.*
>
> *Ich heule dir dann die Ohren voll,*
> *Wie andre gute Christen—*
> *O Miserere ! Verloren geht*
> *Der beste der Humoristen !*

Oh God, foreshorten my affliction
Wherefore I soon interred must be ;
Thou knowest well I have no talent
For martyrdom eternally.

Through Thy inconsequence, Oh Lord,
Permit that I may be surprised
That Thou hast shaped the happiest poet,
And steal'st the good moods he'd apprised.

The hurt doth overcast the hot mind,
Makes me Oh so sad to be,
And does not finish off the jest
That Catholic in the end I be.

I cry to Thee, then, cry aloud,
As other Christians ever do —
O Miserere ! We have lost
A humorist, so good and true !

Little Weil, faithful secretary and friend, shook his head when he read this prayer of Heine's, which he considered blasphemy. This former pupil of a Rabbinical school, and partisan of reform for the Jewish religion, asserted in his writings that the Mosaic religion, purged of its anthropomorphic element and antiquated rites, was predestined to become the religion of modern man.

Under the influence of the Bible and Weil's arguments, Heine revised his conception of the Jewish religion. While in his earlier writings he had opposed Judaism as the most perfect expression of spirituality in favour of Greek philosophy, which represented a cult of life, he now discovered "the wisdom and fecund humanism" of the religion of his ancestors. The Greeks were *ephebi*, beautiful, gay and happy, whereas the ancient Jews—and Moses in particular, who represented all the virtues and capacities of his race—were *men*, initiates, who knew all the secret arcana of life. The dominant figure in the Jewish religion was for him not Jehovah but Moses, that "superman," that great artist—perhaps the greatest of all artists—who had created, by raising himself to the level of his own idea of God, a people in his own image. Weil would have liked to strip the Jewish religion of its anthropomorphic elements. He, on the contrary, loved in God that which He had in common with Moses. If humanity were obliged to attach itself to a belief, and if it could not subsist without God and Divine Grace, dreamed Heine, it should have the faith of Moses, who did not expect heavenly manna, did not discount happiness in the next world, did not preach resignation, but urged his people to conquer a fatherland on earth, to transform the desert into an orchard and to become free and indomitable. Let humanity choose the faith of Moses, who did not separate religion from society, the duties towards God from the duties towards men, and who by his efforts "to endow private property with a moral character" anticipated by several thousand years Heine's contemporaries, the Socialists.

He had the impression that he had treated religious and moral questions in his philosophical works too superficially. In his pride he had over-estimated the intelligence, and lacked humility and comprehension towards morality, which represents— as he wrote in a codicil to his revised testament—"the very essence of monotheism." He decided that in the new edition of his works, both in French and German, he would make not only corrections of style but basic changes of theory. However, he finally renounced this intention. What is written is written, and nobody—not even he—had the right to alter it. The most he could do was to indicate in a new introduction that he no longer held his old opinions. In any case, the revolution he had advocated and predicted in his writings, the revolt against the powerful on earth and against the worshippers of Mammon, could not be displeasing to God, Who had made of man an ambitious and turbulent being who should detest " . . . servants in black, red and gold, wallowing in their own servility . . ."

The rumour of Heine's recantation spread rapidly among his Parisian friends. Princess Belgiojoso, who too was feeling the weight of the years (this woman who had been so beautiful had become a withered and bigoted dowager), tried to persuade her old friend to take the final step in his religious orientation and submit to the holy canons of the Church. She had recently returned from a pilgrimage to the Holy Land. She called at the apartment in the Rue d'Amsterdam accompanied by her confessor, Father Caron. Heine, jesting amiably, gave her to understand that her efforts were vain : he needed neither an intermediary nor a lawyer ; being a poet, he found himself in the privileged position of being in direct contact with Heaven. Pointing to the Bible on his bedside table he said : " Here is the means of arriving there by the shortest route."

One afternoon Weil was entertaining the poet by chanting old Hebrew canticles in his metallic voice. Mathilde, who had never believed that Heine was a Jew, and was convinced that he was jesting even when he told her so, as he bore so little resemblance to their Jewish friends Weil, Doctor Gruby and Wertheimer, listened with stupefaction to these bizarre oriental melodies, these wails of sadness and desolation.

" What are those songs ? " she called from the neighbouring room.

" They are our popular German folk-songs," replied Heine, winking his eye at Weil.

The former Seminarist laughed uproariously and began to intone a gay psalm to the glory of God, who freed His people from the servitude of the Pharaohs, and continues to help those who know how to help themselves.

CHAPTER FORTY

BEFORE " THE ARISTOPHANES OF THE HEAVENS "

THE visitor who thought to find in the apartment of the Rue d'Amsterdam a dying and miserable repentant met with a great surprise. The poet, although moribund, retained the suppleness and freshness of his wit ; he mocked his own suffering and his agony with the same bitter irony that in his youth he had applied to his love affairs.

No one observed the rule of romantic aestheticism formulated by Tieck more strictly than he : " to take jesting seriously and to treat the serious as a jest ; to accept joy and suffering with equal gracefulness, and to hide sorrow with delicacy behind the mask of gaiety." What had been for Tieck nothing but an aesthetic discovery represented an ever deepening experience from youth to death for Heine. To him the world was a perpetual conflict, a rivalry and incessant contradiction between one's desires and one's potentialities, between illusions and reality. One can despair of the tragedy of one's life and also smile at it. This smile—the smile of Aristophanes, Cervantes and Heine—offers to man the only means of conquering the tragedy of his destiny. The world is badly constructed, says this smile—but it is, all the same, good to live in. Under Heine's irony we discover Pascal's definition : " Man is a reed, the weakest of all nature, but a reed who thinks." On his death-bed he understood that it is not we who mock destiny, but destiny that mocks us. It is not harmony that rules our relations with destiny but a lamentable and ridiculous discord.

In his youth Heine had run after glory and riches, and had not obtained them. Now that he could no longer savour anything, " . . . glory, that sugared manna, sweet as pineapple and flattery . . ." was brought to him on a platter. The French edition of his works brought him a great material and moral success. His melancholy and nostalgic verses and his prose writings corresponded with the taste of the day. After the *coup d'état* of Napoleon the disillusioned public turned its back on politics and sought an escape in poetry, music and irony. The critic of the *Revue des Deux Mondes*, Saint-René Taillandier, said of him that, after Goethe, he was the most important figure in German literature. In Germany, the poems of the *Buch der Lieder* became popular songs, and editions followed one after another. If Goethe had been able to boast that even the Chinese " painted ' Werther ' and ' Charlotte ' on glass with a trembling hand " Heine had even more reason to be proud, since the *Buch der Lieder* was the first European book to be published in Japan. Poets, enthusiastic readers and translators wrote to him from every corner of Europe, America, Africa and even Siberia. The young Empress, Elizabeth of Austria—as her brother Gustav, who had arrived from Vienna to see him, reported, preferred him to all other poets ; and they were his poems that the German workers, who had reorganised after the failure of the revolution, sang as they went to their clandestine meetings.

" I find myself at present in front of a huge pot—but I have no spoon." He thought of Firdusi, the Persian poet, about whom it was related that caravans laden with royal presents had arrived at the Western gate of his little town at the very moment when his funeral procession was passing through the Eastern gate. "Alas, the malice of God weighs upon me ! " he wrote in his *Confessions*.

" . . . the great Author of the universe, the Aristophanes of the sky, has wished to make the little earthly author, the self-styled German Aristophanes, feel to what degree his wittiest sarcasms have been but pinpricks in comparison with the thunderbolts of satire that Divine Humour alone knows how to hurl at puny mortals."

And the poet, struggling against his cramps, quotes before the tribunal of Reason this cruelly ironic Author, who has written the text of his role to reproach him for his protracted calvary that has become almost tiresome and useless.

The time passed with appalling slowness in the darkened room. No ray of sunshine penetrated there, no ray of hope. He knew that he would only exchange his downy bed for a grave in the cemetery.

He listened. Through the closed doors of the neighbouring room he could hear Mathilde's regular breathing. How long would the morning take to appear ? He could hardly wait for the moment when he would hear sounds of movement from the other room, the creak of the bed, the rustling of stuffs, and Mathilde putting on her dressing-gown ; a clatter of crockery, a noise of footsteps . . .

Outside a vendor cried, and then he heard the creak of the grocer's iron shutters. Through the closed Venetian blinds the light stole gently into the room ; the familiar contours of the furniture outlined themselves in the shadow. At long last the door opened and Mathilde entered, carrying his breakfast on a tray. Placing it on the table, she opened the window, arranged his pillows and planted a kiss on his forehead. She was usually good-tempered. She sang, chattered and laughed as she poured out his coffee ; " in the whole of Christendom no mouth ever smiled so sweetly." Her good temper seemed in some way to give him an appetite. Then, lifting the shrunken invalid in her strong arms she bathed him, twittering all the time like a little bird.

Visitors who had been present during one or other of Mathilde's rages have defamed this beautiful, healthy and devoted woman. Heine himself was always grumbling, and often complained to his friends and relations of the " constant changeability of Mathilde," and of her " extravagant tastes." But the testimonies of little Weil and Madame Jaubert, who were habitués of the house, and whom no one could accuse of favouritism for Mathilde, may be taken as more reliable. They both maintained in their memoirs that she had cared for her husband with patience, devotion and serenity for eight years. And this was by no means an easy task : Heine proved to be a most tyrannical invalid, demanding constant attention and service ; and he was more jealous than ever of Mathilde. He wanted to be informed of all her errands, meetings and thoughts, and he pushed his inquisitorial mania even to the point of importuning her about her dreams.

One day Gautier brought a young journalist, Henri Julia, to the house in the Rue d'Amsterdam, who offered to help Heine translate the articles he had written between 1840 and 1843. The elegant dark-haired young man sometimes accompanied Mathilde on her shopping expeditions, to the theatre, and even helped her with the household tasks. Heine was at first pleased to see that Mathilde had company, but soon he began to get suspicious. One evening the journalist had stayed late with them after dinner, and Heine thought that they had exchanged looks of complicity. Mathilde accompanied the young man downstairs and was absent for some time—too long. Heine was suddenly seized with the conviction that Julia had not gone, and that, making a pretence at going, he had glided along the corridor to Mathilde's room. Had not Mathilde just turned the key in the lock—or was it an hallucination? He was seized with an impotent rage ; he wanted to cry out, but no sound came from his lips. Then, gathering all his strength and with the help of his cord, he slipped out of bed and, struggling against asphyxiation and wringing with sweat, dragged himself to the door and knocked. Mathilde leaped from her bed in a panic, lit the candle and opened the door. It had not been locked. She looked with terror-stricken eyes at the wasted figure struggling at her feet. Shamefaced and sobbing, he confessed : "I thought there was someone in your room." The following day Mathilde engaged a nurse to watch day and night at Heine's bed.

CHAPTER FORTY-ONE

DEATH, A PREJUDICE

DAYS, weeks, months and years passed in this manner for the incurable man, divided between work, suffering and ironical outbursts. Haussmann had constructed the broad avenues of Paris, the accession to the throne of the " adventurer-emperor " had silenced the Socialists and Republicans, the bourgeoisie, overcoming their fear of the red bogy, had begun to gamble on the Stock Exchange, build factories and rentable properties, to construct railways and erect shops. The workers, flouting interdicts and police persecution, organised themselves, and strikes broke out here and there ; in England, Parliament passed the first social laws ; in the Rue d'Amsterdam children were taken to be baptised, and funeral processions slowly made their way to the Montmàrtre Cemetery.

The life of the living went on, and the dying passed away. There were days when Heine was almost free from pain. But soon, as though in revenge, griping pains would pierce his stomach and he would endure terrible attacks of uraemia. After one of these attacks, when he thought—as he had done so many times before—that his end·had come, Mathilde, whose parrot had died of congestion that very morning, flung herself on the bed and begged him in tears : " No, Henri, you can't do that. I've just lost my parrot, and if you died now too, I really should be too unhappy." Heine smiled despite his pain, and later, when the crisis had passed, said jestingly to her :

" You see, I have obeyed you ; I am still alive. When one is given a good reason . . ."

Meanwhile Gérard de Nerval had been transferred to a clinic for his nervous disorders. The indulgent Doctor Blanche allowed him to come and visit Heine from time to time, accompanied by his nurse, to show him his latest translations. The dying man and the maniac spent strange, sweet and intimate hours together. One day Heine recounted a curious dream that he had had the previous night to his friend : the tombs of Montmartre were shining in the sun, and at the foot of each tombstone there was a pair of beautifully polished shoes, as in the corridors of any hotel . . .

With wide-open eyes Nerval listened to this singular dream. Suddenly he started to weep, and his whole body trembled. Heine motioned to Mathilde, who was standing near the window. She left the room on tiptoe and called the nurse, who came in at once.

" Listen, Monsieur Nerval ; Monsieur Dumas is very ill. You must come and see him."

Nerval brushed away his tears, rose like a somnambulist and, without saying farewell, followed the nurse.

And all the time on Heine's table, beside his old poems, new pages continued to pile up, covered with agonised poems proclaiming his desire to live. He compared himself with the mediaeval poet of whom the Limburg Chronicler speaks who, while the whole land was singing his love poems, wandered through the streets covered with leprosy and whirling his " rattle of St. Lazarus " to warn off the passers-by. One day, when Mathilde was out, the cook announced that a man who would not give his name wished to see him.

" What is he like ? " the sick man asked.

" He is large. His head is round like a full moon. He is wearing a frock-coat buttoned high, a tiled hat and a beautifully knotted white scarf."

" That conveys nothing to me. Is he young ? "

" Not exactly. No, he's not young : his hair is quite white. But he has no wrinkles on his face."

" Did he say what he wanted ? "

" No, he just wants to see you, Monsieur."

" Well, show him in."

The door opened, and Campe, his old publisher from Hamburg, whom he had not seen for eight years, entered. He was scarlet with emotion.

" House-to-house visits are very common in Germany these days—I was curious to see whether a search in Paris would give me any results," he said jovially.

For several months they had been discussing an edition of Heine's new poems by correspondence—for the new volume required an additional large payment, over and above the normal annuity. Campe wanted to keep to the terms of their old contract. He first gave Heine news of Hamburg, and messages from his mother and Lotte (his sister was preparing to come to Paris with her son Maurice, who was studying law at the Berlin University), and then they started to drive a hard but friendly bargain. After several hours they reached an agreement : Campe was to pay six thousand marks for the volume entitled *Romancero*. Goethe, during his whole life, had never gained as much for all his works.

The following month his brother Gustav paid him a surprise visit. He had built up a great career for himself in imperial Vienna. Heine found him self-sufficient, pretentious and unsympathetic.

" Is it true you have become a bigot, Heinrich ? " Gustav asked in passing.

Heine raised his left eyelid. " More a ' devot ' than a bigot," he replied ; " every day I ask God to convert me to a better political conviction."

Gustav laughed and showed his gold teeth.

" Joking apart—the cause of God would gain much if you made a public confession."

" It should be a matter of complete indifference to the great elephant of the King of Siam if a little mouse of the Rue d'Amsterdam in Paris believed in his size and wisdom or not."

Heine had divined his brother's intentions : he would have liked to publish a document on the solemn conversion of Heinrich Heine in the clerical and monarchist journal which he directed in Vienna, and which had triumphantly hailed the crushing of the insurrection in Hungary. As he had done many times before in their youth, Heinrich thwarted his brother's plans. He diverted the conversation to their mother, whom Gustav had also just visited. Perhaps he would do better to return home to die in Hamburg, in their little house near the Dammtor . . . But how could he get there ? A special carriage would have to be built, which would be far too expensive, and " . . . the merchandise is hardly worth the expenses of carriage . . ." After all, he might just as well be buried in Paris, and once dead he had no wish to be disturbed in his last repose. One day they would place Mathilde at his side, for he wished to lie next to the woman who had loved and cared for him until the Last Judgment. If Germany had not wanted him alive, he added bitterly, she could well dispense with him dead. They spoke, too, of Carl who, without waiting to be asked by his cousin, had generously doubled his pension to defray the expenses of his illness.

After Gustav left, other visitors took his place at the bedside of the sick man ; old friends and unknown admirers, men of flesh and blood, and ghosts. Sometimes Heine thought that Death had forgotten him—or was Death simply that monotony of suffering, work and decrepitude ? " Is Death only a prejudice ? " he asked one day of a visitor. The leaves blackened with scribbling piled up on his little table, the fire died out in the fireplace, and the air once more filled with sunlight.

One day in June, while Heine dozed and Mathilde was resting in her arm-chair, they were startled by an unusual crackling sound. Cries came up to them from the street. Mathilde leaped up, flung aside the taffeta curtains and quickly opened the window. The passers-by pointed to the neighbouring house, from which flames were bursting.

" The house is on fire ! "

Mathilde did not lose her presence of mind. Calling the cook, they carried the sick man between them to the porter's lodge, whence they could move him further if necessity demanded. The firemen arrived and placed their ladders against the burning house. The neighbours, when they heard that the dying man had been carried downstairs, crowded round the front of the lodge to look through the glass at the man who had been jesting and writing and dying for six years. The boldest of them entered to examine this extraordinary individual more closely.

" Do you suffer a great deal ? " a young girl asked with compassion.

" Not in the least," replied Heine smiling. " My doctors swear that my malady is not very serious, but only very prolonged. One cannot recover from it, but it appears, too, that one cannot die from it. A soothsayer once foretold from the lines of my hand that I should become immortal."

The poet's words were passed round in a whisper. The fire was soon put out, and the firemen went home ; the crowd dispersed and the porter and the grocer carried Heine back upstairs.

" You can write to my mother," he told Weil, who appeared at that moment, " that the Frenchmen love me so much that they carry me in their arms."

" Yes, you can say that," agreed the fat porter in his heavy Auvergnat accent. " We love Monsieur ' Enne.' "

CHAPTER FORTY-TWO

POLITICAL TESTAMENT

DURING the following year—1854—the Heines left noisy Montmartre and went to live at 51 Grande-Rue, Batignolles, not far from the capital. The house had a large garden, where Heine was installed under the shade of the fruit trees. "I have no need even to raise my hand, for ripe and juicy plums fall straight into my mouth," he wrote to his brother Max.

The change, fresh air, bird's song, and the hum of the bees did him good. He had the impression that he was recovering. He still felt weak, but perhaps one day to the astonishment of his doctors he would be on his feet once more. Mathilde and her bosom friend Pauline, in their light summer dresses, played and rolled in the grass, frolicking like young animals.

It was in this charming spot that Heine finished collating his articles about 1840, which were collected in one volume under the title *Lutetia*. He wrote the preface to this work there, and also the single chapter of his *Confessions* that has survived. Both these writings are among the most important of his works, and serve the same purpose : to clarify the misunderstandings created by his often inconsequential articles. He tried to recapitulate as exactly as possible, without doing violence to his contradictory sentiments and old and new sympathies, by writing a kind of political testament. Above all, he wished to refute the accusation that he had pitted himself against the Republicans. On the contrary, he affirmed, he had never lost an opportunity of stressing their moral superiority, the sincerity of their convictions and their heroism. But the republican idea in itself had never satisfied him. While still young and inexperienced he had already felt that the new epoch would impose a new doctrine, more universal, deeper and more logical than that of the Republic. And when the theory which renounced legitimism and private property had arisen he was one of the first to lend his ear, to attribute to it the importance it deserved, and to make propaganda for Communism.

The " eternal moribund " showed himself proud of having been the first to point out in a German newspaper : " . . . it is the Communists who represent the most vigorous party, and the future is in their hands." And, even now that he had repudiated his youthful atheism, and sickness had transformed him into a bourgeois attached to the *status quo*, fearing change, revolution, troubles and disturbance, he had no reason to deny what he had written. He believed that his prophecies were on the point of realisation. The revolutionary ideas of Feuerbach, Marx, Engels and Lassalle, which had appeared strange some years before, had now become popular and had spread across the Rhine.

" The German workers form the core of a well-indoctrinated, if not disciplined, proletariat. These German workers nearly all profess atheism, and in truth cannot dispense with a complete negation of the religious ideas of the past without coming in conflict with their principles . . ."

And Heine added with an almost patriotic pride :

" These cohorts of destruction, these terrible demolishers, who menace our old and decrepit society, are far superior to the English Chartists and to the levellers and equalitarians of other countries . . . The more or less recondite leaders of the German Communists are great logicians, the best of whom derive from the school of Hegel, and they are without doubt the most capable heads and the most energetic characters in Germany. These Doctors of Revolution and their ruthlessly determined disciples are the only men in Germany who are bursting with life and energy . . ."

The future belongs to them. In the cool shade of the Batignolles garden Heine thought of Marx with his glittering eyes, of the burning Lassalle, and of Engels, more suave, more subtle, but just as resolute. These young men represented a new type of man, of a hard and proud race who had no time for compromise, had no need of heavenly consolation, were content with the visible world but wished to remake it in their own image. Compared with them he was a man of another century, another race, another civilisation—or rather, a man of the interregnum, the transition between two shining worlds. The Communists were men of action, knowing nothing outside their goal, but pursuing it with a savage discipline. His own life had been spent in vacillation and in chasing shadows and phantoms. The Communists would raise the proletariat to power. He would probably have felt ill at ease in this world of workmen in blouses, which would come to replace the bourgeois era, so confused and rich in contradiction. He did not fear the loss of fortune, for he possessed none ; he only feared for the fragile values created by humanist civilisation, and for that interior liberty that the sage and the poet had torn from Church and State after a thousand-year struggle. He feared too, that the liberty of criticism and satire and the impunity of revolt and contradiction would founder at the same time as the turpitudes of the bourgeois world. But even if that did happen, *let it !* If it could not be any other way, thought Heine, let it be *thus*. There is something more important and higher than individual and spiritual liberty— which are often only pretexts for irresponsibility and cowardice— and that is *Justice*.

It was through the idea of Justice that Communism had been able to seduce the poet into their ranks, he who guarded so jealously his independence. Let the era of justice come at last ! Let the old world crumble that has reduced man to a misery worse than death ! Let there arise in its place a new world where men will become generous and united, a world where the love of one's neighbour will become a reality !

Heine saw above all in the Socialists and Communists, who were obsessed with justice, the most resolute enemies of all inequality and usurpation of right. And for this reason he hailed them on his death-bed. From earliest youth until his death he had fought the "Teutomaniacs," the Pan-German Nationalists, whom Marx and his companions loathed with the same ferocious intensity. That was an additional reason for supporting his young revolutionary friends.

"Now that the sword falls from the hand of the dying man," wrote Heine, speaking of these Teutomaniacs in his preface to *Lutetia*, "I feel consoled in the certain knowledge that they will be the first to fall in the path of Communism, and receive their death-blow."

The disciples of Hegel were cosmopolitan like himself, and bore no trace of national prejudice. They loved all nations equally, and despised equally all oppressors, opposing not only the exploitation of man by man, but of one race by another. They aimed at erecting on the ruins of thrones and privileges an alliance whose benefits would be enjoyed by the liberated citizens of the whole world.

The brotherhood of free peoples . . . Life, history and the future belong to those for whom this formula is not merely a pious wish, but a will as concrete and ardent as the desire of a hungry man for bread, the thirsty for water, the lover for a kiss. And Heine, ever young, ever intransigent, reaffirmed in his last writings his faith in Marx, Engels and Lassalle, who were continuing with the substantiation of his ideal.

CHAPTER FORTY-THREE

THE LAST LOVE

THE villa at Batignolles was damp and difficult to heat, and in the autumn the Heines were obliged to abandon it and take refuge in No. 3, Rue des Batignolles. Béranger, who was now seventy-five years old, came there to visit his sick friend. Although his hair was silver, he had retained his good humour and love of jest ; he boasted that age had left him untouched, and that he always felt full of strength. And when Mathilde threw a sceptical and coy look at the old scamp, as Heine called him, he drew himself up and threw out his chest : " You are wrong, Madame, and if you would allow me to give you proof, you would admit that you were wrong . . . "

When the weather became milder Heine was carried out on to the balcony, where a screen protected him from the wind. He watched the life of Paris through a telescope. He could see the cake-sellers offering their wares with happy cries to ladies in crinolines, children playing, news-vendors and strolling lovers . . .

One afternoon, while Mathilde was out an unknown lady called upon him. She had just arrived from Vienna with some pages of music that an Austrian composer had asked her to deliver to the poet. She was a charming young woman of medium height with delicate features set in a frame of brown curls, an upturned nose and twinkling eyes. He looked at the attractive visitor with relish, and when as she crossed her legs in the arm-chair she displayed a slender ankle, he gave a start. As though understanding Heine's embarrassment the woman blushed, adjusted her skirt and fell silent. A short time after, Camille Selden—for this was the charming visitor's name—rose to depart. " I did not wish to disturb you," she murmured. Heine quickly collected himself. " You're not going, surely ? I should like you to stay with me for ever."

" For ever ? "

Camille sat down again, and at the poet's request drew her chair nearer. She spoke of Vienna, the opera and a new play by Hebbel, and of Heine's *Romancero* which she knew by heart. Her voice was velvety and caressing, and her manner was at once shy and coquettish. Heine noticed with great emotion that the young woman did not speak to him as to a paralysed and dying invalid, but treated him as though he were a man in good health. Camille Selden seemed to refuse to acknowledge the gravity of his condition. She raised her eyebrows sceptically when he spoke of his pain, and under her influence he began to doubt the reality himself. "Mouche," as she had asked him to call her, saw in him only—through the magic of his poetry—the young Heine of the *Buch der Lieder* : greedy for tenderness and beauty, for the scent of the blue flower and spiritual communion, the man on whom time and disease had left no trace, and who had on the contrary become more chaste and more serene. Mouche had no need of explanations and words : she understood him completely by a look, a gesture or his silence. And now Heine, who had abandoned all hope of ever knowing the sweetness of " celestial love," and of ever meeting a woman who could be to him what Laura had been to Petrarch, Beatrice to Dante, Dorothea to Friedrich Schlegel, or Sophia to Novalis, covered with pustules and with one foot in the grave, had found at the age of fifty-eight the woman who could have made him happy—who did make him happy.

Mouche left, promising to return soon. During the night Heine could not sleep, but he made no complaint. He relived all the moments of the afternoon, saw again in his mind's eye the feline movements of the girl, and felt the contact of her fingers. A violent rain beat against the window-panes, and the autumn wind wailed in the chimney like a soul in pain.

The next day he donned his camel-hair dressing-gown, wrapped the lower part of his body in blankets, and installed himself in an enormous arm-chair to await the young woman's visit. What a marvellous change in his life—to wait again for someone ! He who had for so long been reduced like the old to ransacking his past in search of memories. Now he trembled at every footstep. But she did not come. The days went by in this agony of waiting, and still the young woman did not appear. Would he never again see his " pretty lotus flower," as he called her in his dreams ?

But an idea occurred to him. On her departure Mouche had written something on the back of the music score that she had brought. He reached out for the folder, and discovered that it was her address. " She wanted me to call her," he said to himself. With trembling hands he scribbled a few lines : she must come quickly, he was waiting for her, his days were numbered . . . He instructed his friend Weil to take the letter to her hotel, and a few hours later a messenger brought him a reply. On the seal he found a little fly—her sign, her symbol ! Her mother had given her the name of " Mouche."

The following day she arrived. She had on a simple cloak over her dress. Her face was pale as she entered the sick man's room. She hardly dared to look Heine in the eyes—but the poet knew that he had conquered. No need to declare their love : the miracle had been achieved. " Silence is the choicest blossom of love." Little by little the girl unfroze, and they began to chatter and jest like old friends. She did not wish to speak of her past, which she said had been banal and filled with sadness ; but when the poet insisted she consented to relate her life story. Her family had married her at eighteen to a Frenchman who had quickly tired of her, and who, in order to be rid of her, had taken her to England and had her confined in a madhouse. " . . . but I was not mad," she added. " In actual fact, I very nearly did lose my reason as a result of his cruel injustice and the misery of the confinement. After the first shock of the realisation of my plight, I no longer had the desire to speak . . ." She was finally released and completely recovered. At present she was earning her living as a companion and teacher of languages. She travelled a great deal, but had no friends. A few years previously she had met Alfred Meissner in a train, and he had given her a copy of the *Buch der Lieder*. From that moment her sorrows had disappeared, and she began to find an outlet for expression in music. Meissner had promised one day to introduce her to the poet whom she admired so much, but he must have forgotten. One day a long time ago she had stood before Heine's house, and had recognised the poet as he was leaving—in company with a woman. She had taken refuge in a café on the boulevard, and in a dark corner begun to weep. " It was the greatest disillusionment of my life," she admitted with a gentle smile. Then, in the company of an old Countess, she had left for Vienna, where she had spent several years. A young musicián who was a great admirer of Heine's, learning that she was returning to Paris, had asked her to bring his compositions to the poet. " *Verfehltes Leben, verfehlte Liebe . . .*" With these, the poet's own lines, she brought her tale to a close.

They sat in silence as twilight fell. For several strange and exquisite hours they remained thus, dreaming side by side and exchanging occasional words of tenderness. Under the dark shadow of his approaching death the poet felt transported by an incredible and fantastic happiness. And from this happiness were born those magnificent verses so redolent of mystic sensuality. " Oh, final days of fingers filled with mortal desire, my greedy fingers moist with delight." Their love was innocent and vicious like that of children and old men. It was a sulphurous and shadowy love, that might have been born of the heated imagination of Hoffmann.

LOTOSBLUME

Wahrhaftig, wir beide bilden
Ein kurioses Paar.
Die Liebste ist schwach auf den Beinen,
Der Liebhaber lahm sogar.

Sie ist ein leidendes Kätzchen,
Und er ist krank wie ein Hund,
Ich glaube im Kopfe sind beide
Nicht sonderlich gesund.

Sie sei eine Lotosblume,
Bildet die Liebste sich ein ;
Doch er, der blasse Geselle,
Vermeint der Mond zu sein.

THE LAST LOVE

Die Lotosblume erschliesset
Ihr Kelchlein im Mondenlicht,
Doch statt des befruchtenden Lebens
Empfängt sie nur ein Gedicht.

THE LOTUS

In truth, we two do paint
A very curious pair :
The loved one weak on her legs,
He with a cripple's air.

She is an ailing kitten,
He as ill as a hound ;
I do believe their heads
Are not completely sound.

That she's a lotus flower
Fancies the lady soon ;
He with his visage pale
Supposes he's the moon.

The lotus does unlock
Her chalice to the moon ;
But instead of fruitful life
She receives a poem soon.

Did Mathilde know what was taking place ? When she returned home, noisy and bustling, her arms full of parcels and brimming over with news, she was received with embarrassed looks in the still room of the invalid. She treated Mouche without ceremony, with contempt even, never inviting her to dinner or addressing a pleasant word to her. She did not conceal from Heine's friends that she detested this importunate intruder, whom Heine had presented as an old friend whom he had engaged to read to him in German. She was jealous of Mouche ; but she would send the nurse to fetch her on days when she did not arrive, when she observed how depressed and peevish her husband became.

One afternoon Lotte arrived unexpectedly with Gustav. She had not seen her brother for twelve years, and now when she saw his condition she flung herself on the bed and sobbed. Mouche wanted to retire, but Heine made a sign to her to stay. Once her emotion had passed Charlotte began to talk of old times and childhood memories.

"Do you remember, Gustav," said Heine, "when we found papa's uniform? We shared it : I put on the plumed helmet and said, 'I am Napoleon,' and you buckled on the sword and said, 'I am Murat.' It was Max who donned the uniform itself, and became the Emperor's doctor. And, you see, you have become a Hussar officer, Max a doctor, while I—I am waiting for the visit of Death at St. Helena . . ."

DEATH AND IMMORTALITY

Aт the beginning of 1856, perhaps as a result of overwork and the excitement of his new love, the poet's condition worsened. For nights on end he could not sleep, and suffered from attacks of asthma, stomach cramp and vomiting. Was this at last the end ? He must finish the editing of his poems . . . In spite of an incessant ringing in his head and the express orders of his doctor, he would work five or six hours at a stretch. Mathilde, Mouche and the nurse all implored him to spare himself. It was useless. " I still have four days' work to finish. I must hurry," he replied.

On February 15 the crisis reached its peak. Mathilde sent for Gruby, but as he was not at home, was obliged to call in another doctor, who prescribed laudanum drops and Vichy water mixed with an infusion of orange blossoms. Gruby arrived in the evening and administered other medicines, and ordered iced compresses on the stomach.

" Doctor, you have always been so kind to me," whispered the invalid ; " tell me the truth : it is the end, isn't it ? "

Gruby sat down on the edge of the bed without a word. Heine took his hand. " Thank you."

The medicaments had no effect on his suffering. The world grew dark, and only the shooting, rending pains remained.

Between four and five o'clock the following afternoon Heine whispered to the nurse : " I want to write. I must write . . . write . . ."

" Presently," answered the nurse.

A little later Heine spoke again. " I am dying . . . I am dying . . ."

Mathilde, on her knees by the bedside, held his hand. She had not allowed Mouche to see her husband that day. Towards midnight she could no longer keep awake, and the nurse sent her to her room. The poet watched her leave with a long loving look : he would never see her again. Then his spasms took hold of him once more. The nurse tried to give him relief, but Heine turned his head away. It was useless, he had ceased to struggle. The terrible agony made the approach of death bearable. A final paroxysm and his heart ceased to beat.

.   *   *   *   *

The stars that the poet had so often sung were paling. On the pavement in front of the house the milk carts were rumbling noisily. Mathilde, who had been wakened by the nurse, came and knelt by the bed. Her eyes were dry ; she had no more tears left to shed. The nurse sank into an arm-chair and stretched out her legs.

That morning in Hamburg old Betty Heine, her hands folded on her breast, lay awake in her bed listening to the hoot of a steamboat. Mouche was sleeping tranquilly in her Parisian attic, and young Frenchmen were dying before the walls of Sebastopol. Old Lamartine was putting the final touches to his *Cours Familial de la Litterature*. The *Würzburger Neue Zeitung* announced that the future of foreign troops stationed in Turkey would not definitely be decided until after the conclusion of peace ; the situation in New York on the contrary was favourable, capital issues were increasing. The people of Madrid had spent a calm night despite the fact that a police perquisition had discovered more than a thousand subversive tracts written in a democratic tone. In London, in the House of Lords, Lord Lansdowne had made an eloquent speech affirming that better education for the working classes presented a grave danger ; he did, however, add that " . . . it was impossible to establish an absolute ruling on this question . . ." Mathilde sent for Henri Julia to help her with the burial formalities. Theophile Gautier, turning over the pages of the *Journal des Débats*, read the brief announcement :

> " The illustrious poet, Heinrich Heine, has died as a result of a painful illness, of which he has been the victim for eight years. His obsequies will take place on Wednesday, 20th February, at ten o'clock."

The unassuming hearse was followed by Mathilde and a few writers and artists, Gautier, Royer, Dumas, Baudelaire and little Weil, who walked by the side of Mouche, whose face was hidden by a thick veil. Behind them came the solemn porter and a few shopkeepers of the district ; the inevitable old women who follow in the wake of every funeral brought up the rear.

Mathilde, although it was painful to her, respected the last wishes of her husband : the coffin was lowered into the grave without ceremony or discourse.

Detractors and scandalmongers claimed that he had been buried at seven o'clock and that by eight his wife—as though to fulfil her husband's ironical prophecy—had been drinking red wine and enjoying herself, and then had gone away to the country to live with Henri Julia. When Weil repeated this rumour to her some time after, she was very indignant. The truth is that she had left immediately after the funeral, as she had promised Heine, for Asnières, where she had hired a small house. Henri Julia had only helped her to move and to collate her husband's writings, which she could not do herself. Shortly afterwards this young man made a rich marriage and embarked on a fine administrative career in the South of France.

Mathilde lived at first in Asnières, and later at Batignolles with Pauline, a parrot and a white long-haired dog. She received Heine's friends—charming Alfred Meissner, Gautier, and the correspondents of the German newspapers. Several years later, when Gustav Heine announced with much bluster that he intended to erect a tombstone to his brother, she protested furiously and said that as she had been the only one who had bothered to care for him while he was alive, she refused to allow anyone to share in the expense of a memorial.

*   *   *   *

Heine was dead, but his *avatars* continued. As he had written in a proud and cruel poem to Amelie, in the shape of a farewell :

> *Die Schönheit ist dem Staub verfallen*
> *Du wirst zertrieben, wirst verhallen*
> *Viel anders ist mit dem Poeten*
> *Da kann der Tod nicht gänzlich töten . . .*

The poet's lips were closed, but his melancholy and tender songs, ironical romances, satires and laments continued still to echo, his revolutionary writings still to stir up revolt, and his malicious wit indefatigably to persecute hypocrites, "Pan-German lackeys," bad poets, false idols and thick-skinned "Atta Trolls." There are poets, writers and revolutionaries who find peace in death, and who in some way make a posthumous reconciliation with their erstwhile enemies. Heine was not one of these conciliatory dead. As his malady had been unable to quench his spirit, so death did not diminish his aggression. He remained what he had been when alive—a free spirit who conquered his own contradictions with inflexible irony, and warred against false grandeur without respite. This aggression explains why official Germany had never been able to come to terms with him ; the poet made too many demands for such a reconciliation, and the Germany of Bismarck was not disposed to renounce its inner structure. His apparent irony and intellectual superiority were a challenge to the convictions of the German ruling class.

Heine's lucidity and penetrating gaze unmasked—even from the tomb—the will to power of Wilhelm's Germany. But he had not criticised and railed at the Germans alone ; the Jews, the English and the French also came in for a good deal of castigation. His irony knew no racial prejudice. But the English, the French and the Jews, bowing before his immense talent, forgave him because of his sincerity ; only the Pan-Germans, the German professors and the Junkers continued to hate him, never understanding the poet's tender and profound love for his own country, which the German philosophers and musicians knew so well how to express.

The professors, the *literati* and the priests styled Heine frivolous and anti-national, and made every effort to alienate German youth from his work—that "dangerous poison". But the sweet songs of the *Buch der Lieder* always won the hearts of young lovers, and many of these poems were transposed into popular songs ; the workers considered Heine as their poet, and declaimed his verses àt their celebrations.

The Municipal Council of Düsseldorf overruled the majority who proposed to erect a statue to the famous poet ; but the stiff-necked patricians soon perceived that the thousands of Austrians and Swedes, Spaniards and Italians, Hungarians and Rumanians only halted in their town in order to make a pilgrimage to the house where the author of *Leise zieht durch mein Gemüt* was born, and to cast a glance at the garden where the infant Heine had played with Lotte.

Menzel, Gödeke, Hehn, Bartels and Treitschke spoke with disdain of his writings, whereas Baudelaire hailed him as one of the greatest poets of the century ; the Italian, Carducci, wrote a solemn ode in memory of the " great German," and the Englishmen, Meredith and Arnold, proclaimed him one of the masters of modern poetry.

The Norwegian, Georg Brandes, an authority on German culture, refuted Karl Hildebrandt, who maintained that the foreign cult for Heine was based on a misunderstanding, inasmuch as they took him more seriously than he had taken himself. The humorous and mocking Heine, said Brandes, was at heart a pathetic creature.

The first German who dared to contradict Heine's official detractors was Nietzsche—who had come under his influence. Nietzsche proclaimed his admiration for " . . . the sweetly passionate music of Heine's verses and the divine malice of his wit . . ." and placed him both as a creator and thinker and as a good European among the greatest figures of the century—in the same rank as Napoleon, Beethoven, Goethe and Stendhal. His disciples, however, wishing to present their master as the prophet of Pan-Germanism, ignored his admission of Heine's genius.

During the first world war Heine's works were once again put on the Index. He was reinstated under the Weimar Republic, but when those elements in Germany whose forerunners, like the demagogues of 1812—Turnvater Jahn, the Nationalists obsessed with the *Burschenschaft*, Massmann and his kind—came to power, his works were thrown on the bonfire. They went so far as to erase his name from the curriculum of Literature. But once again Heine's work escaped its persecutors : banished from Germany, it remained curiously alive wherever the spirit of liberty breathed. His predictions and fiery poems were remembered ; they inspired contempt and anger against the common foe.

Now the demons of Germanic night have been defeated. The old Germany has disappeared. We cannot help but think of Heine's poem :

> *Es wächst heran ein neues Geschlecht*
> *Ganz ohne Schminke und Sünden*
> *Mit freien Gedanken, mit Freier Lust*
> *Dem werde ich alles verkünden . . .*

Will there emerge from the chaos into which we have been plunged that world of brothers in which he never lost faith ?

THE END

BIBLIOGRAPHY

HEINE'S WORKS

HEINRICH HEINE *Sämtliche Werke*, Adolf Strodt-mann, 12 Bde. in 6, Hamburg, Hoffmann u. Campe, 1861–1869.
Gesammelte Werke, hg. Gustav Karpeles, 9 Bde. Berlin, G. Grote, 1887.
Memoiren, hg. Gustav Karpeles, 3 Auflage, Berlin, K. Curtius, 1909.

HENRI HEINE *De l'Allemagne*, Paris, Renduel, 1835.
De la France, pref. Henri Julia, Paris, 1857.
Drames et fantaisies, pref. Saint-Réné Taillandier, Paris, 1858.
Autobiographie, hg. Gustav Karpeles, Berlin, R. Oppenheimer, 1888.

CORRESPONDENCE AND DOCUMENTS

ENFANTIN *De l'Allemagne*, Paris, Duverger, 1836.

HENRI HEINE *Correspondance inédite*, 3 t. Paris, Michel-Lévy frères, 1866–1877.

HEINE-BRIEFE *ges. v. Hans Daffis*, 2 Bde. Berlin, Pan-Verlag, 1906–1907.

HEINE-RELIQUIEN hg. Heine-Geldern u. G. Karpeles, Berlin, K. Curtius, 1911.

BIOGRAPHIES, CRITICISMS AND WRITINGS ON HEINE

BARTELS, ADOLF *Heinrich Heine*, Auch ein Denkmal, Dresden, A. Koch, 1906.

BASTARD, JEAN *Un malade de talent*, Lyon, 1930.

BETZ, L. P. *Die französische Litteratur im Urteile H. Heines*, Berlin, Gronau-Verlag, 1897.

BRANDES, G. *Das junge Deutschland*, 5 Bde. Berlin.

BROD, MAX   *Heinrich Heine*, Amsterdam, A. de Lange, 1934.

BROWNE, LEWIS   *That Man Heine*, McMillan's, New York, 1927.

CABANÈS   *Grands névropathes*, t. 3, Paris, Albin Michel, 1935.

CHANTAVOINE   *Musiciens et poètes (Heine et Liszt)*, Paris, 1912.

CHARLÈTY   *La Monarchie de Juillet*, Paris, Hachette, 1921.

Essai sur l'histoire du Saint-Simonisme, Paris, Hachette, 1896.

CLARKE, MARGARET A.   *Heine et la monarchie de Juillet*, thèse, Paris, 1935.

FERRAN, ANDRÉ   *L'ésthetique de Baudelaire*, Paris, Hachette, 1935.

GUILLERME, MARC I.   *Les amours tourmentés de Heine*, Ed. de France, 1937.

HIRTH, F.   *Henri Heine à Granville*, Mortain, 1938.

HOUBEN, H.   *Henri Heine par ses contemporains*, trad. B. Netter-Gidon, Paris, Payot, 1929.

Gespräche mit Heine, Frankfurt, Rütten u. Lönnig, 1926.

JAUBERT, CAROLINE   *Souvenirs*, Paris, 1881.

KARPELES, GUSTAV   *H. Heine und seine Zeitgenossen*, Berlin, F. und P. Lehmann, 1888.

Heinrich Heine. Aus seinem Leben und aus seiner Zeit, Leipzig, 1899.

KAUFMANN, DAVID   *Aus Heinrich Heines Ahnensaal*, Breslau, Schottländer, 1896.

KIEFT, PIETER   *H. Heine in westeuropaischer Beurteilung. Seine Kritiker in Frankreich, England und Holland*, Zutphen, 1938.

KOHN-ABREST   *Les coulisses d'un livre*, Paris, 1887.

LEGRAS, JULES   *Henri Heine, poète,* Paris, Calmann-Levy, 1897.

LICHTENBERGER, HENRI   *Henri Heine, penseur,* Paris, Alcan, 1905.

LINDEN   *Das Heine-Grab auf dem Montmartre,* Leipzig, Barsdorf, 1898.

LIPTZIN, SOL   *Heinrich Heine, " blackguard " and " apostate " ;* a study on the earliest English attitude towards him, Publications of Modern Language Association, 1943.

MARCUS, LUDWIG   *Ein Leben zwischen Gestern und Morgen,* Berlin, Rodwalt, 1932.

MARX-ENGELS   *Briefe,* 3 Bde. 1844–1853.

MATTHEW, ARNOLD   *Essays in criticism,* London, 1912.

MAUCLAIR, CAMILLE   *La vie humiliée de Henri Heine,* Paris, Plon, 1930.

MELCHIOR, FELIX   *H. Heines Verhältnis zu Lord Byron,* Berlin, Felber, 1903.

MOOS, EUGEN   *Heine und Düsseldorf,* Marburg, 1908.

NASSEN, J.   *Heinrich Heines Familienleben,* Fulda, 1895.

NERVAL, GERARD DE   Notice du traducteur de " La Mer du Nord " 15 Juillet, 1848, dans *Revue des Deux Mondes.*

Notice de traducteur de " l'Intermède," 15 Septembre, 1848, dans *Revue des Deux Mondes.*

OTT, BARTHELEMY   *La querelle de Heine et de Börne,* thèse, Lyon, n.d.

PIERRE-GAUTHIEZ   *Henri Heine,* Paris, 1935.

PROUDHON, J.-P.   *De la Justice dans la Revolution et dans l'Eglise,* Tome II, Oeuvres complètes (Jugement sur Heine, p. 433), Paris, 1931.

BIBLIOGRAPHY

PÜTZFELD, CARL   *Heinrich Heines Verhältnis zur Religion*, Berlin, Grote, 1912.

ROCCA, PRINCESS DELLA   *Souvenirs de Henri Heine*, Paris, 1896.

SCHILL   *Les traductions françaises de Henri Heine*, thèse, Paris, n.d.

VALLENTIN, ANTONINA   *Henri Heine*, 9 ed. Paris, Gallimard, 1934.

WENDEL, H.   *Heinrich Heine und der Sozialismus*, Berlin, 1919.

WERNER, F.   *Ein öffentliches Heine-Denkmal auf deutschem Boden? . . . Fort mit der Schmach eines öffentlichen Heine-Denkmals*, Leipzig, Hedeler, 1913.

WINTERFELD, ACHIM VON   *Heinrich Heine, sein Leben und seine Werke*, Dresden, Pierson, 1903.

INDEX

INDEX

INDEX

INDEX

INDEX

INDEX

INDEX